D1140672

BRITISH BATTLES

ENGLISH HERITAGE

BRITISH BATTLES

THE FRONT LINES OF HISTORY IN COLOUR PHOTOGRAPHS

KEN AND DENISE GUEST

HarperCollins*Publishers*

ACKNOWLEDGEMENTS

The authors wish to express their gratitude to Dell Computers for the loan of computer equipment (not least the 'quantam fireball'); Val Horsler of English Heritage Publications for supporting this project from its inception; David Smurthwaite and colleagues at the National Army Museum whose diligent research for the English Heritage Battlefield Register was an enormous aid to our own efforts; Sarah Dupuy, Barbara Hamilton, Anita King, Liz Munro, Gail Pilkington, and Nicola Scully of Swanage Library who put in much hard work behind the scenes tracking down obscure tomes in an impossibly short timescale; Howard Giles of the English Heritage Special Events Unit for organising access to various re-enactment events; Paul Williams Photographic for help with the processing; Paul Meekins, Richard Brown and Victor Sutcliffe for providing endless lists of essential books; the Society of Authors and the Authors' Foundation for their generous support, Araminta Whitley, our agent, for her sound guidance; Ian Drury, our long suffering editor, for his endless patience and good humour; and Jan and Peter Guest for their essential rearguard action on the home front.

Thanks are also due to Ian Allen, Chris Baker, Ian & Trudy Barret, Phil Berthon, David Blackmoor, George & Betty Blake, Dan Bolaney, Nick Blloe, Andrew Brown, Bob Carruthers, David Cree, Dave Chambers, Brendan Cronin, Chris Broome-Smith, John Cole, David Cubbage, Melanie Davis, Rachel Dreher, John & Tessa Drury, Richard Dunk, Adrian Elliston, Ken Evans, Phil Fenwick, Martin Philips, Mark Griffin, Barry Hanson, David Hardwick, Sue Hewitt, Ann Hemus, Rosemary Hills, Paul Hitchin, Alex Hook, Karin Kelly, Derek Watkins, Alan Jeffrey, Alan Larsen, Colin Levick, Michael Loades, David Logan, Paul Lydiate, Ian & Mary MacDonald Watson, Jane May, Dougie McCall, Dave McGrath, Bruce MacLellan, Mark Meltonville, Keith Piggot, Jonathan Prickett, Stewart Pryde, Chris Pullen, Heath Pye, Pete Ross, Chris Scott, Alex Summers, Julian Tillbury, Jonathan Taylor, Chris Thomas, Stuart Reid, Liz Roberts, Dave Ross, Dave Ryan, Judy Smith, Kim Siddorn, Les & Amanda Thomas, Paul Thompson, Philip Vaughan, William Wake, Veronica Wallace, John Washbourne, James Wilson, David Wilson, Mike and Lynda Woodhouse.

Last, but not least, we would like to place on record our indebtedness to all of those anonymous pikemen who demonstrated their drills; the Highlanders who performed endless charges for us to photograph; the knights who answered obscure questions about armour; the archers who drew their bows time and again; the musketeers who fired volleys; the smoke-begrimed gunners who revealed the mysteries of their devilish art; and all of the many other re-enactors without whom this book would not have been possible. To each and every one we unreservedly express our thanks.

This edition produced for Bookmart Limited
Desford Road
Enderby
Leicester LE9 5AD
Registered number 2372865

HarperCollins*Publishers*
77-85 Fulham Palace Road
Hammersmith
London W6 8JB

First published in Great Britain by HarperCollins*Publishers* 1996
This edition published 2002
Text and photos © Ken and Denise Guest 1996
The authors assert the moral right to be
identified as the authors of this work

ISBN 0 00 765126 0

Maps: Peter Harper

Editor: Ian Drury
Design: Rachel Smyth
Production Manager: Bridget Scanlon

Colour reproduction by Saxon Photo Litho, Norwich, England
Printed and bound in Spain by Graficas Estella

CONTENTS

FOREWORD

If battles are, as Winston Churchill wrote, 'the punctuation marks of history', then battlefields are fragmentary pages on which those punctuation marks are written in blood.

Some represent turning points in our history, on many others, great leaders' reputations were made or lost; and on many more, the tactics and skills of war which have moulded the course of our country's fate were developed and honed.

Every battlefield is a testament to unknown soldiers who fought and died in the making of Britain's history. It is vital that those battlefields that still remain should be recognised and should survive.

English Heritage's Register of Historic Battlefields, published after extensive public consultation in 1995, identifies 43 areas of historic signifcance in England where important battles took place. The Register gives those sites some protection and encourages expert advice on their conservation and enhancement for future generations.

This fascinating new book complements our Register by calling on contemporary records and modern photographs to recapture vividly the heat, clamour, toil and pain of each significant conflict as seen through the eyes of fighting men down the centuries.

English Heritage and HarperCollins responded enthusiastically to Ken and Denise Guest when they proposed this format. They are combat photographers of great standing, with expertise acquired in many of the war zones of the late 20th century, such as Afghanistan and Cambodia.

Their stunning pictures vividly capture the feel of the battles, almost suspending belief that the scenes we see took place in recent years, as part of English Heritage's annual Special Events programme of historic re-enactments.

As Chairman of English Heritage I commend *British Battles* as a remarkable work of record and authority which I am sure will appeal to a wide audience. This book is bound to stimulate and encourage further the need for the conservation of our battlefield heritage.

Sir Jocelyn Stevens CVO
Chairman, English Heritage

INTRODUCTION

Ajournalist covering one of the modern world's many guerrilla wars has an option. He can choose either to go with the side which has the helicopters, or the side which can't afford shoes. The correspondent with the helicopters covers more ground and has better photo-opportunities. Conversely his colleague down in the scrub with the men without shoes, endures more walking, bigger blisters, less food, more fear and perhaps, for a few brief moments, looks more deeply into the face of war.

During the eighties we accompanied the Afghan Mujahideen on forced marches for many footsore miles over the Hindu Kush. The lack of food, the search for water, the absence of proper shelter or any modern convenience, the fear of ambush, and the nagging worry about wounds in an environment devoid of medical back-up were sobering experiences. Travelling beyond the reach of the twentieth century in this way is like journeying in time, and our experiences in such environments have inevitably helped to shape our perceptions of period warfare. Certainly life is just as spartan, the meals just as frugal and the fleas just as voracious, for the Afghan guerrillas as they were for, say the Saxons who fought an invading Norman superpower for their Wessex homeland in 1066.

In twentieth century Britain the majority of us take democracy and peace for granted. The battles in this book provide a glimpse into the fiery furnace in which these basic human rights are forged. While the names of kings and great commanders inevitably loom large, it is the ordinary footsoldier who mans the front lines of history. Throughout this work we have endeavoured to convey something of the experience of battle from his standpoint; whether it be in the shield wall at Maldon or the Highland charge at Culloden.

When the Last Post is blown
And the last volley fired,
When the last sod is thrown,
And the last foe retired,
And the last bivouac is made under the ground –
Soldier, sleep sound.

[Joseph Lee, b.1876, Ballads of Battle]

Ken and Denise Guest

SOLDIERING IN ANGLO-SAXON BRITAIN

In AD 980, two years into the reign of King AEthelred II, the Vikings fell on Southampton. It was a generation since these seaborne raiders had last prowled along English shores and the sight of their dragon-carved prows cresting the waves was ominous indeed. AEthelred's England was ripe for plunder: a thriving and comfortable land, inadequately defended. The standing field army once mobilised by Alfred the Great was but a memory, and the old town defences had fallen into disrepair. Despite AEthelred's efforts at diplomacy and military rebuilding, the Viking successes of 980 were to establish a pattern of summer raiding which was to last for the next 36 years.

In the whole of AEthelred's prosperous little realm, there could have been few more tempting prizes than Maldon: a coastal town housing a royal mint. The task of guarding this Saxon bank-without-a-safe fell to the King's thegn, Brihtnoth, Ealdorman of Essex. In 988, Brithnoth's East Saxons successfully thwarted a Viking raid. Withdrawing to their cold homeland, the Norse marauders brooded over this defeat through three dark winters. In the spring of 991 they decided to return.

Close quarter battle in Anglo-Saxon times: a desperate struggle with axe, sword and spear. With relatively light body armour, soldiers mainly depended on their shields to protect themselves.

MALDON
⊰⊱ 10 August 991 ⊰⊱

The Danish King, Svein Forkbeard set sail with an army of 4,000 men in 93 ships. His Vikings had already blooded their swords at Sandwich, Folkestone and Ipswich, before their dragon ships glided up Pante's Stream (the Blackwater River estuary) to the Isle of Northey.

Linked to the mainland by a causeway navigable only at low tide, this island was an easily defensible base from which to ravage the treasure chambers of Maldon. The planned combination of vengeance and profit gladdened many a Viking heart. While some gathered wood for camp fires and others fished in the hot August sunshine, Svein Forkbeard 'at once sent word that they had come to avenge' those killed in the preceding raid and would regard Brihtnoth 'a coward, if he would not dare to battle with them'[1].

In 991 Ealdorman Brihtnoth was an aging warrior, easily distinguished by his 'tall stature' and the 'swan-like whiteness of his head'[2]. The size of the Viking army, considerably larger than usual, must have come as a shock to him. Nonetheless, 'neither shaken by the small number of his men, nor fearful of the multitude of the enemy'[3], he responded by rushing the East Saxon fyrd to confront the foreign invaders. As yet the state of the tide had prevented Forkbeard from establishing a bridgehead on the mainland. While the 'the flower of the East Saxons and the shipmen's host'[4] waited, a bow-shot apart, for the causeway to emerge from the sinking waters of the estuary, they exchanged insults.

Forkbeard warned the Saxons 'it will be better for you all that you buy off an attack with tribute, rather than that men so fierce as we should give you battle'[5]. Undaunted, Brihtnoth parried this verbal assault with mockery of his own: 'Hear

Left: *Contrary to later legend, the Vikings did not sport horns on their helmets. They wore very practical headgear which was sometimes fitted with eye pieces like this.*

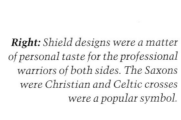

Right: *Shield designs were a matter of personal taste for the professional warriors of both sides. The Saxons were Christian and Celtic crosses were a popular symbol.*

you, searover, what this folk says? For tribute they will give you spears, poisoned point and ancient sword … It seems to me too poor a thing that you should go with our treasure unfought to your ships, now that you have made your way thus far into our land.'[6]

Despite his brave words the proud Saxon was no match for the sly Viking. Forkbeard had quickly realised that his superiority in numbers would count for nothing if his men were forced to fight their way across the narrow causeway. With the emerging passage held fast against him by only three of Brihtnoth's warriors, the silver-tongued Danish King changed tactics. Conceding that the Saxons were a formidable foe, he meekly requested that his Vikings be allowed to cross unmolested for a more even battle on the far shore. Astonishingly Brihtnoth agreed.

As the Viking 'wolves of slaughter pressed forward … over the gleaming water'[7] Brihtnoth's front line linked their wooden shields to create the defensive Saxon 'shield wall'. To counter this Forkbeard ordered his men into a tight-packed wedge formation known as

For both Saxons and Vikings, heroic fighting and heroic drinking were strongly connected. Great warriors were commemorated in verse and song and Brihtnoth's epic last stand was justly celebrated.

'svinfylka' (swine array). Then, screaming their war cries as they came, the Vikings 'rushed with one resolve'[8] upon the Saxon line and locked with it in vicious, close-quarter combat. The elite warriors of Brihtnoth's 'hearth-troop', deployed in the centre of his line, absorbed the brunt of this attack. Despite his advancing years,

FIGHTING IN THE SHIELD WALL

Hunched low behind their interlocked shields, with their spears held in an overarm grip, the warriors stabbed at the faces of their enemies while attempting to dodge spears directed at themselves. When two shield walls fcollided, the front rank no longer had room to manoeuvre their spears and resorted to close range weapons such as axes, maces or swords. Now, in the violent, shield-locked shunt, those in the rear ranks did what they

could to add to the mayhem. Heavy, long-handled axes rained splintering blows on any enemy shield within reach; often severing the arm which held it. Meanwhile other combatants were furiously thrusting spears beneath the shield wall, at the shins and calves of the opposing ranks.

In this press, braced hard against the blood-smeared shields of ones foes, it was possible to physically feel the ebb and flow of battle. Where deaths or crippling wounds created gaps in the wall, the line would flinch back to heal itself. Such retrogressive movements were instantly sensed by the other line, which surged forward to increase the pressure.

The drumming of swords on wooden shields, the screams of the wounded and the battle cries of the desperate, all combined to make the air tremble. Eventually, the will of one side would collapse and their shield wall would burst apart; an event often triggered by the death of a leader. Once this happened all united defence was over. It was now, with the broken side fleeing for their lives, that the slaughter really began.

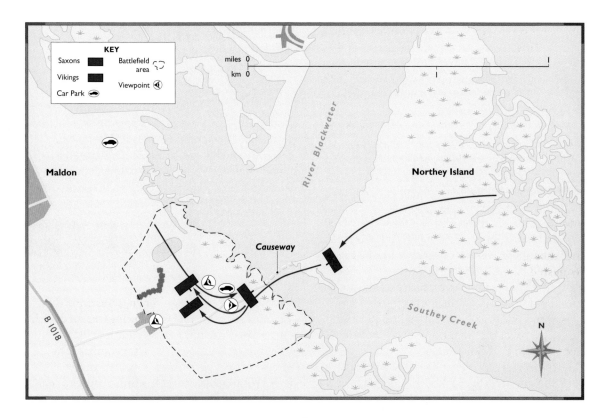

the Ealdorman also fought in the front rank of his army as befitted a man of his rank.

Naturally, the Saxon leader was a marked man in the eyes of his enemies. In the bloody cut-and-thrust which followed he was wounded three times by a Viking 'strong in battle' before he finally 'took the life of his deadly foe'[9]. As he despatched his second Viking however, the Saxon lord received a wound from a javelin. Though the young warrior next to him withdrew the point and hurled it back at the enemy, Brihtnoth had been 'pierced all too deeply'[10] Seriously weakened, he could not hope to survive for long. The end came quickly: as he struggled to defend himself an enemy blade sliced through his sword-arm.

The old warrior's snow white hair melted from view as he sank to his knees: 'his golden-hilted sword fell to earth; he could not use his hard blade nor wield a weapon'. He was now at the mercy of his enemies. As the Norsemen closed in to deliver his death-blow, King AEthelred's thegn 'looked up to heaven and cried aloud: "I thank thee, Ruler of Nations, for all the joys I have met with in this world" … Then the heathen wretches cut him down'[11], striking his head from his shoulders.

With the horror of their commander's death, the bulk of the Saxon levy lost heart and began to run from the field of slaughter. Only Brithnoth's loyal hearth-guard remained, vowing 'to avenge the one they loved'[12]. They proceeded to honour this oath with their lives, extracting a heavy price for the now inevitable Viking victory. In consequence Forkbeard's raiders were so mauled it was recorded that they 'could scarce man their ships'[13] after the battle.

SPEARS

The standard weapon for the armies of this era was the spear. Unlike the javelin, which was exclusively designed for throwing, the spear was usually retained for close combat as a far-reaching stabbing weapon. It remained the dominant weapon on British battlefields for a considerable period of time; surviving (albeit as a minority weapon) as late as the 1698 Jacobite uprising.

THE INVASIONS OF 1066

King Edward the Confessor died on 5 January 1066, leaving no issue. His realm was not destined to be leaderless for long. Four powerful and ambitious men coveted the crown of England: Duke William of Normandy, to whom the Confessor had promised the throne; Harold Godwineson, Earl of Wessex, to whom he had purportedly willed it on his death-bed; Harold's brother Tostig, the banished Earl of Northumbria; and Harold Hardraada, King of Norway.

Harold Godwineson wasted no time. Arranging the King's funeral with indecent haste, he was crowned in Westminster Abbey the day after the Confessor's death. Sadly for Harold the rival claims of Harold Hardraada and William of Normandy proved somewhat harder to bury. In September, while he was fruitlessly preoccupied guarding the south coast against William, Hardraada landed near York with an army of Vikings.

Although they usually dismounted to fight, Harold's Housecarls rode to the battlefield and some may have fought on horseback at Stamford bridge. The hard core of professional soldiers on both sides wore similar armour and fought with the same types of weapons.

STAMFORD BRIDGE
⋙ 25 September 1066 ⋘

Hardraada arrived with a Norwegian force of about 300 ships to join forces with Tostig who had been busy raising troops in Scotland. On 20 September 1066 this combined army defeated an English force led by the Northumbrian Earls Edwin and Morcar at the battle of Gate Fulford

The road to York now lay open and the city capitulated without a fight; agreeing to hand over hostages to ensure a peaceful transition of authority. Believing that he had nothing more to fear in the north, Hardraada graciously withdrew his troops to rejoin his fleet at Ricall. This was a mistake for which he was to pay with his life. On the morning of 25 September the Viking King set off towards Stamford Bridge to collect his hostages.

The Viking force which marched towards York on that bright September day tramped along casually in the autumn sunshine, shields over their backs and helmets dangling from their belts. Convinced that the nearest English army was 200 miles away in London, they had '... no thought of any attack'[14] and few had bothered to wear their mail shirts.

The first warning that all was not right was a strange, dancing light which reminded them of the sun reflecting off the ice-fields in their far off northern homes. As they drew closer to Stamford Bridge they realised that the light was caused by the 'bright shields and shining mail' of a great army. Cautioned by Tostig that '... the king himself must be with such an army'[15], Hardraada sent three men on horses to ride like the wind to the fleet for reinforcements and mail shirts. Then he marshalled his men into lines behind his, aptly named, 'Landwaster' standard.

King Harold had made an epic six-day forced march in order to confront Hardraada before he

Left: The straps on the back of the shields enabled them to be slung over the back when not in use.

Right: The mail shirts worn by both sides were made up of hundreds of metal rings, linked together and backed by a stout leather jerkin.

THE 'BERSERKER'

The steps of that most dangerous of the Viking breed, a berserker, echoed off the planking of Stamford Bridge. Spreading his feet for balance, he planted himself in the centre of that narrow span and 'stood firm against the English forces, so that they could not cross the bridge'. The Vikings had been caught unawares by the sudden arrival of King Harold's army and their champion on the bridge was determined to buy precious time for Hardraada to organise their defence.

One after another all who challenged the berserker were hacked down and hurried on to the afterlife. At length, a lone Anglo-Saxon decided to try guile. Creeping unseen beneath the wooden bridge, he bided his time until he saw the Viking above him. Then, with a mighty shove he sent his spearpoint through a gap in the planking, up under his enemy's mail coat, and deep into the most vulnerable part of his defences, between the legs. This painful achievement is still commemorated at Stamford Bridge on the anniversary of the battle in the consumption of 'spear pies'.

could consolidate his position in the north. Now, in the word-war which preceded the battle, he attempted to win his brother Tostig's allegiance back to the English crown; offering to reinstate his Northumbrian earldom. To Hardraada however, Harold said that he would offer only 'seven feet of English earth, or perhaps a little more as he is something tall'[16]. There was no 'Danegeld' to be had from this English king.

When the time for talk was over the huge English army advanced upon the Viking lines, beating their spears upon their shields as they came on. Though the Vikings were determined to show 'more fight … than flight'[17], they were heavily outnumbered. Unable to hold their line, knots of combatants were quickly broken away, splintering the action into a series of separate engagements. According to one contemporary account '… there was such difference in numbers that the English could pick out bands and surround them and go at them from all sides'[18].

If Hardraada could not hope for victory, he was determined at least to die as befitted a Viking king. Beset on all sides, he 'gripped the hilt of his sword with both hands in front of himself'[19] and carved a pathway through the living flesh of his foes. Only when he had killed many men was he stopped by an English arrow; which sliced through his windpipe '… so that blood straightaway gushed from his mouth. That was his death-blow and he fell at once to the ground and when this happened the

Marching with no scouts ahead of them and without much of their equipment, the Vikings were stunned to see the English army emerge into view.

Although the Vikings fought with desperate courage, their king died in hand-to-hand fighting and his men were scattered. The first and last Norwegian invasion of England was decisively repulsed.

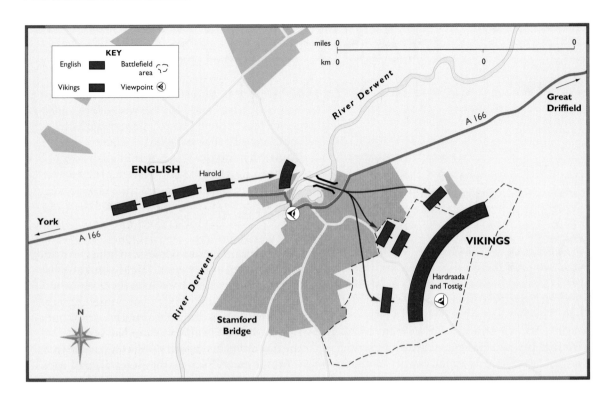

English attacked so strongly that all those who had stood near the king were killed'[20].

With no chance of escape, the remaining Vikings fought with desperate ferocity until Eystein Orri arrived with reinforcements from the ships. Now, as Harold urged his exhausted English army to drive home another charge, 'it was actually in the balance whether the English would fly'. In the end Eystein's intervention served only to prolong the slaughter. Beneath the crushing weight of Harold's next and final charge, the heroic Viking resistance broke at last. The survivors scattered before the English blades. Those who made it back to the coast filled only a fraction of the 300 ships which had brought them to English shores.

Hardraada's invasion had won him, not a kingdom, but the seven feet of English soil he had been promised. Tostig was also dead. Only one man now remained to threaten Harold Godwineson's hold on the crown: Duke William of Normandy.

THE SAXON SHIELD

The standard Saxon round shield, constructed from wood planking, averaged a yard in diameter. For extra strength, sun-dried, stretched leather might be added to the outer surface; which could then be adorned with the sort of geometric designs seen here.

HASTINGS
⋙ 14 October 1066 ⋘

Three days after the battle of Stamford Bridge, William 'the Bastard', Duke of Normandy, landed with a 7,000-strong army at Pevensey on the East Sussex coast. The English immediately turned about and marched south to confront the new threat.

On the night of 13 October, Harold's army of around 6,000 men camped about 12 miles from Pevensey, close to Hastings. At dawn the next morning the Normans marched out to meet them. The Norman army included a large contingent of cavalry, possibly as many as 2,000. Although his soldiers seldom fought mounted, Harold had seen the Norman cavalry in action in Brittany and knew how dangerous it could be. To counter this threat, he deployed his army on top of the steep-sided Senlac Hill.

Duke William's army included contingents of Bretons and Franco-Flemish mercenaries. Positioning these on his left and right wings respectively, he retained the hard corps of his Norman divisions in the centre. Trumpets pierced the morning calm and the Duke's forces began to roll forward; archers at the front, followed by the heavy infantry, with the cavalry bringing up the rear. Watching in silence from the other side of the valley, the English shuffled together until their shields overlapped. Twelve ranks deep, with the elite housecarls in front and some fyrd (militia) behind, they formed a solid shield-wall for 800 yards along the brow of Senlac Hill.

William began his assault with a shower of arrows. Once Norman archery had softened up the objective, his infantry passed between their bowmen and headed up the slope. Then it was the turn of William's men to endure a hail of missiles: javelins, spears, and skull-cracking hammers (thrown by those in the English rear ranks). The steepest part of the assault was the last twenty-five yards. Weighed down by their heavy mail 'hauberks', and burdened with shields and weapons, the Normans were unable to generate sufficient momentum to burst through the English shield-wall. In this deadly encounter, all advantage lay with those on the crest. Eventually the exhausted Bretons on William's left flank gave way and fled back down the hill. As the demoralised Norman centre began to follow them, Duke William

Above the English line floated the standards of Harold and his chieftains. The fall of Harold's own standard was to be a turning point in the battle.

THE TWO-HANDED AXE

The two-handed battle axe, with its four foot haft, had originally been devised by Danish Vikings for boarding ships. In expert hands it shattered shields and sliced through opponents from crown to hip. Having received a brutal introduction to this lethal close-quarter weapon, the Saxons adopted it as part of their own arsenal. In time this Viking legacy was to become a common feature of Anglo-Saxon warfare.

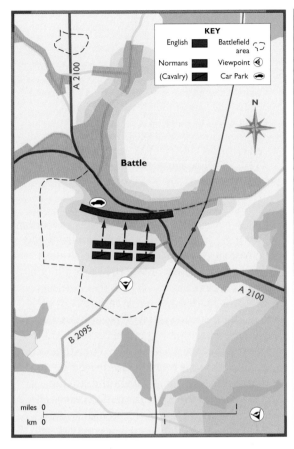

immediately embarked on damage limitation; urging his men to stand firm. At this critical moment he was unhorsed and the rumour flashed through the ranks that he was dead. Before the panic could spread, the Duke scrambled back into his saddle, lifted his helmet to reveal his face, and shouted, 'Look well at me. I am alive and shall conquer through Grace of God'. Though this prompt action saved his centre from rout he was forced to withdraw in order to regroup.

By now the panic-stricken Bretons were in danger of total disintegration. Chased down the slope by a large number of the triumphant English on the right flank, they had been pursued

The charge of the Norman cavalry was legendary throughout eleventh century Europe: few armies could withstand it. But from their hilltop position, the English warriors repulsed a series of attacks, some Housecarls managing to bring down both horse and rider with smashing blows of their two-handed axes.

Dismounted knights and Norman foot soldiers advanced after the mounted charges had failed.

The English line readied itself for the next attack, which was repulsed after heavy fighting.

THE WARRIOR CLERGY

Eleventh century clergymen had no scruples about participating in combat, often considering it their duty. In order to circumvent awkward biblical injunctions against taking up the sword, informed ecclesiastical warriors favoured the mace (not mentioned in the bible). Armed with this fearsome battle tool, clerics such as Bishop Odo at Hastings did not so much forgive their enemies, as enthusiastically splatter out their brains.

into some swampy ground at the foot of Senlac Hill. However, the sudden arrival of the Norman cavalry (led by Duke William himself) on their flank gave the fyrd cause to regret their unauthorised counter-charge. Though a desperate knot of them rallied on a prominent knoll half way up the slope, their rash advance had cut them off from all help and they were overwhelmed.

Despite this localised reverse, Harold was still in possession of his hill. The midday sunshine rippled across Norman armour and weapons as they began a second assault up the steep incline; now littered with the broken bodies of their own dead. This time the advance was supported by mounted Norman knights; riding close enough behind their infantry to stab at the English with lances. The English countered this annoyance by lunging with long war-axes. Swinging their wide blades over the shields of those in their own front

Norman knights rode down several bands of English warriors which pursued their enemies down the hill. Rallied by William, the knights prepared to attack again after the archers had done their work.

LEADERSHIP

The crush of the Saxon shield-wall formation restricted King Harold's field of vision and prevented him from exercising any real command. He was unable to turn local advantages into decisive victories, or to prevent the suicidal charge of his right wing in pursuit of the fleeing Bretons.

By contrast William's mobile command allowed him to intervene personally where most needed; a feature which staved off imminent defeat more than once during the battle. Moreover the Duke led by example, bidding his men 'to come with him more often than he ordered them to go in front of him'. Adapting to the constraints imposed on him by Harold's choice of ground, he applied the principles of combined arms assault to smash the foundation on which the Saxon defence rested: the shield-wall.

ranks, their hacking blows could severe the leg of a horsemen and disembowel his mount with surgical ease.

In the midst of this mayhem Duke William's horse was killed by a javelin thrown by one of Harold's brothers. Untangling himself from his dead mount, the Duke 'rushed upon the young man like a snarling lion and hewed him limb from limb'[22]. Then, looking for a way to escape the English spears, he spotted a Norman knight from Maine riding through the slaughter and called for help. When the knight (who was afraid for his own life) refused to give up his mount, William seized him 'furiously by the nasal of his helmet … tumbled him head over heels to the

ground and rushed to mount the horse thus left to him'[23]. Rank had its privileges!

King Harold had chosen both his ground and his strategy well. Despite William's best efforts the Normans once again lost heart and fell back. Frustrated by the failure of his infantry to break through the shield-wall, the Duke now had little choice but to fully commit his cavalry, with the exhausted infantry in support. Screaming their war cry 'Dex Aie' (God's Help), the wave of Norman horse led the way forward against the unyielding English line. As William of Poitiers observed, it was 'a strange manner of battle,

Left: *Norman archers came forward and subjected the English to a merciless storm of arrows. With few archers of their own, the English were unable to retaliate.*

WOMEN

As in so many wars it was left to the women to pick up the pieces; to wander among the dead and dying littering the battle field, desperate to find a loved one and terrified they might succeed. After the violent dismemberment of King Harold at Hastings his body could only be identified by his wife, Edith Swan Neck.

The distinctive Norman kite-shaped shields protected the warrior's side when he was on horseback.

The shield was held on the arm and manoeuvred with the left hand.

where one side works by constant motion and ceaseless charges, while the other can but endure passively as if rooted to the sod'[24].

By now the English had also suffered serious losses, and the depth of their formation was considerably diminished. Amid the carnage of the third assault the first cracks appeared in Harold's stout defence and a few of William's mounted knights were at last able to penetrate the frontage of shields. The hard-pressed English responded like battle-crazed berserks; screaming 'Out! Out! Out!' as they hacked the Normans from their saddles. This ferocious defence once again pushed the Duke's forces over the lip of Senlac; forcing them to tumble back. This time no howls of abuse or showers of missiles followed the Normans down the hill. The battle-weary English merely leaned on their shields and watched them go.

Time was running out for William. Isolated in a foreign land he knew that anything less than a total victory would be fatal. Up on Senlac Hill the English watched the Norman divisions regrouping in the golden light of late afternoon and braced themselves for what they knew must

be the last round. By now fresh supplies had arrived for the Norman archers and William's men took heart at the drumming rattle of arrows showering down onto English shields and heads. Nonetheless, it was no mean feat to launch a fourth assault up the same steep slope, slippery with blood and gore.

Once more the Norman trumpets brayed as their lines rolled forward. This time there would be no pulling back until one side or the other was destroyed. Looking up, William spotted Harold's personal banner, 'The Fighting Man', bobbing above the wall of wooden shields on the English right flank. There was his chance. If he could kill the king, the day might yet be his. With Eustace of Boulogne by his side the Duke led a cavalry charge directly towards Harold's standard. It was desperate and bloody work; each yard bought with the lunge of a spear or the slice of sword.

Unknown to William, the king was already wounded, struck by an arrow above the right eye. Faint with pain, blinded by the free-flowing blood, he leaned against his shield desperate to remain on his feet and prevent a panic. Though the wound was serious, it was possibly not fatal. Closing around him, Harold's housecarls attempted to extract him from the press. However, hemmed in by their own lines, they were unable to manoeuvre more than a few yards. In this crush even the dead 'could not be laid down ... each corpse though lifeless stood as if unharmed and held its post.'[25] Meanwhile, twenty mounted Norman knights inched

Ranks thinned by the rain of arrows, the English struggled to maintain their line against the renewed Norman assault.

William led his personal retinue directly against Harold and the death of the English leader signalled the beginning of the end. As the shield wall collapsed, so the real butchery began.

relentlessly closer to the helpless king, supported by their blood-spattered infantry. At last they were close enough to hack down the royal standard bearer and 'the Fighting Man' sank from sight.

With the king's banner down, English morale collapsed. William's knights hewed a bloody swathe through their enemies to deliver Harold's death-blow. Four knights were finally close enough to strike at the wounded king: 'the first, cleaving his breast through the shield with his point, drenched the earth with a gushing torrent of blood; the second smote off his head below the helmet and the third pierced the inwards of his belly with his lance; the fourth hewed off his thigh and bore away the severed limb'[26].

Hastings was one of the most important battles in British history and it lasted almost all day. Casualties were heavy, with the estimated 4,000 dead fairly evenly divided between the sides. It had been a close-run thing, but William 'the Bastard' was now William 'the Conqueror'. After a period of mopping up he was crowned King of England on Christmas Day 1066. The rule of the Normans had begun.

With one battle, William of Normandy had won the crown of England and created an empire spanning both sides of the Channel.

ARROW IN THE EYE

There has been much debate over the manner of King Harold's death, particulary the question of whether or not he was hit in the eye by an arrow. However the tradition that the King received such a wound was firmly established in early chronicles. According to Guy, Bishop of Amiens, William had instructed his archers to aim at 'the faces of the English'. In addition there is the evidence of the Bayeux tapestry; although even here there is room for debate over the exact point of the arrow strike (eye or forehead). On the tapestry 24% of all arrow hits are head wounds, making Harold's wound not untypical of those suffered by many of his companions.

SOLDIERING IN MEDIEVAL BRITAIN

Lacking sons, Henry I wished to leave the crown of England to his daughter Matilda. This was not a universally popular choice and when Henry died in 1135, the powerful English barons offered their allegiance to Matilda's second cousin, Stephen of Blois. The subsequent reign of King Stephen (1135–54) was so bedevilled by revolts, invasions, border incursions and wars against the Scots and the Welsh that this period was dubbed 'the Anarchy'! Not the least of the King's problems was Matilda's refusal to accept the loss of her inheritance without a fight. In the ensuing struggle her interests were represented by her maternal uncle, King David of Scotland. The Scottish monarch was not wholly motivated by avuncular concern: the succession crisis also represented a heaven-sent opportunity for Scotland to annex Northumberland.

After several cross-border incursions, the Scots returned in force in July 1138. With King Stephen preoccupied by a rebellion in the south, the defence of northern England fell to the aging and bedridden Thurstan, Archbishop of York. This unlikely champion set about raising an army by declaring the forthcoming conflict a crusade, in which there would be heavenly rewards for the participants and eternal damnation for the less enthusiastic. As an added inducement he provided the banners of four Yorkshire Saints to act as standards. Thurstan's recruiting methods proved inspired and the resultant army was a healthy mix of Normans, Anglo-Normans, English and even a few Scots.

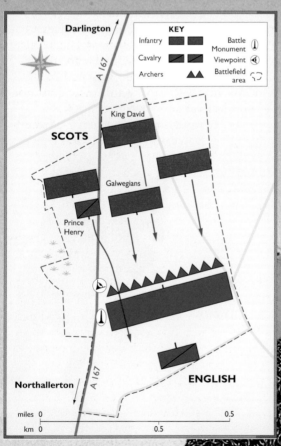

NORTHALLERTON
⋖⋗ 22 Aug 1138 ⋖⋗

As the Scots deployed near Northallerton on 22 August 1138, they must have been bemused by the sight of a ship's mast rising from the centre of the opposing English lines.

Nailed to the cross-spar were the banners of Thurstan's four Yorkshire saints while, sparkling at the top, was a silver vessel containing communion bread. It was hoped that this would not only inspire the English soldiers, but provide 'a sure and conspicuous rallying point, by which they might rejoin their comrades in the event of their being cut off'.[1]

Drawn up on a slight rise, Thurstan's forces were arrayed in a single large division rather than the usual three. The horses had been stationed well to the rear 'lest they should take fright at the shouting and uproar of the Scots'[2] and the knights had dismounted to fight on foot. In the front rank of this deployment, blocks of archers were interspersed with the armoured men-at-arms so that the army 'could with equal vigour and security either attack or receive ... [an enemy] attack'[3].

Six hundred yards away, on another shallow rise, the Scottish deployment had prompted a heated argument. The King's attempt to place his best-equipped troops in the front rank had greatly

The English knights dismounted to form the front rank of the army. The levies stood behind them, inspired by the saints' banners which led to the battle being known as 'The Battle of the Standard'.

offended the unarmoured contingent from Galloway. Insisting that they had 'iron sides, a breast of bronze [and] a mind void of fear'[4], they demanded the honour of being first in battle.

When the Scottish trumpets finally signalled the advance, the men of Galloway 'gave vent thrice to a yell of horrible sound'[5], drummed their spears on their shields, and charged across the field. At close quarters the English archers, sheltering behind their armoured front rank, made every arrow count. This was not battle but a merciless baiting, in which many a Galwegian might be seen 'bristling all round with arrows, and nonetheless brandishing his sword and in blind madness rushing forward now [to] smite a foe, now lash the air with useless strokes'[6].

Prince Henry attempted to steady his father's army by leading a cavalry charge from the right. Screaming his battle cry of 'Albany, Albany'[7] he 'hurled himself, fierce as a lion, upon the opposing wing ... scattering that part of the [English] army like a spider's web'[8]. Had the Prince's effort been supported by infantry, the day might yet have been saved. However, he was thwarted by English chicanery. As the outcome of battle wavered in the balance 'a certain prudent man ... raised aloft the head of one of the killed and cried out that [King David] was slain'[9]. Scottish morale plummeted and the Galwegians, unable to endure any longer 'the shower of arrows, the swords of the knights ... took to flight'[10]. Fortunately some of David's men realised (from the sight of the royal banner, 'blazoned like a dragon'[11]) that their King still lived. Rallying to his standard these troops enabled him to make a fighting withdrawal.

LEWES
⇜ 14 May 1264 ⇝

Exasperated by the baronial opposition centred
around Simon de Montfort, Henry III unfurled his
dragon standard in April 1264. Another Civil
War loomed.

On 13 May the opposing baron's army reached Fletching (9 miles north of Lewes). Outnumbered by 10,000 to 5,000, Simon de Montfort made a final attempt to reach a negotiated settlement. The King rejected his overtures. There was now no other option but trial by battle. However, the ensuing conflict was not destined to go according to the plans of either commander. Before Henry had a chance to respond to the challenge, battle was accepted by his eldest son Prince Edward. Discovering the enemy drawn up close to his camp, he launched the 3,000 royal cavalry in an impulsive charge without troubling to wait for the rest of the army. According to a contemporary account Edward, 'thirsted for … blood because [the baronial faction] had insulted his mother'[12].

In consequence Edward's cavalry hit de Montfort's left wing 'with such violence that he compelled them to retreat … for four miles, slaughtering them most grievously'. King Henry now had little choice but to commit his infantry to an attack on the remaining baronial army. With 'standards unfurled and preceded by the

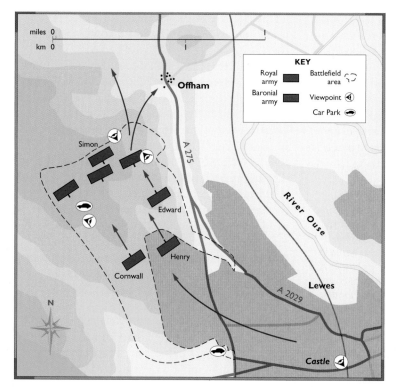

The King's army was quartered in Lewes with no idea the rebel barons were so nearby, until de Montfort's messengers arrived with a peace offer. Prince Edward rejected the terms and led his men out of the town, leaving their followers behind.

royal banner, portending the judgment of death'[13] the royal army advanced; albeit 'considerably diminished'[14] by the absence of their cavalry. However, the advantage of the ground lay with de Montfort. Charging down the slope, the baronial troops were able to push the King back into Lewes. There, after a desperate struggle, the royal forces were forced to fall back to the castle and the priory.

By the time Edward had returned, the main battle was over. Although he was willing to engage in further fighting, wiser council prevailed. The King (having suffered in the region of 2,700 casualties against approximately 1,300 on the baronial side) agreed to terms of surrender.

By the 13th century most knights wore helmets with some degree of face protection. Shields were now flat-topped, losing the tear-drop shape of Norman times.

EVESHAM
⤐ 4 August 1265 ⤐

After the battle of Lewes in 1264, Simon de Montfort, Earl of Leicester, governed England in the name of the King Henry III. To ensure the King's compliance, Prince Edward was held hostage in Hereford.

However, far from the 'government by consent', which de Montfort envisaged, he found himself forced to behave with increasingly dictatorial authority. Rebellion in Wales and the defection of many of his supporters demanded stern measures. From the safety of their castles, many barons began to doubt the wisdom of replacing Henry's crown with de Montfort's sword. Finally, on 28 May 1265, all that the Earl was striving to achieve was placed in jeopardy by a horse race at Hereford Castle. Prince Edward, who was held captive there, had persuaded his gaolers to allow him to compete. Not surprisingly, having won the race, Edward sank his spurs deep into his mount and kept going, shouting a valedictory 'have now [a] good day'[15].

Once free the Prince lost no time in forging alliances with disaffected barons, foremost among whom was Gilbert de Clare, Earl of Gloucester. Together they assembled an army of 8,000 men and began a campaign to restore the royal authority of the King.

On 1 August Edward turned his attentions to de Montfort's son, Simon, who was preparing to come to his father's aid with reinforcements. Swooping upon young Simon's camp at Kenilworth while most of the force were still asleep, the Prince removed the baronial reinforcements from the equation. Three days later, having marched through the night, his army trapped de Montfort's force of 6,000 at Evesham in Worcestershire.

Left: *For 12 months, Simon de Montfort had controlled the King and, through him, England. But Prince Edward's dramatic escape led to another pitched battle between the baronial faction and forces loyal to King Henry.*

Right: *Mail coats were now being supplemented by sections of plate armour. Knights wore surcoats bearing their insignia, but identification during battle was fraught with difficulty, especially when fighting the contingents of other English nobles.*

De Montfort's supporters took refuge with their families in castles all across England. One-by-one they made their peace with Edward I, whose ambitions in Wales would soon demand their support.

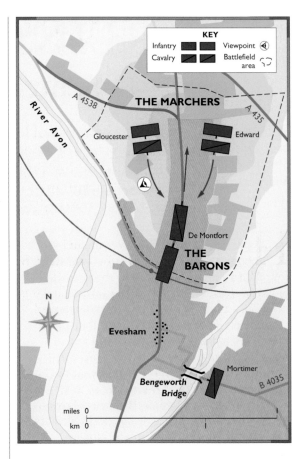

Caught in a loop of the River Avon, de Montfort was surrounded to the east, west and south by water. His troops were not only outnumbered, but tired and dispirited by weeks of constant marching and short rations. Moreover, the prospect of a battle had prompted a steady trickle of desertions from his disaffected Welsh troops.

Prince Edward's faction held all the cards. Despatching Roger de Mortimer's force to hold Bengeworth Bridge (which crossed the Avon south-east of the town), the Prince and Gloucester closed the trap by occupying Green Hill on the route north. De Montfort's only chance was to come out fighting. Aiming his forces at a gap between Edward's lion standard and the chevroned banners of Gloucester, he advanced up the hill.

Only as he gained the brow, did the beleaguered Earl fully realise the extent of the force arrayed against him. He had staked all on the hope that he could burst through the enemy line with a powerful charge. Now, even as he launched his army forward, de Montfort was heard to mutter, 'May God have mercy on our souls, for our bodies are the foe's'[16].

The desperate impetus of the baronial army carried them deep into the ranks of enemy spears and swords. As their charge finally expired amid a gory frenzy of hacking and thrusting, the cavalry flanks of the opposing line swung around and enveloped them. At the same moment the heavens above unleashed solid sheets of rain. Amid this grisly weather, a slaughter ensued the scale of which was rarely seen in Medieval battle.

Somewhere amid that crowd hurrying to oblivion, fell the brave de Montfort. As he was cut down and his body cruelly mutilated, '… lightning occurred and darkness prevailed to such an extent, that all were struck with amazement'[17]. With him perished a large part of his army (the dead, wounded and captured were later estimated to be in the region of 3,000). 'Such was the murder at Evesham, for battle it was not'[18].

Though their field army was destroyed, the rebellious barons retreated behind their tall castle walls and refused to submit. Ironically, it was Edward who, a decade later during his reign as Edward I, was finally to bring about a reconciliation. In 1275 he enshrined some of the elements of 'government by consent' in the Statute of Westminster. If de Montfort the man was dead, the seeds of reform which he had planted were not.

STIRLING BRIDGE

⋘ 11 September 1297 ⋙

While Edward I stayed in England to quell a baronial revolt, he sent an army into Scotland to crush Wallace's rebellion. Under the command of John de Warenne, Earl of Surrey, the English army reached Stirling. Wallace's army was waiting on the slopes of Abbey Craig.

With the Scottish flanks protected by a loop in the River Forth, the only direct approach lay over Stirling Bridge and along a causeway flanked by meadows. Wallace had some 5,000 men under him, almost entirely infantry. The English force included 300 men-at-arms and several thousand supporting infantry.

By now, the Scots were formed up and waiting on the other side. Sir Richard Lundie, (a Scottish knight in the Earl's service) desperately tried to warn the English officers of their folly, cautioning 'My Lords, if we cross that bridge now, we are all dead men. For we can only go over two abreast, and the enemy are already formed up: they can charge down on us whenever they wish'[19]. His advice was to abandon the narrow bridge and cross the river in force via a ford two miles upstream.

Dismissing this laudable plan on the grounds that it would delay the battle, 'all these experienced men, though they knew the enemy was at hand, began to pass over the bridge … until the vanguard was on one side of the river and the remainder of the army on the other'[20].

Events now progressed with sickening inevitability. With impeccable timing, the Scottish army poured down the slopes and flooded across the meadows like a spring tide. As they fell upon the English vanguard, the rear of the English army surged forward in support; stampeding onto the flimsy bridge. Groaning beneath this sudden weight, the wooden

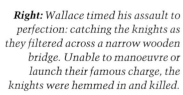

Left: *The English knights arrived at Stirling Bridge expecting to exterminate the Scottish army. No force of infantry had ever defeated mounted knights, let alone one mainly consisting of rebellious farmers.*

Right: *Wallace timed his assault to perfection: catching the knights as they filtered across a narrow wooden bridge. Unable to manoeuvre or launch their famous charge, the knights were hemmed in and killed.*

Left: *With many of Scotland's noble families imprisoned by Edward I, Wallace's army was desperately short of mounted troops. His tactics at Stirling Bridge more than compensated for this weakness.*

Right: *Only the unarmoured archers and a few retainers managed to escape by swimming back across the river. The followers of many knights waited in vain for their return as Wallace's men took no prisoners for ransom.*

structure gave way and collapsed into the water. The vanguard were now trapped against the bend in the river by the Scottish advance, with little room to manoeuvre and no hope of reinforcement. Powerless to intervene, de Warenne could only watch from the far bank as they were swamped by Scottish spearmen.

A few lightly clad English and Welsh foot soldiers escaped by swimming the river, but many more drowned in the attempt or were butchered on land. For the mail-clad knights escape across the water was not an option. Before the Earl's horrified gaze, over a hundred were speared and dragged from their saddles even as they lashed out desperately with maces, battle-axes and swords.

After this débâcle, de Warenne fled to the safety of Berwick and King Edward I resumed command. Wallace was rewarded with a knighthood and the custodial title 'Guardian of Scotland'.

THE SCOTTISH WARS OF INDEPENDENCE

On the night of 18 March 1286 the ink-black sea in the Firth of Forth was lashed by a violent storm. Behind wooden shutters rattled by a rain-soaked wind Yolande, wife of King Alexander III of Scotland, waited patiently for her husband of only five months. It was an appointment the King was not destined to keep. As Alexander hurried the last few miles homeward he became separated from his guides and plunged over the cliffs to his death.

As his sons had predeceased him, Alexander's crown passed to his three-year old grand daughter Margaret. She died four years later and the King of England, Edward I was asked to arbitrate between the numerous distant relatives claiming the throne of Scotland. The strongest claimants were Robert Bruce of Annandale and John Balliol, both descended from the younger brother of King William I. Edward decided in favour of John Balliol, who he then treated as a vassal, commanding him to supply soldiers for Edward's next war with the King of France. Balliol defied Edward and signed a treaty with France, but Edward reacted with typical speed and ruthlessness. By 1297, Balliol was lodged in the Tower of London and an English army remained in Scotland to enforce Edward's will. Many Scottish nobles were imprisoned or went into exile.

Under the leadership of William Wallace, the second son of a minor noble, a new Scottish army assembled in 1297, determined to defy the English King.

FALKIRK I
⤞ 11 July 1298 ⤝

During the summer of 1298 King Edward I laid waste
numerous Scottish villages but he was unable to
bring Wallace's elusive army to battle.

The King was about to abandon the campaign when two Scottish Earls brought him just what he needed to turn the tables upon his elusive foe: precise information about Wallace's position and detailed knowledge of his plans. On 21 July Edward made a rapid night-march towards Falkirk where the Scottish army of 10,000 infantry and 200 cavalry were encamped. The Scots were now forced to do the one thing which they had hoped to avoid: fight a pitched battle.

The Scots deployed in four schiltrons: circular formations, each 'made up wholly of spearmen, standing shoulder to shoulder in deep ranks and facing towards the circumference of the circle, with spears slanting outwards at an oblique angle'[21]. Between the schiltrons Sir John Stewart

of Bonkill deployed his few archers; while the small Scottish cavalry force was commanded by Sir John ('the Red') Comyn of Badenoch. Having made the best use he could of the terrain, Wallace informed his army: 'I have brought you into the ring, now see if you can dance'[22].

Undaunted by the light fall of Scottish arrows, 2,000 English knights, in their great helms and coats of rippling mail, pressed on up the slope. Faced with this awesome mass of mounted mayhem, the resolve of the vastly outnumbered Scottish cavalry was wholly overturned. They fled from the field, leaving their lightly armed bowmen to be ridden down.

Having removed the threat posed by Wallace's cavalry and bowmen, Edward was able to bring up his own archers. Beneath the heavy

Heavily-armed and armoured knights formed the backbone of Edward's army. Riding horses trained to kick enemy foot soldiers, they were supported by a large force of archers.

Wallace's infantry were formed up in deep formations (schiltrons) and stopped the knights' first charge. For the first time in medieval history, foot soldiers had withstood charging knights.

Left: The Scottish infantry beat off the knights, but their own small force of cavalry was driven from the field, allowing the English archers to move forward. The Scottish formations presented an easy target.

***Below:** Survivors of Falkirk regrouped later that summer and carried on a guerrilla war against the English army of occupation. Edward I only triumphed by offering a large reward for Wallace's capture.*

concentration of English arrows, the close-packed ranks upon which the schiltrons relied for defence became a death trap. The Scottish spearmen 'fell like blossom in an orchard when the fruit has ripened … bodies covered the ground as thickly as snow in winter'[23].

When his archers had reduced the Scottish formations to a shambles, Edward ordered his knights to charge again. This time the schiltrons broke and fled. For this conclusive victory the English King had suffered barely 200 casualties, around half of which were mounted knights speared from their saddles in the first unsuccessful charge. By contrast, during the battle and the rout which followed, the English had killed perhaps as many as 4,000 Scots.

William Wallace resigned as Guardian of Scotland, but did not give up the struggle. While others more equipped by birth and wealth to lead their nation yielded and collaborated with their foes, Wallace continued to wage a guerrilla war. He was finally betrayed to the English by fellow Scots in 1305. After a show trial at which the verdict was never in doubt, he was convicted of treason. On 24 August 1305, at Smithfield in London, William Wallace was hung, drawn, quartered and beheaded. Afterwards his head was displayed upon Tower Bridge so that all who passed might tremble at King Edward's justice.

ROBERT THE BRUCE

By the beginning of the fourteenth century Scotland was a powderkeg with a lit fuse. The erstwhile King, John Balliol, had died in exile and the vacant throne consumed the thoughts of Scotland's powerful nobles. A crisis point was reached at Grey Friar's Church in Dumfries on 10 February 1306. There Robert Bruce, Earl of Carrick (grandson of the Bruce whose claim to the throne had been passed over by Edward I), plunged a dagger into his major rival: John 'the Red' Comyn. Shortly afterwards Bruce was crowned King Robert I of Scotland in the Abbey of Scone. However, by June, having been defeated in battle by the English at Methven, Scotland's newly crowned King was forced to flee to the Highlands. With a price on his head as well as a crown, he was now forced to wage a guerrilla war.

The upswing in his fortunes began in 1307. A significant victory at Loudon Hill in May was followed by the death two months later of King Edward I, 'the Hammer of the Scots'. Edward II lacked his father's iron will and aptitude for war, and English strongholds in Scotland began to fall to Bruce's audacious guerrilla tactics. If the Scottish King had begun his career as a political opportunist, he was now very much the nationalist hero.

BANNOCKBURN
⫷ 23–24 June 1314 ⫸

In 1313 Robert the Bruce's brother, Edward, made a typically medieval compromise with the English governor of Stirling Castle. Rather than the Scots continuing to besiege the castle, he agreed to a year's truce on condition that if the castle was not relieved by 24 June 1314, it would surrender.

Bruce was furious: faced with this challenge an English invasion was now a certainty and he would face the sort of pitched battle he wished to avoid. Although he left his preparations very late, Edward II duly invaded Scotland at the head of over 1,000 superbly-equipped knights and supporting foot soldiers. The Scots prepared to give battle at Bannockburn two miles east of Stirling. Bruce's forces numbered less than 500 cavalry and perhaps 10,000 infantry, but at least a third of the latter were 'small folk' – local freemen, chiefs and their retainers – poorly equipped and untrained. Falkirk had been the first occasion that medieval foot soldiers had stood up to the charge of mounted knights, but it had still ended in defeat. None of Edward's

Even after the first day's fighting, the knights' confidence was unbounded. Some knights rushed into action so quickly, they did not don all their protective armour. The defeat of Edward's professional soldiers by Bruce's volunteers astounded medieval Europe.

hardened professionals doubted they could repeat the performance.

King Edward divided his force. The Earls of Gloucester and Hereford were to advance straight up the Stirling road, driving the Scots into another force of knights under Sir Robert de Clifford and Sir Henry Beaumont. Gloucester and Hereford squabbled over precedence and set off, riding side-by-side in frosty silence. Gloucester's frame of mind was in no way improved by the aggravating sight of Hereford's nephew, Sir Henry de Bohun, prancing back and forth upon his richly caparisoned mount fifty yards ahead of everybody else. De Bohun soon came upon another lone rider inspecting the Scottish troops half hidden in the woods beyond. As this stranger trotted along on a 'grey palfry litill and joly'[24] the sun flashed from a gold circlet on his helmet. It was none other than Bruce himself. Without hesitation the young English knight couched his lance and spurred his war-horse forward.

Bruce was unwilling to retreat from such a challenge before the massed ranks of his entire army, and as Sir Henry thundered towards him, the Scottish King swerved his nimbler horse aside, rose up in his stirrups and dealt his opponent a mighty blow with his battle axe. It fell with such ferocity that the blade 'cleft de Bohun to the brisket'.[25] Inspired by their King's example, his troops surged towards the English vanguard emerging from the trees. The English fell back in disarray. Meanwhile, the detachment commanded by Lords Clifford and Beaumont had

Full helms like this became popular during the 13th century. Edward II's knights were superbly equipped and clearly expected to crush Bruce's army with a single all-out charge.

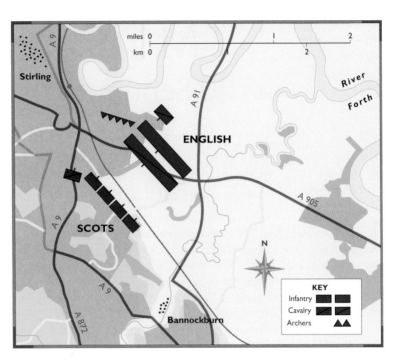

encountered the Earl of Moray's spearmen on Bruce's left flank. The Scottish schiltron proved impervious and, as Sir James Douglas approached with Scottish reinforcements, they too withdrew, ending all hostilities for the day.

As the sun rose on the morning of 24 June, King Edward was amazed to see the Scottish formations advancing: 'What, will yonder Scots fight?' he asked of no one in particular. A little over a hundred yards away the schiltrons stopped and the Scots began to kneel. Edward II exclaimed: 'They kneel for mercy!'[26]. 'For mercy yes ...' replied one of his knights, '... but not from you. From God for their sins. These men will win or die'[27].

As the realisation dawned that the Scots truly intended to fight, the English knights hurried to make ready and mount their horses. In their arrogance, the knights did not bother to form up properly and attacked piecemeal. Again, to the knights' astonishment, the Scottish foot soldiers stood firm. Gloucester, who had not bothered to don his surcoat, died unrecognised among the Scottish spears. Soon, the Earl of Moray and Sir James Douglas were pressing their schiltrons forward, penning the English between the waters of the Bannock burn and the Pelstream.

Edward II proved incapable of co-ordinating his forces. Though some English archers crossed the Pelstream, from where they could pour arrows into Douglas's left flank, they were unsupported by any knights and were ridden down by Scottish cavalry. On the other side of the Pelstream, sweating in the summer heat, the English knights were attempting to fight their way out of the death-trap in which they found themselves. 'So great was the spilling of blood that it stood in pools on the ground ... knights and horses [might be] seen tumbling on the ground and many a rich and splendid garment fouled roughly underfoot'[28]. Realising that all hope was lost, Edward's personal bodyguard drove a path through the press to drag him to safety.

In the wake of his victory at Bannockburn 'Robert de Bruce was commonly called King of Scotland by all men, because he had acquired it by force of arms'. All that is, except the English King. Edward's pride prevented him from ever acknowledging Scottish sovereignty. Further invasions followed, the with English returning to Edinburgh in 1321. It was not until 1328 that Edward's successor, Edward III, finally recognised Robert Bruce as King of an independent Scotland.

MYTON
⤜✥⤛ 20 September 1319 ⤜✥⤛

After the battle of Bannockburn in 1314 the English were ignominiously expelled from Scotland. Four years later, the Scots had captured Berwick-upon-Tweed. Edward II moved to York, ready for war.

In 1319 Edward II laid siege to Berwick. In response an army of several thousand Scots, commanded by the Earl of Moray and Lord James Douglas (both veterans of Bannockburn), marched through the north of England torching all in their path. Their secret objective lay in Edward's court at York; from whence they hoped to abduct his 21-year old Queen, Isabella, and hold her hostage. By the time the English learned of this plan from a captured spy, the Scots were already at Myton only thirteen miles from York. Forced to improvise an army from whatever sources were at hand, the local Mayor and Bishops hastily co-opted 'laymen, clerks and men of religion'[29]. As they set out towards their objective, this band of unlikely warriors did not so much march, as stroll: 'all scattered through the fields, and in no kind of array'[30]. After a casual picnic lunch, they finally arrived at the stone and timber village of Myton.

For their part the Scots could hardly believe their eyes. Rapidly concluding 'these are not soldiers but huntsmen; they will not achieve much'[31], their main concern was not to frighten off their unsuspecting English foes before they could bring them to battle. To this end they 'set on fire three stacks of hay; and the smoke thereof was so huge that [the] Englishmen might not see …'[32]. Under this blinding screen they prepared for battle. Slightly unnerved by this development 'the Englishmen came on sadly'[33] only to discover that, lurking on the other side of the smoke lay their worst nightmare. Among the veteran Scottish army were men 'picked … from the whole of Scotland for their fighting ability'[34]. By contrast, most of the 'sad' English soldiers in the

Raid and counter-raid followed Bannockburn, with parties of Scottish cavalry penetrating far into northern England. In 1318 the Scots captured the major English fortress of Berwick.

Perhaps hoping to achieve a second battle of Otterburn, the clergy assembled local forces in Yorkshire and marched to intercept the Douglas's raiding party.

KEY

English
Scots
Battlefield area
Viewpoint
Car Park

N

Myton Bridge

Myton-on-Swale

miles 0
km 0

field that day were entirely 'untrained in the art of war'[35]. Faced with its reality they suddenly found themselves far 'readier to flee than fight'[36].

The outcome of this unequal contest was never in doubt. Formed up 'according to their custom in a single [division]', the Scots 'uttered together a tremendous shout to terrify the English, who straightaway began to take to their heels at the sound'[37]. Unfortunately they had failed to secure their escape route over the River Swale. 'Alas! What sorrow for the English husbandmen'[38]: if they knew nothing of war when the day began, their ignorance was soon put to rights by the Scottish 'hobilars' [mounted infantry] who now cut off their retreat to the bridge. Ruthlessly harried by the spears of their enemies, 'about one thousand … were drowned in the water of the Swale'[39].

By the onset of darkness the total death toll at Myton had reached a reputed 4,000, of whom by far the majority were English. By contrast most of the Scots 'returned unharmed to Scotland'[40]. For Edward II already at odds with many English nobles. It was another disaster. Afterwards he was forced to raise the siege of Berwick and ultimately agreed to a two year truce.

Left: *The Douglases were professional warriors, as heavily-armed and equipped as the English knights. It was the reverse of Bannockburn: Scottish professional soldiers fighting English peasants-turned-soldiers.*

Right: *With few knights or other professional warriors with them, the Yorkshire militia lasted only a matter of minutes once the Scottish army charged.*

BOROUGHBRIDGE
⪼ 16 March 1322 ⪻

Edward II was as tormented by his barons as his father and grandfather had been. Of all these troublesome lords he detested none more fervently than his cousin, Thomas, Earl of Lancaster, killer of the notorious Piers Gaveston.

Lancaster was the most powerful of the English nobles, but he failed to secure much support when he finally instigated a rebellion. Most nobles stayed neutral, watching and waiting. Lancaster had left his rising too late. He had mustered only 3,000 men when he encountered the King at Burton-on-Trent. Greatly outnumbered by the royal army, he fled northwards through Yorkshire. Meanwhile, the King's Warden of Carlisle, Sir Andrew de Harcla, had 'summoned, under very heavy penalties … knights, esquires and other able men of … [the Border region]'[41]. Having thus assembled a force some 4,000-strong, he marched through the night to block Lancaster's retreat at Boroughbridge. When the Earl arrived the next morning, Sir Andrew had stationed all 'his knights and some pikemen on foot at the northern end of the bridge, and other pikemen he stationed in schiltron [a defensive block] … opposite the ford … to oppose the cavalry wherein the enemy put his trust'[42].

Lancaster himself took command of the rebel cavalry at the ford. However, as the narrow bridge 'afforded no path for horsemen in battle array'[43] it would have to be stormed by men on foot. This task he delegated to his son-in-law, Sir Roger de Clifford: a man much admired for his physical strength. With the arrows of de Harcla's archers already singing through the air in 'a constant discharge'[44], Clifford advanced. At his side were a handful of knights including the Earl of Hereford: a 'worthy knight of renown throughout all Christendom'[45].

De Harcla's Border levies were taking no chances. As the Earl of Hereford laid about them with his sword, 'a worthless creature, skulked under the bridge, and fiercely with a spear smote the noble knight into the fundament, so that his bowels came out there'[46]. Thus impaled, Hereford 'fell immediately and was killed'[47]. The remaining knights were unable to make headway against the unyielding pikes of the Borderers.

Left: Lancaster's knights had seen their master execute the King's lover Piers Gaveston. Now Edward II had a new favourite, Hugh Despenser, and the rebellious nobles looked forward to disposing of him the same way.

Right: The men of the borders had no compunction about fighting Lancaster's supporters. By the time Lancaster's army reached Boroughbridge, it was obvious he had failed to attract enough other nobles to his cause. The rebellion was doomed.

Eventually, Sir Roger de Clifford was 'grievously wounded with pikes and arrows, and driven back...'[48].

At the ford, Lancaster's cavalry were faring little better. Though they attempted to force a passage, they could not enter the water 'by reason of the number and density of arrows which the archers discharged upon them and their horses'[49].

The Earl sent messengers to Sir Andrew, requesting an armistice until morning, when he would either give him battle or surrender to him'[50].

Amid the arrow-studded carnage of battle, with the weeping of the wounded in his ears, Sir Andrew was in no mood for soft words and bellowed his reply across the water: 'Yield, Traitor, Yield!'. The negotiations were not going as well as Lancaster had hoped. Moreover, the charge of treason hung heavy with him and he replied 'Nay ... Traitor be we none, and to you will we never us yield while our lives last'. Nonetheless, with darkness drawing in, both sides were reluctant to force the issue further that day and the overnight truce which Lancaster had requested was eventually accepted.

With two or three hundred of the Earl's small force already dead, his soldiers knew that the odds were mounting against them and many fled under cover of darkness. By dawn, Lancaster no longer commanded a sufficiently large force to contemplate battle. Feeling the hangman's noose closing about their necks, the remainder of the rebel force now 'left their horses and putting off their armour looked round for ancient worn-out

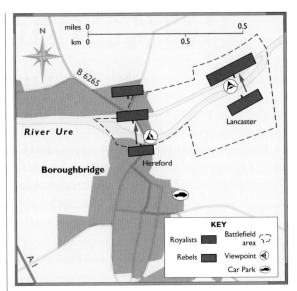

garments and took to the road as beggars. But their caution was of no avail, for not one single well-known man among them all escaped'[51].

Lancaster himself was found in a nearby chapel 'kneeling down upon his knees, and turning his face towards the Cross', where he sought solace in a higher authority than that vested in Sir Andrew de Harcla. As he prayed aloud, "Almighty God! To you I yield myself, and put myself into thy mercy" ... the base worthless creatures leapt upon him, on every side ... and despoiled him of armour, & clothed him in ... his squire's livery, and forth led him unto York'[52]. There he was 'confined in the castle to awaite ... the pleasure of my lord the King'[53]. Edward II was not in a generous mood. His 'pleasure' was to have Lancaster's head struck from his shoulders.

The border levies and de Harcla's men-at-arms blocked both the bridge and the ford. Lancaster's army failed to break through at either point, and his men began to desert during the following night.

HALIDON HILL
19 July 1333

The death of Robert the Bruce provided a perfect opportunity for Edward Balliol. In 1332 he returned from exile at the head of an invading army, defeated the royal Scottish forces and was crowned King of Scotland. Deposed only four months later, he took refuge with King Edward III.

Seeing a chance to undermine the hard-won Scottish sovereignty which he had been forced to recognise in 1328, Edward III offered Balliol English support in order to regain his lost crown. In return Balliol was pledged to reward Edward with a large slice of Scotland. The icing on the cake was to be the return of Berwick, which had been in Scottish hands since 1318. Accordingly, in May 1333, Edward and Balliol laid siege to Berwick with 10,000 men.

Sir Archibald Douglas, commander of the Scottish Royal army, attempted to draw off the English by raiding the surrounding countryside. It was to no avail. Steadfastly ignoring the bait, Edward continued his siege. In July the

The Scots advanced slowly across marshy ground and up the hill. The English archers took steady aim and let loose a storm of arrows.

exhausted citizens of Berwick finally appealed for a truce. Under the terms of this agreement they agreed to surrender Berwick if Douglas's relief force had failed to attain one of three goals by 19 July. Accordingly, Douglas was informed that within four days he must either: win a pitched battle; cross a given stretch of the river Tweed; insert 200 troops into Berwick itself; or accept the loss of the city. Edward then settled comfortably into position on Halidon Hill, dominating the approach to Berwick, and waited for Douglas to arrive.

On the morning of the deadline a Scottish army of 1,200 men-at-arms and 13,500 spearmen drew up to the north of Halidon Hill. Before them lay an area of boggy marshland which proved impassable to their horses. Around midday, having waited for the rising tide on the Tweed to cut off any possibility of English retreat, they advanced on foot through the treacherous mire and began to ascend the slopes of Halidon Hill.

King Edward's army were formed up on foot in three divisions to receive them; the King commanding in the centre, with the Earl of Norfolk on his left and Balliol on his right. However, despite the strength of the English deployment, 'the Scots had so great an army and such a great force that when the English saw them they were down cast'. Alarmed by the sullen attitude of his army King Edward 'rode about everywhere … and encouraged his men well and nobly, and generously promised them a good reward provided that they conducted themselves well against the great multitude of

In 1330, at the age of 17, Edward III had seized power from his mother, Queen Isabel and her lover Roger Mortimer. Three years later, he led the English army to victory at Halidon Hill.

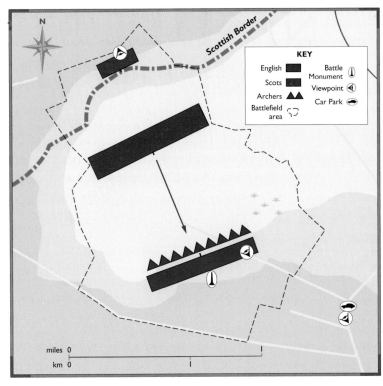

their Scottish enemies'. The Scottish forces ploughed heroically up the hill into a savage shower of arrows. Realising that Balliol's division was on the right of the English line they had 'diverted their course in order that they might first meet and attack the division of him who … laid claim to [their] kingdom'. However, before they could come to grips with the usurper, hundreds 'were so grievously wounded in the face and blinded by the host of English archery … that they were helpless, and quickly began to turn away their faces from the arrow flights and to fall'[54].

Though Sir Archibald Douglas personally led the Scottish vanguard, the English troops of Edward Balliol had every advantage. In this desperate and 'prolonged struggle there perished 500 of the strongest and choicest of all the people in Scotland'[55]. With the death of Douglas himself, the vanguard finally broke and the remaining Scottish divisions were forced into disorderly retreat. As they ran for their lives 'there might be seen many a Scotsman cast down onto the earth dead, and their banners displayed, and hacked into pieces, and many a good halberd of steel

bathed in their blood'[56]. With an estimated 4,000 Scots killed on Halidon Hill, Edward III had regained Berwick and inflicted a crushing defeat on his enemies.

Balliol was eventually installed upon the Scottish throne as a puppet King. True to his bargain, he ceded a large part of his new kingdom to Edward; thereby condemning his people to another century of cross-border warfare as they battled to recover their lost territory.

The power of the longbow demonstrated at Halidon Hill made a profound impression on Edward. Within a few years he was at war with France, and his armies would include large contingents of archers from Wales and England. At Crécy in 1346, they would defeat the flower of French chivalry.

NEVILLE'S CROSS
⪼ 17 October 1346 ⪻

David II regained the Scottish throne while Edward III of England was fighting for the throne of France. On 26 August 1346, Edward III destroyed the French army at Crécy, but David was already assembling a Scottish army to invade England in support of his allies.

King David led an army of 15,000 Scots across the English border. However, England was not entirely unprepared. Anticipating an attack while he was in France, Edward III had appointed Sir Ralph de Neville, Sir Henry de Percy, and the Archbishop of York to guard his northern marches. At the head of 700 men-at-arms supported by 10,000 archers and hobilars, they set out to confront him.

On the morning of 17 October, Sir William Douglas and a detachment of 500 Scottish hobilars were busy plundering the town of Merrington. As a heavy mist had descended, they were oblivious to the proximity of the English army. The first sign that the enemy was upon them was 'the trampling of horses and the shock of armoured men'[57] emerging from the fog. This unexpected interruption threw the Scottish raiders into 'such a spasm of panic that William and all those with him were utterly at a loss to know which way to turn'.[58] In consequence, less than half of Douglas's force made it back to King David's camp to raise the alarm.

Having announced their presence, the English deployed on a narrow ridge near Neville's Cross, one of several ancient crosses which encircled the city of Durham. There they waited for the Scots to march out to meet them. As the ground was not ideal for cavalry, the knights and men-at-arms were stationed in the rear, while the three

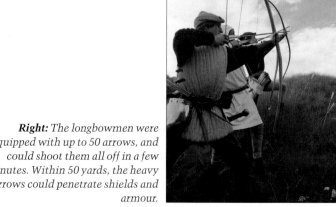

Left: The terrain was not particularly suited to mounted action, and the bulk of the English army consisted of archers. Most of the knights dismounted to fight alongside them, just as they had done at Crécy.

Right: The longbowmen were equipped with up to 50 arrows, and could shoot them all off in a few minutes. Within 50 yards, the heavy arrows could penetrate shields and armour.

divisions of infantry were drawn up with archers to the fore.

The Scottish King received the news calmly. Ordering 'his breakfast to be made ready, [he] said he would return to it when he had slain the English at the point of the sword'.[59] It was only as the Scots set off over Crossgate moor that the full strength of the enemy position became apparent. Earl Patrick, whom King David had appointed to lead the Scottish vanguard, surveyed the terrain and asked to lead the rearguard instead!

Command of the vanguard thus fell to the Earl of Moray, who pressed forward on the Scottish right and immediately ran into difficulties. Funnelled into an increasingly narrow front by a ravine, the vanguard became tangled with the central division of the army, commanded by the King. The resultant mass of struggling Scots presented an ideal target for the 'archers of England [who] were quick and light, and shot with good aim and skill, and so fiercely that it was a terror to see'.[60] The Scottish left, under Robert the High Steward and Earl Patrick, charged home with spears and 'great axes, sharp and hard' and gave the English 'many great strokes',[61] but they were forced back by the arrival of the English cavalry. When Moray, on the right, also gave ground to a cavalry charge, the King's division was left perilously exposed. Here was a small patch of hell: 'the trumpets

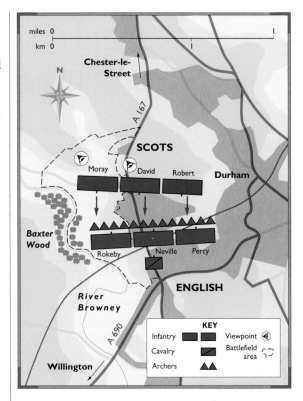

blaring, shields clashing, arrows flying, lances thrusting, wounded men yelling and troops shouting'.[62] By dusk the Scots could endure no more. A thousand of their number lay dead, including the Earl of Moray. Abandoning their King amid the 'sundered armour, broken heads, and … many laid low on the field'[63] they fled. King David was cut-off and surrounded in the rout. The wounded King was captured by John of Coupland, although not before knocking out two of his would-be captor's front teeth.

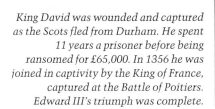

King David was wounded and captured as the Scots fled from Durham. He spent 11 years a prisoner before being ransomed for £65,000. In 1356 he was joined in captivity by the King of France, captured at the Battle of Poitiers. Edward III's triumph was complete.

OTTERBURN

⊰⊱ 19 August 1388 ⊰⊱

In 1388 England's young King Richard II was preoccupied by a peasant revolt. The powerful Douglas clan seized the opportunity to launch more ambitious raids into English territory.

Sir Archibald Douglas marched a large column of Scots to Carlisle while James, the second Earl of Douglas, led a smaller raiding force of around 300 mounted men-at-arms and 2,000 infantry into Northumberland: the territory of the Percys. The Earl of Northumberland duly sent his sons Sir Henry Percy (known as 'Hotspur') and Sir Ralph Percy to block Sir James Douglas's progress at Newcastle.

During one of several skirmishes outside the gates of Newcastle, Sir James Douglas snatched Sir Henry Percy's lance pennon. The Scots then departed for home, but not before Douglas had mocked Percy by promising to display the captured pennon before his tent. When young Hotspur swore to recover it, the Scot tauntingly offered to wait and give him battle at Otterburn.

The moonlit night of 19 August did indeed find Sir James Douglas camped near Otterburn. However, he was waiting, not for Henry Percy, but for 'Market Thursday' at nearby Elsdon.

At that very moment, Hotspur was surveying the Scottish camp from the shadows on the other side of the valley. With the rear of his column still spread out for some three miles along the Newcastle road, he and his knights were debating their options. It might be possible to manoeuvre some forces behind the Scots and launch a twin-pronged attack. However, it would take time to bring up the column, and with every moment that passed they risked discovery by Scottish picquets. The distant lowing of stolen Percy cattle carried on the gentle night air from the Scottish camp made up Hotspur's mind for him.

With the moonlight glinting off their spears, the English crept through the shadowy undergrowth. Gathered around the warm circles of their fires, the Scots were relaxing: cooking suppers, cleaning weapons, playing dice, telling stories, and tending to small domestic tasks.

This peaceful scene was shattered

The town of Elson was busy in late August, preparing for the regular cattle market. Out in the hills near Otterburn, a Scottish raiding force was assembling, commanded by Sir James Douglas. Already weighed down with plunder, this was to be their last raid before returning to Scotland.

The English nobles assembled an army outside Newcastle, but were defeated in a series of skirmishes before the Scottish raiders withdrew. By stealing his cattle, and parading his captured pennon, the Scottish commander made a bitter personal enemy of the English commander, Sir Henry Percy.

when the rampant blue lion on Hotspur's shield sprang forward into the firelight and the air was rent by his war cry, 'Percy! Percy!'. The Scots scrambled to their arms, but the murder was already upon them. Vats of scalding stew were overturned, carts were upended in the panic, and tents were set ablaze, their screaming occupants fleeing from the hot flames onto the cold steel waiting outside. Through this mayhem of flashing blades and dancing flames, Hotspur's banner pushed ever forward as he searched for Douglas. As chance would have it, the English attack had fallen upon the baggage train rather than among the rich pavilions of the knights further up the valley. Provoked beyond endurance as the banner of the hated Percys bore down upon him, Sir James Douglas determined to encourage his men by example. Taking 'his axe in both his hands [he] entered so into the press ... that none durst approach near him, and none was so well armed that he feared him not for the great strokes that he gave'.[64] Thus, with his war axe devouring his foes, he 'went ever forward like a hardy Hector, willing alone to conquer the field and to discomfort his enemies;

but at last he was encountered with three spears all at once – the one struck him on the shoulder, another on the breast and the stroke glinted down to his belly, and the third struck him in the thigh'.[65]

Even as Douglas took his death blows, Hotspur was also wounded and captured by the Scots. The rest of the English quit the field by dawn.

Sir Henry Percy ('Hotspur') led the pursuit. Finding the Scottish forces at Otterburn, he ordered an immediate night attack, despite the obvious handicap that his archers would be ineffective in the darkness.

HOMILDON HILL

ᐳ 14 September 1402 ᐸ

In 1399, the Percy family helped Henry Bolingbroke
depose King Richard II of England and become Henry
IV. While the Percies aided Henry IV against a series
of rebellions, the Scots raided England in force.

In 1402, Sir Archibald Douglas's men laid
waste to a large swathe of northern England,
while Henry IV was dealing with the revolt of
Owen Glendower in Wales. The task of dealing
with the Scots fell to the Douglas's arch-rivals,
the Percies. It was the scale of his success which
was to prove Douglas's undoing. Having
exhausted their energies appropriating
everything of value between Scotland and
Newcastle, his men were hauling their plunder
homewards when they came upon Henry Percy
(senior), Earl of Northumberland, barring their
escape. The Earl and his men were positioned
some five miles north-west of the town of
Wooler. Realising that he had little option but to
fight a battle, Douglas deployed on the
precipitous slopes of nearby Homildon Hill and
waited for the English to attack.

The Earl of Northumberland drew his army up
on the plain at the base of the hill and
thoughtfully surveyed the Scottish position. His
knights and men-at-arms were backed by a large
contingent of longbowmen, whose devastating
archery had won so many battles over the
previous century. The question was, how best to
deploy them. His son, the ever impetuous
Hotspur, recommended a suicidal frontal assault.
Dismissing this suggestion (many a soldier must
have heaved a sigh of relief that Hotspur was not
in command) Northumberland ordered a large
contingent of archers to ascend nearby Harehope
Hill. This feature, a short distance to the north-
west, rose almost to the same height as
Homildon Hill. There the archers would be
protected from enemy cavalry by the steep slope
and yet remain within bow-range of the Scots.
The Earl's remaining bowmen formed a deadly
frontage for his infantry on the plain.

Even before the archers on Harehope Hill were
fully in position, they had 'smothered [the Scots]
in arrows'.[66] Though Douglas's much smaller
contingent of archers retaliated, there was no

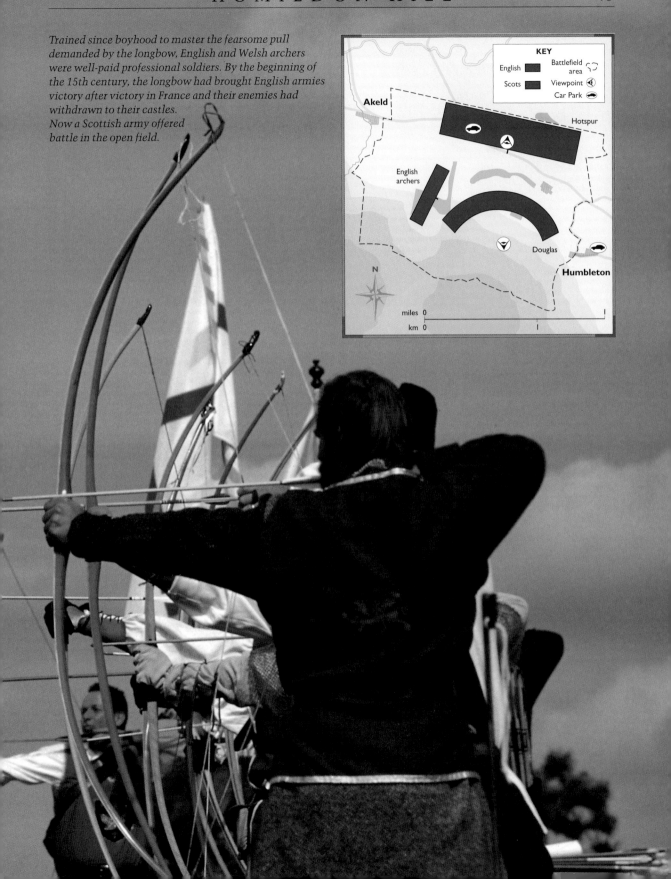

Trained since boyhood to master the fearsome pull demanded by the longbow, English and Welsh archers were well-paid professional soldiers. By the beginning of the 15th century, the longbow had brought English armies victory after victory in France and their enemies had withdrawn to their castles.
Now a Scottish army offered battle in the open field.

KEY

English

Scots

Battlefield area

Viewpoint

Car Park

Akeld

Hotspur

English archers

Douglas

Humbleton

N

miles 0

km 0

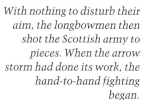

Left: The battle began with the English archers driving off the much smaller number of Scottish bowmen.

With nothing to disturb their aim, the longbowmen then shot the Scottish army to pieces. When the arrow storm had done its work, the hand-to-hand fighting began.

escape from the greater volume of English arrows, which 'fell like a storm of rain'[67] transfixing 'the hands and arms of the Scots to their own lances'.[68]

This long-range culling provoked the Scottish knight Sir John Swinton to an absolute fury. This was not war as he knew it and his voice raged against such unchivalrous tactics: 'Illustrious comrades! Who has bewitched you today … Why do you not join in hand-to-hand battle nor as men take heart to attack your enemies who are in a hurry to destroy you with their flying arrows as if you were little fallow-deer … Those who are willing should go down with me and we shall move among our enemies in the Lord's name, either to save our lives in so doing or at least to fall as knights with honour'.[69]

Although he could not have known it, Swinton was railing vainly against the future face of warfare. Nonetheless, his rousing words prompted Adam de Gordon to kneel before him and attest for all to hear that in his opinion Swinton was the bravest knight in the land. As Swinton and Gordon were rivals of long standing, this protestation had considerable impact; inspiring 'a band of a hundred respected knights to follow these leaders'[70] into battle. Knowing that they were advancing to certain death, this small band of knightly brothers-in-arms marched down the hill to teach their enemies the meaning of chivalry.

Sir Archibald Douglas himself was no less gallant. Seizing a lance, he 'rode down the hill with a troop of his horse … and strove to rush on the archers. When the archers saw this, they retreated, but still firing, so vigorously, so resolutely, so effectively, that they pierced the armour, perforated the helmets, pitted the swords, split the lances, and pierced all equipment with ease. The Earl Douglas was pierced with five wounds, notwithstanding his elaborate armour'.[71] At this point the remainder of the Scottish army, which had not descended the hill, 'turned tail and fled … for fear of the death-dealing arrows'.[72] Eventually, trapped by the River Tweed, most of the survivors surrendered. Of those who chose to attempt the swim 'the waters devoured, so it was said, five hundred'.[73]

It was a medieval custom that the ransoms raised on prisoners of noble birth belonged to the victorious commanders. Having captured an unusually high number of knights at this battle, including the wounded Earl of Douglas, the Percies now calculated that they stood to collect a king's ransom. Unfortunately for them, King Henry IV agreed with this assessment. Tempted beyond endurance by the size of the prize, he broke with tradition and demanded that the prisoners be turned over to him. This was a terrible mistake, an insult that would not be forgotten. The honour of the Percies demanded vengeance.

SHREWSBURY
❧ 21 July 1403 ❧

Complaining that the Henry IV expected them to
subsidise the defence of his northern borders, the
Percy family disobeyed his command to hand over
all prisoners held for ransom after Homildon Hill
and began to plot a coup d'état with the Welsh
patriot, Owen Glendower.

In July 1403, as Hotspur rode south to link up
with Glendower, Henry IV was already
marching north with an army of about 5,000
men; not to crush the Percies, but to lend them
support against an expected Scottish invasion!
Stunned by news of their rebellion, Henry
cancelled his march north, and raced eastward to
intercept Hotspur's army of 4,000 rebels at
Shrewsbury.

In his heart of hearts the King found it hard to
accept that things had come to such a pass. The
rebel forces were drawn up on a ridge three miles
to the north of the town, but before marching out
of Shrewsbury, he sent the local abbot to offer
'peace and pardon' if Hotspur would 'desist from
his adventure'.[74] In response, Hotspur despatched

his trusted uncle, Thomas Percy, with demands
for a reformation in the government of the realm.

Having no real wish to make war upon his
most powerful barons, the King agreed. All was
in order for both sides to down arms and part as
friends. The only fly in the ointment was 'Uncle
Thomas', whose blood still seethed over the lost
ransom money. Returning from the peace talks
two hours before sunset, he informed Hotspur
that the King flatly refused all conditions! The
dispute was to be settled by combat.

Hotspur's vanguard was led by none other
than his former enemy, Sir Archibald Douglas,
who the Percies had fought and captured at
Homildon Hill a year earlier. The veteran
Cheshire bowmen under his command began the

Left: *Loyal to the nobles who
recruited and paid them, the Percies'
archers had no hesitation in fighting
the King's army. For the first time,
two hostile units of longbowmen
prepared to do battle.*

Right: *The archers sometimes carried
small shields (bucklers) which they
used in hand-to-hand fighting after
expending their ammunition.*

fight, drawing their bows 'so fast that … the sun which at that time was bright and clear then lost its brightness so thick were the arrows'.[75] Although the King's side reciprocated with 'a shower of sharp points against their adversaries',[76] the smaller, rebel force got the better of this murderous exchange. In Henry's ranks, men fell 'as fast as leaves fall in autumn after the hoar-frost'[77] and to prevent the spread of panic, he moved the main part of his army up in support.

Now, with the arrows of both sides exhausted, the combatants 'put their hands to swords and axes with which they began to slay each other, and the leaders of the advance guards … with lances couched struck each other. And the men and horses were slain in such wise as it was pitiable to see'.[78]

In the thickest part of this cruel combat,

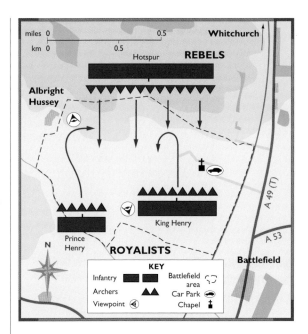

Fabulously wealthy, controlling their own armies and fortresses, the great English nobles sensed new political opportunities. These 'overmighty subjects' could only be kept in check by a strong King.

Hotspur was pressing forward with thirty mounted knights in a bid to kill the King. Striking left and right from their saddles, they hacked limbs and cracked skulls, carving a grizzly 'lane in the middle of the host til [Hotspur] came to the king's banner'. There his intended regicide was confounded by the presence of several decoys all wearing the royal surcoat and 'he slew the earl of Stafford and sir Thomas Blount [the King's standard bearer] and others'.[79]

Meanwhile, elsewhere amid the brutal mêlée, the fifteen-year-old Prince of Wales (later Henry V) who was 'then fighting his first battle, was shot in the face by an arrow: boy though he was, he did not falter, but with courage beyond his years, disregarding his wounds, cheered on his troops to vengeance'.[80] The young Prince's counter-attack passed like a bloody arrow straight through Hotspur's line and, turning about, struck them again in the rear. The rebels were now pinioned between two forces: with the King in front and the Prince behind. As neither side wore uniforms the 'rebel army fell into a state of great perplexity, not knowing whether they were fighting against the king's party or their own'.[81]

In the midst of this confusion, the rumour went around that the King had been slain and the

With full plate armour now in widespread use, two-handed swords became popular again. Developed in France and Germany, they survived in Scotland until the 18th century.

THE MEDIEVAL ARCHERY DUEL

Late medieval battles invariably began with an archery duel. In the bloody minutes that this arrow storm lasted, the knights, squires, billmen and other, less well-equipped levies could only stand and endure it. The veterans among them were careful to keep their heads well down, and urged others to do the same. Only a novice would allow his curious eyes to wander upwards in order to watch the dark wooden cloud descend. A man whose face was exposed to the heavens during those lethal moments stood to loose not only his sight, but his life.

At long range the bowmen used 'flight-arrows' with elongated shafts designed for distance. For closer targets they swapped to 'sheaf-arrows'. At short range the heavier 'pile' (or head) on a sheaf arrow was capable of punching through armour. The bowmen on both sides worked furiously to keep six arrows in the air at any one time. At this rate of fire they quickly exhausted the buckets of arrows which had been prepared for use and so 'retrievers' were sent forward. It was the retriever's task to run between the front lines of the opposing armies and pick up undamaged arrows. This required some nerve. As fast as the arrows were snatched up, a new crop would fall from the sky to replace them.

For those who could only stand and wait to be hit, the archery duel was galling indeed. To keep up their nerves and drown out the ominous rattle of arrow heads striking armour, the billmen shouted abuse or battle cries at the enemy. Meanwhile the wounded, walking or crawling according to their injuries, would begin trailing away to the rear. Among them went the newly blinded, screaming for guides to lead them away. The faint-hearted, where not restrained by their companions, were only to quick to oblige. This torment would only end when one of the opposing commanders judged that his bowmen had inflicted enough damage, or that his men could endure no more. At this point the only thing left to do was attack, advancing rapidly to cross the killing zone as quickly as possible.

When the trumpets sounded the signal to advance the billmen passed forward between the ranks of bowmen in order to form a new frontage of steel for the next brutal phase of the battle. The bowmen then shouldered their bows and, arming themselves with swords or falchions and plate-sized bucklers (shields), formed the new rear ranks.

cry went up among Hotspur's men: 'Henry Percy king!' None on the field that day was more startled to hear this than the King himself, still very much alive. To encourage his own men and deter the rebels, he immediately retaliated by shouting 'with all his might, "Henry Percy is dead!"'.[82] To the shock of all within earshot, there was no reply. With his failure to roar denial, came the heart-stopping realisation that the dynamic Harry Hotspur must indeed be dead. Some of the rebels 'began to retire, seeing that their only hope lay in flight'.[83] However, the action had become so widespread and the din of battle so great that 'many of the combatants', unaware of Hotspur's death, 'struggled with such obstinacy that when night came on they did not know which side had won; and they sank down in all directions a chance-medley of weary, wounded, bruised and bleeding men'.[84]

Hotspur was indeed dead, killed by an arrow in the face. His father submitted, only to die in another rebellion five years later. The bitter contest at Shrewsbury heralded a new form of warfare in England: concentrated archery followed by savage hand-to-hand fighting. There were to be many more such brutal actions before the last arrow of the bloody fifteenth century was shot. Henry V's death in 1422 created a power vacuum that led to Civil War.

SOLDIERING IN THE WARS OF THE ROSES

In an era when kings still ruled by personal charisma and political skill, the reign of Henry VI was a disaster. Only nine months old at the time of his succession, his long minority was to foster dangerous ambitions among the aristocracy. Powerful nobles vied for influence in the King's council. By the time Henry finally came of age in 1444, his realm was desperately in need of a strong and stabilising hand but the young King lacked the ability to control the council and halt the growing anarchy and corruption. According to an anonymous chronicler of the period '… the realm of England was out of all good governance … for the king was simple and led by covetous counsel, and owed more than he was worth'.[1]

Overgenerous, indecisive, lacking in military awareness, Henry made virtually every conceivable mistake and then compounded them by a sudden descent into madness in August 1453. The resultant power vacuum provided an opportunity for Richard Duke of York, whose rival claim to the throne dated back to the death of Richard II in 1399. Despite the opposition of the Queen, Margaret of Anjou, who was convinced that the Duke represented a major threat to the succession of her son, the ruling council of nobles awarded him the office of Protector of England during the King's illness.

York seized the opportunity to take action against his powerful rivals in the ruling House of Lancaster. The King's favourite, Edmund Beaufort, Duke of Somerset, was despatched to the Tower of London, only to be released when the King regained his sanity at the end of 1454. Fearing retribution, the Duke of York prepared to defend his position by force. The result was the first battle of St Albans in 1455, at which first blood went to the Yorkists. Somerset was cut down, King Henry relapsed and York was reinstated as Protector.

By 1456, Henry was sufficiently recovered to resume his position. However, although he had sufficient wit to placate York by making him chief of the ruling council, it is doubtful that he ever made a complete recovery. From this point onwards, the hand behind the ruling House of Lancaster was increasingly that of Queen Margaret. It was soon to become evident that the velvet glove of Anjou contained a fist of steel.

In 1458 Henry VI made one final effort to reconcile the feuding between the nobles of York and Lancaster with the bizarre spectacle of the 'love-day' parade. In order to symbolise peaceful accord, these bitterest of enemies were induced to plod behind the King, two by two, through the streets of London to St Paul's Cathedral. The Duke of York's partner was none other than the Queen herself. If he could but have known it, his smiling companion dearly wished to see his head impaled above the gates of York. Within a year the dynastic power struggle between these two was to propel England into civil war.

By the Wars of the Roses, most soldiers fought on foot with two-handed pole arms. They carried swords and small shields as secondary weapons.

BLORE HEATH

23 September 1459

In the spring of 1459 the Queen presented indictments for treason against the Duke of York and his nephew the Earl of Warwick. The response of the Yorkists was to raise an army.

As the Earl of Salisbury (Warwick's father) hurried his forces south to rendezvous with York at Ludlow, he was intercepted at Blore Heath by the Queen's forces under Lord Audley. Outnumbering the Yorkists by 2:1, Audley augmented his advantages by deploying on a shallow ridge. Although Audley had partially concealed the true strength of his Lancastrian army behind the crest of the ridge, Salisbury could glimpse a formidable number of banners and standards poking up from '… behind a great hedge of trees'.[2] Realising that any attempt to withdraw in the face of such a force could only end in disaster, the Earl made the best of his position. Deploying with his left flank protected by a wood and Hempmill Brook along his front, he drew up his supply wagons to create an improvised field defence for his right wing. Then, having 'prepared themselves for death, his knights and followers all kissed the ground where they stood …'[3] determined that they would live or die upon the spot.

Having made ready, Salisbury's next problem was to bring Audley to battle before the arrival of reinforcements from a second Lancastrian army less than ten miles away. He achieved this by faking 'a sign of retreat'. Obligingly, Audley, who had been given 'the queen's terrible commandment … to bring to her presence, the Earl of Salisbury, quick or dead, … blew up his trumpet...'[4] and charged his vanguard forward. In their rush to close with the enemy, the knights and men-at-arms at the forefront of the Lancastrian assault remained mounted; even though their usual habit was to dismount and fight on foot.

As Audley's knights raced down the hill and floundered across the '… not very broad, but somewhat deep'[5] waters of Hempmill Brook, they were subjected to a concentration of arrow

Knights were better protected than ever, wearing full suits of interlocking plate armour, curved to deflect arrows or sword thrusts.

THE DYNASTIC BACKGROUND TO THE WARS OF THE ROSES

Edward III had seven sons. Of those who survived infancy the four eldest were: his heir – Edward (the Black Prince), Lionel (Duke of Clarence), John of Gaunt (Duke of Lancaster), and Edmund Langley (Duke of York). As the Black Prince predeceased his father by a year, it was his son who eventually succeeded to the throne in 1377, becoming Richard II.

Richard's reign witnessed both peasant revolts and aristocratic conspiracies. Succesive disputes with the nobility eventually led to his downfall. In 1399, Richard's cousin Henry Bolingbroke, the eldest son of John of Gaunt (Edward III's third son), usurped the throne, had Richard executed and founded the ruling dynasty of Lancaster as Henry IV.

Henry's claim to the throne rested on his being the next surviving male heir. Unfortunately for him, there was a rival claim through the line of Philippa, daughter of Edward III's second son – the Duke of Clarence. Philippa had married Edmund Mortimer, Earl of March, by whom she had a son; thus founding the claim of the House of Mortimer.

In 1425, Richard Duke of York, the grandson of Edmund Langley (Edward III's fourth son) was to inherit the Mortimer claim through his maternal uncle. He was to prove a formidable rival to his distant cousin, the weak-minded Henry VI of the House of Lancaster who alienated the Duke by borrowing vast sums of money he never repaid.

---

fire. Indeed, according to a contemporary account, Salisbury's Yorkist bowmen '… began to shoot so intensely that it was frightful, and so violently that everything in range suffered'.[6] Then, as the Lancastrians struggled to climb the bank on the far side of the brook, a rush of Yorkist knights, men-at-arms and billmen ran forward to bludgeon them back into the water. Audley's attack faltered and the Lancastrians pulled back leaving their dead and wounded choking the stream behind them.

Although his second assault on Salisbury's position met with the same fate, Audley was determined to gratify the Queen's wish for Salisbury's head. Changing tactics, he spearheaded his third attack with four thousand

Lancastrian infantry rather than the twice-defeated cavalry. Back down the slope they went, enduring the Yorkist arrow storm once more as they slithered through the mud and blood and plunged into the cold waters of Hempmill Brook. Many lost their footing and were drowned in the fury of the ensuing mêlée in which the opposing sides 'fought hand to hand for a good half hour'.[7]

Fighting at the head of his men, Lord Audley made it part way up the slope on the Yorkist side of the brook before he was brought down and killed. This was the turning point of the battle. The Lancastrian cavalry were by now so thoroughly demoralised that most fled the field and some even changed sides. Having lost their leader and their horse, the remainder of Audley's

Left: For the previous hundred years, English armies had included a high proportion of archers. They had proved very effective against the French, but now they were fighting each other. At Blore Heath, the Yorkist archers inflicted heavy losses on the Lancastrians before they could close with their opponents.

Right: Most soldiers, especially archers, carried small daggers. While mainly used for mundane chores in the field, they also served to despatch wounded knights, stabbing between the joints in a suit of armour.

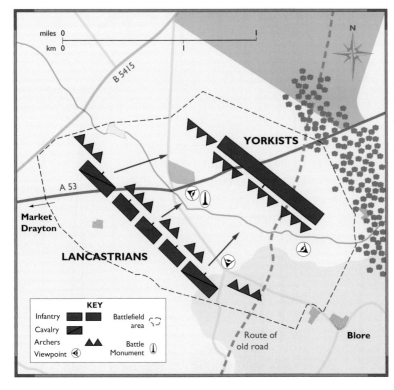

Arrow heads carried large barbs, making them difficult and agonising to extract. Since archers tended to stick them in the ground for rapid re-loading, they often caused incurable wound infections.

The bulk of the soldiers in the Wars of the Roses were professional troops retained by the most powerful noble families. These private armies would dominate English politics for the next 30 years.

army broke and routed, pursued by the Yorkists to the banks of the River Tern. Now began the real slaughter typical of medieval battles.

While Salisbury's force had sustained minimal losses, they had wrecked terrible devastation upon their enemies. The blood of the 2,000 Lancastrians who lay dead upon the field was reputed to have dyed the waters of Hempmill Brook red for three days afterwards.

THE ROSES MOTIFS OF YORK AND LANCASTER

Sir Walter Scott is credited with having coined the description 'Wars of the Roses' in 1829. However, Scott's imposing title owes more to that arch-propagandist of the Tudors, William Shakespeare, than to historical fact. In Shakespeare's famous Temple garden scene (I Henry VI, II IV) the quarrelling nobles pluck red and white roses to symbolise their allegiance to York or Lancaster. In fact, although the standards of Edward IV and Henry VII did incorporate roses, they were by no means the most important motif of the period. Margaret of Anjou for example, favoured a swan, Henry VI an antelope and Richard III a white boar.

NORTHAMPTON

◆◆ 10 July 1460 ◆◆

The summer of 1460 found the King gathering forces
in the Midlands in anticipation of an Irish invasion
led by the Duke of York. In his absence London
capitulated to York's eighteen year old son, Edward,
Earl of March, who had advanced through Kent
supported by the Neville family (the Earls of
Warwick and Salisbury and Lord Fauconberg).

THE LATE MEDIEVAL FOOT-SOLDIER

Although the common foot-soldier was not fully armoured, he was better provided for than infantry of the eleventh and twelfth centuries. Improved armour filtered down the ranks and the open-faced sallet helmet became very popular. Cheaper to buy than the more complex visored helmet it was also cooler. Helmets were sometimes painted, both as a means of rust control and a method of unit identification. Alternatively, some units knotted a coloured scarf around their helmets as a battlefield insignia.

The helmet was complemented by a 'jacque': a tunic stuffed with tow. According to Dominic Mancini, writing in 1483, '... the softer the tunic the better do they withstand the blows of arrows and swords, and besides that in the summer they are lighter and in winter more servicable than iron'. Alternatively, the better-off might have a brigadine, which offered the added protection of hundreds of steel plates stitched into the fabric. Leg armour was rarer and the legs of the common soldiery remained for the most part exposed, although the use of steel 'genouillières' (knee guards) was widespread.

The principal tool of the foot soldier's trade was a polearm or staff weapon, averaging six to eight feet in length. The long ash shaft was often hexagonal in shape to improve grip. At the business end it was protected by metal strips (in order to prevent the blade being hacked off by the enemy). The most common polearm was the bill, incorporating a lethal combination of hook, spike and blade.

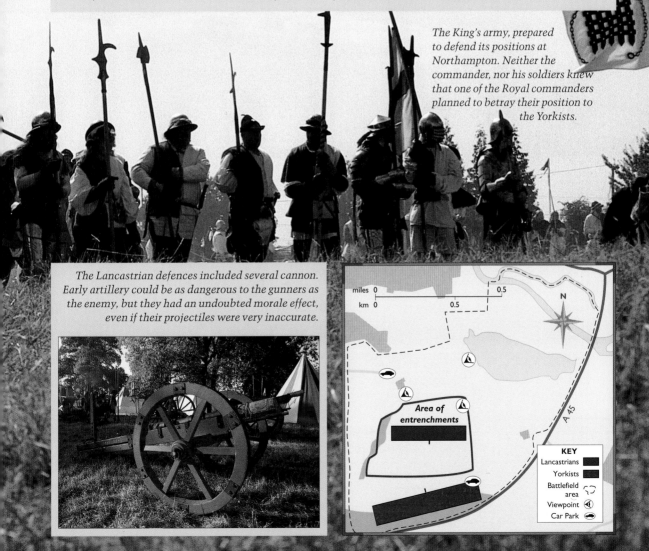

The King's army, prepared to defend its positions at Northampton. Neither the commander, nor his soldiers knew that one of the Royal commanders planned to betray their position to the Yorkists.

The Lancastrian defences included several cannon. Early artillery could be as dangerous to the gunners as the enemy, but they had an undoubted morale effect, even if their projectiles were very inaccurate.

miles 0 — 0.5
km 0 — 0.5
N

Area of entrenchments

A 45

KEY
Lancastrians
Yorkists
Battlefield area
Viewpoint
Car Park

WOMEN IN THE WARS

The armies were accompanied by whole families, but some women played a more active role. Queen Margaret became the real Lancastrian leader and others were not shy of command. In February 1461 an armed force under Sir Gilbert Debenham set out to eject the small garrison defending Buckingham castle in Norfolk. He was to meet with resistance from an unexpected quarter. Arriving at the raised drawbridge he demanded that the castle should surrender at once. In response, Lady Knyvet leaned out of an upper window and replied, 'if ye begin to break the peace or make any war to get the [castle] of me I shall defend me, for [rather] I had in such wide to die than to be slaine when my husband cometh home, for he charged me to keep it'.

Faced with such obvious determination to hold out against the lesser evil of his attacking force, Sir Gilbert abandoned his attempt on Buckingham castle and marched away!

Realising that it was essential to bring the King to battle before his army had time to reach full strength, the Yorkists decided not to wait for the landing of the Duke, but to press on towards the Midlands. As they approached Northampton they found the King's forces waiting for them, under the command of the Duke of Buckingham. Although the Yorkists outnumbered the Lancastrians by about 7,000 to 5,000, Buckingham was well prepared to receive them. With the River Nene at his back and his front and flanks protected by ditch, ramparts and cannon, his field fortification was a formidable prospect.

Not surprisingly, having marched through unseasonably heavy rain to be confronted by a camp bristling with engines of war, the Yorkists decided to venture diplomacy before duress. Warwick sent a herald with a message that he would either speak to the King before 2 p.m. or die in the attempt. Buckingham, convinced of the strength of his defences, rudely dismissed him. His confidence was misplaced. Unknown to Buckingham, the treachery of Lord Grey of Ruthin was to decide the battle almost before it had begun. To make matters worse, rain had already spoiled the gunpowder, rendering his cannons ineffective.

Wasting no more time, the young Earl of March led the Yorkist divisions straight towards the point in Buckingham's defences manned by Lord Grey's contingent. As they

The sallet was the most popular helmet of the Wars of the Roses, some having face pieces like this one, others were solid. The back of the helmet sweeps outwards to protect the back of the neck, while the front offers maximum protection to the face. Its disadvantage is the narrow vision slit, restricting your field of view.

approached the formidable ramparts, Grey's 'men met them and seizing them by the hand hauled them into the embattled field'.[8] The remaining Lancastrians, shocked to find the enemy suddenly at close-quarters, were quickly overcome. The walls of their fortified camp had become a death-trap. Within half an hour the Duke of Buckingham lay slain and the Yorkists had taken possession of the hapless King Henry.

Having seized the King, the Duke of York now pressed his claim to the throne, and the Act of Settlement was passed in 1460 declaring him to be King Henry's heir and disinheriting the Prince of Wales. It was a compromise the Queen would never accept. Storming through Wales, the West Country and the north of England, she raised a new army. In the following months the family feud was to become an increasingly desperate and bloody vendetta.

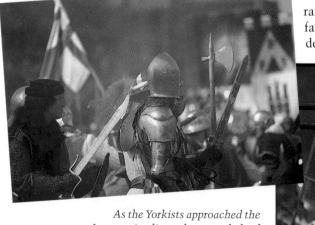

As the Yorkists approached the Lancastrian lines, they were helped into the defences by Lord Grey and his treacherous contingent.

TOWTON
⤙ 29 March 1461 ⤚

The Duke of York was killed by the Lancastrians at the battle of Wakefield in December 1460. But London defied Queen Margaret and welcomed York's son Edward. The Lancastrians withdrew to their northern strongholds. Edward led the Yorkist army in pursuit.

As the new Duke of York, Edward knew that he must now win the throne or die. He entered London in February 1461, where the political establishment, considering him a better prospect than Margaret of Anjou, declared him King Edward IV. However, the Queen had defeated Warwick at the Second Battle of St Albans and rescued Henry VI. It was clear that Edward would not long have a head upon which to wear the crown unless he could defeat Margaret's army decisively in battle.

While Edward marshalled support in the south, Margaret was busy increasing her forces in the north. The opposing armies of York and

Both sides deployed their archers in the front line, but the Yorkists had the wind behind them. The Lancastrians' arrows fell short, doing little but providing their enemies with more ammunition.

For the nobles and their senior followers, the stakes were now much higher. Both sides were now habitually executing captured enemy leaders, and each killing demanded vengeance.

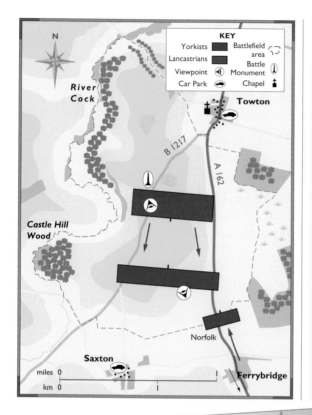

COMPOSITION OF THE ARMIES

The chief missile of the fifteenth century army was still unquestionably the arrow, with an increased ratio of archers to billmen since the preceding century. Although there was also an increasing use of hand-guns, their battlefield numbers were limited by the purse of those sponsoring the army. Lighter and more mobile than in the previous century, hand-gunners were usually deployed in groups, scattered among the blocks of archers.

While late medieval armies possessed increasing numbers of artillery pieces, their destructive power remained limited. They were highly susceptible to the vagaries of weather. Nonetheless, the morale boosting value of such a loud weapon could be immense. The formidable booming of their own guns greatly bolstered the courage of the soldiery; an asset in the bloody hand-to-hand combat which invariably followed.

The close-quarter, battering power of the army was provided by the foot-soldier wielding a two-handed pole weapon. It was not guns or cannons, but the combination of arrow shower and blade work which rendered late 15th century armies so deadly.

The Duke of Warwick's contingent provided the bulk of Edward's Yorkist army. Warwick had beaten the Lancastrians twice in February, preventing a serious attack on London.

The Yorkist ranks were swelled by volunteers from the Welsh Marches, traditional followers of the Duke of York, galvanised by his death at Wakefield. The massacre of a Yorkist detachment at Dunstable in January ensured that future battles would be fought to the bitter end.

Margaret's soldiers were mainly recruited from the north of England and had become notorious for their ruthlessness. Twenty miles south of York, they turned on their pursuers.

SIZE OF ARMIES

Contemporary descriptions of the battle of Towton in 1461 have earned it a reputation as the largest and bloodiest engagement ever fought on English soil. Surviving accounts cite armies numbering in the region of 100,000 men, while the lowest estimate of the casualties involved is 28,000. Although the evidence suggests that the numbers involved in this battle were unusually large, fifteenth century chroniclers were prone to exaggeration. A fact which in 1460 caused Prospero di Camulio (attempting to assess the Battle of St Albans) to comment in exasperation to his sponsor: 'My lord, I am ashamed to speak of so many thousands, which resemble the figures of bakers, yet everyone affirms that on that day there were 300,000 men under arms, and indeed the whole of England was stirred, so that some even speak of larger numbers'.

An informed guess would suggest that armies in this era ranged from 3,000 to 20,000 (the latter being a rare exception).

Lancaster finally confronted each other on the morning of 29 March 1461, on a plateau between the villages of Towton and Saxton. According to contemporary chroniclers there were over 100,000 men in the field. Even allowing for their exaggeration, it was probably the largest medieval battle fought on British soil.

Lancastrian archers continued to shoot at their enemies, but as the weather closed in, they could not see that most of their arrows were falling short.

It had been a bitterly cold night and the grey light of dawn brought fresh snow carried on a biting wind. There were two Kings of England in the field that day and there could be no peace in the realm until one or the other was dead. Yet

while King Edward was giving orders that 'no prisoner should be taken, nor one enemy saved',[9] Henry VI was asking for the battle to be postponed because it was Palm Sunday. His request fell on deaf ears. The Queen's enormous army, commanded by the twenty-four-year-old Duke of Somerset, was the first to move forward.

Edward's vanguard was commanded by his uncle Lord Fauconberg, a wily and experienced soldier who ordered '…every archer under his standard, to shoot one flight and then made them to stand still.' Driven on a tail wind,

invisible in the flurrying snow, the shock arrival of the Yorkist arrow storm stung the Lancastrians into a foolhardy response. Although half blinded by the snow and shooting against the wind they fired all 'their sheaf of arrows as fast as they might'.[10] Not surprisingly, the Lancastrian volley fell short and the Yorkist archers now moved forward to fire the reminder of their sheaves and gather the spent arrows of their enemies.

Undaunted by the Yorkist arrow storm, Duke of Somerset's contingent pressed forward. A desperate close quarter battle began.

The Duke of Norfolk led his contingent up from Ferry Bridge while the battle raged. Arriving on the Lancastrian flank, his attack effectively decided the battle.

The retreating Lancastrians were hemmed together, struggling to cross the river. Most of the casualties occured after the battle was lost.

With their enemies fleeing in panic, the Yorkists pressed forward to avenge the death of Richard, Duke of York. Towton was to be the largest, and bloodiest of England's medieval battles.

Despite losing the archery duel, 'the chieftains of King Henry's vanguard'[11] launched a furious charge. Six or seven 'thousand Welshmen led by Andrew Trollope and the Duke of Somerset with seven thousand men more'[12] powered home like an iron-gloved fist. Edward's left flank reeled and broke. Had the Duke of Northumberland, on the opposite Lancastrian flank, charged at the same time it might all have been over. But he failed to advance and the Yorkist right wing still stood intact.

King Edward knew that the fate of his army hung in the balance. Riding along the lines to his standard-bearer, he '… dismounted and, sword in hand, affirmed that this day he wished to live or die with [his men] …' Then, with the banners of Henry VI bearing down on him through the snow, '… he put himself before his standard facing his enemies'.[13]

For hour after hour the two armies were locked together in hand-to-hand combat. Bills, halberds, glaives and other assorted blades hacked, pierced and stabbed with equal ferocity on both sides. Only when the Duke of Norfolk arrived with Yorkist reinforcements did the balance finally swing in favour of King Edward. Then, at last, the Lancastrian fight became flight and their exhausted lines fragmented.

With the Yorkists snapping at their heels, many fled towards Tadcaster, only to find their escape obstructed by the River Cock 'not very broad, but of great deepness'. Here the slaughter was terrible. Trapped in the narrow river gully, the frantic Lancastrians could find no escape

The 'Wars of the Roses' was a Shakespearean invention: actual battle standards incorporated all sorts of medieval icons from Warwick's bear on a ragged staff to Richard of Gloucester's boar. Some symbols were similar, leading to 'friendly fire' incidents not helped by the prevailing atmosphere of treachery.

BAR ROOM BRAVADO

Although weapons, uniforms and methods of warfare have changed greatly since the Wars of the Roses, human nature has remained little altered. The bar-room bravado expressed in the following lines, written by a young soldier in the Middle Ages, would certainly be understood by his modern counterparts:

'When we are in the tavern drinking strong wine, and the ladies pass and look at us with those white throats and tight bodices, those sparkling eyes resplendent with smiling beauty: then nature urges us to have a desiring heart. Then we could overcome Yaumont and Agolant, and the others could conquer Oliver and Roland. But when we are on campaign on our trotting chargers, our bucklers round our necks and our lances lowered, and the great cold is congealing us together, and our limbs are crushed before and behind and our enimies are approaching us, then we would wish to be in a cellar so large that we might never be seen by any means'.

from the butchery except to throw themselves into the deep, freezing waters. In the end so many were 'drenched and drowned … that the common people there afirm, that men alive passed the river upon dead carcasses…'[14]

By nightfall on Palm Sunday 1461, thousands of bodies lay strewn across the rolling Yorkshire countryside amid the raw pink mush of the blood-soaked snowdrifts. The heralds who counted the dead affirmed that it had been the bloodiest day in English history. However, despite the massive scale of the carnage, Henry VI and his Queen escaped and fled north to Scotland. The battle of Towton had resolved nothing: two Kings still claimed the English crown. While they both lived, the wars would continue.

BARNET
⨠ 14 April 1471 ⨲

By 1469 King Edward IV had fallen out with the powerful Earl of Warwick who had helped to place him upon the throne. The King had secretly married Lancastrian widow Elizabeth Woodville and advanced the interest of her family at the expense of Warwick's.

Warwick, who had hoped to cement an alliance with France by marrying Edward to a relative of Louis XI, was furious. The simmering resentment between the Earl and the King finally erupted into open war at the battle of Edgecote on 26 July 1469. By 1470 Edward had been forced to flee to the Continent and Warwick, the 'kingmaker', had restored the Lancastrian Henry VI to the throne. However in March 1471 Edward landed in Yorkshire, outmanoeuvred Warwick and took possession of London. Warwick offered battle ten miles outside the capital, near High Barnet. His army numbered 15,000 against Edward's Yorkist force of approximately 10,000. Edward collided with Warwick's pickets at dusk on 13 April. Hoping to launch a surprise attack at dawn, the Yorkists encamped in line of battle and 'kept passing great silence all night … whereby [the enemy] might not know the very place where they lay'. Indeed, although Warwick ordered a night bombardment of Edward's position, his gunners overshot as 'the king's host lay much nearrer than they deemed'.[15]

However, by deploying in darkness, Edward had misaligned his forces. Dawn brought no clarity, only a blinding mist, heavy with the sulphuric whiff of gunpowder. As was customary, each side had formed up in a line divided into three 'battles' or divisions. Thus, when the Yorkists advanced to the attack just before dawn, their right wing overlapped Warwick's left and vice versa.

Most English cannon were single-barrelled, but some Burgundian mercenaries used 'ribaudekins'. These multiple-barrelled weapons were alarming at long range and devastating at close range. However, they were strictly a one salvo affair as they took a long time to reload.

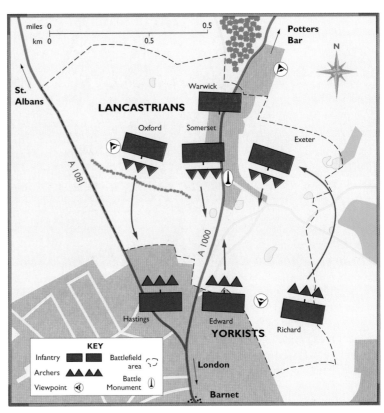

Richard Neville, Earl of Warwick had been dubbed 'The Kingmaker' for putting Edward IV on the throne. His estrangement from the Yorkist camp led to a new round of conflict as he joined the defeated Lancastrians.

Lord Hastings, commanding Edward's left flank, made contact first; advancing over the fog-bound, cobwebbed heath to challenge the Earl of Oxford. Hearing the armoured rattle of Hastings' approach, Oxford's archers made ready to shoot. As soon as the first, faint shapes of the Yorkists began to emerge from the mist, the chill air was filled with a whistling rain of arrows. Added to this, the crackling volleys of Oxford's hand-gunners spat eerie flashes of yellow flame in the dim, blue dawn. As the Yorkist advance faltered, Oxford seized his moment and ordered a charge. Aided by the slope of the ground, his attack buried itself deep in the Yorkist formation, putting Hastings to flight.

By contrast on Edward's right, his brother Richard, Duke of Gloucester, failed to make contact, owing to the misalignment of the lines. This mistake worked in his favour. Realising what had happened, Gloucester was able to swing around in a flanking attack on Warwick's extreme left. Heavily pressed, both by Gloucester and by Edward's own division to their front,

CLOSE-QUARTER COMBAT

When the armies impacted, opposing front ranks were often crushed hard against each other by the press of those behind, lunging with staff weapons over the heads of their comrades. There, in such close proximity, a fatal blow might equally come from a stiletto blade in an unseen hand, as from a poleaxe. In other places the lines stood a bill-length apart, searching furiously with polearms for any crippling strike: a knee-cap, a face, an armpit exposed by an outstretched arm.

In this merciless encounter the soldier feared loosing his footing almost as much as a wounding blow. It mattered little whether he was brought down by the side-swiping, hammer-strike of a poleaxe, or the muscle-tearing cut of a well directed glaive. Once felled, he was horribly vulnerable and likely to be struck again. His only hope lay in scrambling back between the legs of those behind. If not trampled to death, the wounded man left the field of battle as fast as he was able. If his side were to lose, he knew that he stood more chance of being killed in the rout than in the battle itself.

Warwick's left wing began to buckle, and the battle spun on its axis so that the lines now faced east/west instead of the north/south alignment in which they had begun. This was to have unforeseen consequences later. Meanwhile, Warwick was pushed back into Dead Man's Bottom. There, with the opposing billmen locked in hand-to-hand combat, the centre of the battleground became a bloody abattoir.

Unfortunately for Warwick, his victorious right wing under Oxford had left the field in pursuit of Hastings' routing command. Having reached Barnet, they abandoned fighting in favour of looting. Of all his force, Oxford was able to rally only 500 mounted men to return to the main battle. Then, in the confusion of the mist and the shifting lines of battle, Warwick and Oxford mistook each other for the enemy. The

The battlefield of Barnet was enveloped in thick fog, and no-one was certain who might change sides next. Ordinary soldiers prepared to fight anyone not from their local contingent.

HOW TO FIGHT WITH A POLE-AXE

The poleaxe was a brutally effective weapon with an eight-foot shaft and a wide, hacking blade which incorporated a sharp hook (for pulling men out of saddles, or off their feet) and a hammer head designed for brain-smashing blows to the cranium. As English knights preferred to fight on foot by the fifteenth century, it was only natural that they should choose the weapon best-suited to such work. The sword was a secondary weapon, worn suspended from the belt, along with a mace and dagger.

In close-quarter combat the knight held his poleaxe at shoulder height in a two-handed grip (keeping his elbows tucked close to the body so as not to expose the vulnerable underarm). With feet well-spaced for balance, he dodged and parried the lunge of enemy blades while searching for his own crippling strike. The hammer-head might be employed to crack open an unarmoured knee-cap, while the curved hook could be tucked behind an opponent's knee and wrenched forward in a sinew-tearing twist. The most prized hit however, was to bury the stabbing point of the weapon deep into the face of the enemy: guaranteed to drop a man where he stood! Alternatively, if one's intended victim parried the blow, the point could be suddenly reversed for an impaling strike at the feet.

Many Lancastrian soldiers quit the field after fighting broke out between the contingents of Oxford, Warwick and Somerset: all supposed to be on the same side. At this crucial moment, Edward IV launched his attack.

fact that the livery worn by Oxford's men (a 'star with streamers'[16]) was very similar to King Edward's own did not help matters. Consequently 'the Erle of Warwikes men schott and faught ayens the Erle of Oxenfordes menne … and anone the Erle of Oxenforde and his men cried 'treasoune! treasoune!' and fledde awaye from the felde …'[17]

At this juncture Edward committed his reserves to the fray, pushing Warwick's centre further into Dead Man's Bottom. The Earl, realising that the battle had reached its deciding moment, frantically tried to rally his men crying out 'This is our last resource. If we withstand this charge the day is ours'.[18] It was not to be. With his army disintegrating around him, Warwick joined the frightened tide of humanity streaming to the rear. As he attempted to recover his charger, tethered in Wrotham Park, he was recognised by his livery and attacked by a knot of Yorkist men-at-arms. The Earl stood alone as his enemies closed upon him. At last, wounded and knocked to the ground, his visor was torn open and his struggles ended by the thrust of a heavy war blade. In this sordid manner the mighty Richard Neville, Earl of Warwick, left the turbulent stage of the Wars of the Roses. According to Edward Hall, a near contemporary chronicler, '…the common people thought the sun had gone out of the heavens'.[19]

In death, Warwick had plenty of company. Over 1,000 of his own men and perhaps 500 more of Edward's were slain at the battle of Barnet.

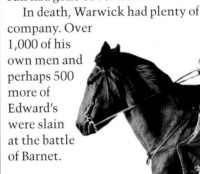

Top and above: Wearing similar equipment and insignia, the Lancastrians briefly fought each other as the battle began.

Left: Primitive 'handguns' reduced the already poor visibility when they opened fire.

Some senior Lancastrians escaped on horseback, but the Earl of Warwick had fought on foot to encourage his men and was killed in the rout.

TEWKESBURY

⊰⊱ 4 May 1471 ⊰⊱

Although he had beaten Warwick's forces
conclusively at Barnet, the troubles of the Yorkist
King Edward IV were far from over. On the very
eve of his victory, Margaret of Anjou landed
at Weymouth with an invasion force of
seventeen ships.

The erstwhile Queen was persuaded that the crown might yet be secured for her son (the Lancastrian Edward, Prince of Wales) by linking up with the Welsh forces of Jasper Tudor. On 3 May 1471, after a forced march from Dorset to Gloucestershire, the Lancastrian army of 6,000 men halted at Tewkesbury. There, with Edward IV's 5,000 strong Yorkist army gaining on them,

Archers prepare to engage their opposite numbers.
Edward IV supported his bowmen with cannon and the
Lancastrians were forced to attack or be shot down.

the Lancastrians decided to make a stand. Early on the morning of 4 May the Lancastrian army deployed within sight of Tewkesbury Abbey, where the difficult terrain formed a natural defensive position. The Duke of Somerset, in overall command, took the right flank, the young Prince Edward shared the centre with Lord Wenlock, and the Earl of Devonshire took the left. Before them were '... fowle lanes and depe dikes, and many hedges, with hylls, and valleys, a right evil place to approche, as cowlde well have been devised'.[20]

The enmity between the dynasties was now so bitter that nobles on the losing side faced execution rather than capture. You could save your skin by changing sides, but Lord Wenlock left it too late at Tewkesbury.

King Edward knew that his best chance of victory lay in catching Queen Margaret before her forces were further swollen by Jasper Tudor's reinforcements. When he reached Tewkesbury he had already marched thirty miles that day. With his army both outnumbered and tired, the King advanced warily, despatching 200 mounted spearmen into the trees beyond his left flank as a precaution. This prudent action was later to reap benefits out of all proportion to the size of the contingent involved.

The banners and pennants were a blaze of colour in the spring sunshine as the opposing armies finally faced each other before the tall stone walls of the Abbey. Clouds of arrows darkened the sky. The Yorkist arrow storm had an extra bite: Edward had the advantage in artillery and was determined to soften up the enemy before launching his assault. Labouring in the heat, his gunners kept up a ferocious barrage of stone cannon balls which screeched over the Lancastrian lines, shredded hedges, and smashed through armour, flesh and bone.

On the receiving end, the Duke of Somerset decided to end this by launching a bold flank

Although Edward IV and his retinue rode to the battle, they dismounted to fight. Footsoldiers were now so cynical about their commanders' ability to escape if the battle was lost that most leaders fought with the infantry – and died if they lost.

FIGHTING IN ARMOUR

The idea that medieval knights were so weighed down by their armour that they had to be winched into their saddles is a myth perpetrated by the Victorians. In reality as knights often fought on foot, their lives in battle were dependent as much on freedom of movement as on armoured protection. A suit of armour had to be light and flexible enough to enable its wearer to run, fight, mount a horse and rise from a fall without the least impediment.

The principal restriction on the use of armour was cost. Though the craft of the armourer reached its zenith in the fifteenth century, only the wealthiest nobles could afford the best. A full suit might cost the equivalent of £50,000 in modern terms. The vast majority of knights and men-at-arms wore older, cheaper styles.

A knight demonstrates the flexibility of his plate armour: it had to be light enough for the wearer to fight on foot or on horseback. Armour only became an impediment at the end of a losing battle, when the wearer might well be exhausted, and unable to outrun lightly equipped archers.

attack. Concealed by the terrain, he took the bulk of his own division towards Edward's left wing to 'set right fiercely upon th'end of the Kings battayle'.[21] Somerset's plan called for Wenlock, commanding the Lancastrian centre,

Thanks to Lord Wenlock's hesitation – or possible treachery – the Lancastrian foot soldiers were engaged piecemeal. Their right flank was left unsupported and was soon crushed by Edward and his brother Richard, Duke of Gloucester.

to add his weight by pressing forward simultaneously on Edward's front. However, Wenlock was a man with a chequered history (having previously fought for the Yorkists at Towton) and the Duke was soon to have qualms about his loyalty.

The Yorkist left reacted quickly as Somerset's men burst from cover and charged towards them. Gloucester, on King Edward's extreme left flank, managed to turn his lines and reach the shelter of a hedge, breaking the Lancastrian momentum.

Part of the King's own division (in the Yorkist centre) also turned to face the attack. As weight of numbers began to tell against Somerset, the Duke looked in vain for support from Lord Wenlock; whose banners failed to move from the 'marvaylows strong grownd' of their original position. Instead, Edward's 200 mounted Yorkist spearmen suddenly emerged from the trees and hit Somerset in the rear. This final shock was too much for the Duke's men who 'greatly dismaied and abasshed ... toke them to flyght'.[22]

King Edward now realigned his forces, '... displayed his banners, dyd blowe up the trumpets; commytted his [cause] ... to Almighty God ... and advaunced, directly upon his enimies'.[23] At the same time the Duke of Somerset, having survived the rout of his division, was also making his way back towards the remaining Lancastrian lines. Although the main bodies of the two armies were finally coming to blows, his Lordship had a more private score to settle. Marching up to Wenlock, he denounced him as a traitor, took up his axe and personally 'strake [his] braynes out of his hedde'.[24]

With victory in the air, and murder in the Lancastrian camp, nothing could stop the advance of the Yorkists. As Edward's men poured over the dykes and hedges and carved into their formations, the Lancastrians' morale collapsed: 'many rann towards the towne; many to the churche; to the abbey; and els where; as they best myght'.[25] Many more, trapped by the impassable barrier of the River Severn, were butchered by the Yorkists upon its banks. The scale of the slaughter was such that the place was ever afterwards known as 'Bloody Meadow'.

Those who tried to take sanctuary in

Tewkesbury Abbey fared no better. Somerset was captured in the Abbey, dragged out and executed in the market place, along with many of his knights. The seventeen-year-old Lancastrian Prince Edward was killed and his mother, Margaret of Anjou, was apprehended. The final casualty was Margaret's husband: the pathetic Henry VI. He had been kept alive in the Tower of London solely in order to weaken his son's claim to the throne. Now, serving no further useful purpose to the Yorkists, he too was executed.

After Tewkesbury King Edward IV never had to fight for his crown again. The only surviving male members in the Lancastrian line were Jasper Tudor, the Earl of Pembroke and his nephew Henry. Forced into exile in France, the Tudors seemed to pose little threat to the House of York.

The Lancastrian cause was lost for ever at Tewkesbury. Henry VI and his heir Prince Edward were executed, his Queen paraded in triumph through London before her confinement in the Tower. Margaret was exiled to France in 1475 and it seemed that the Wars of the Roses were over.

BOSWORTH

⤝ 22 August 1485 ⤞

Edward IV died in April 1483, to be succeeded by his
12 year old son Edward V. By June the boy-King had
been deposed by his uncle, Richard Duke of
Gloucester; the same Gloucester who had fought
so effectively for Edward IV at Barnet
and Tewkesbury.

*Commanded by their
king, Richard of
Gloucester, one of the
most successful Yorkist
commanders, the Royal
archers open fire on the
rebel army of Henry
Tudor.*

The new Yorkist King, Richard III, was never a popular monarch and by 1485 the young Henry Tudor, exiled in France, felt that he could command enough support to risk an invasion. He landed in Wales on 1 August 1485 with 2,000 men. Three weeks later, having gathered 3,000 more, he faced Richard's army of 8,000 near the town of Market Bosworth in Leicestershire. Even as Henry marched along the Sutton Cheny road towards his objective, it was already evident that Richard had outmanoeuvred him. Arrayed in clear sight, on the crest of Ambion Hill, the Yorkist lines stretched 'forth of a wonderful length ... full replenished both with horsemen and footmen'.[26] For Henry's army, toiling along in the midsummer heat below, it was a dispiriting prospect.

KEY

Infantry	
Cavalry	
Car Park	
Battlefield area	
Viewpoint	

The Yorkist army was hastily assembled, with more troops following on behind.

With rumours of treachery rife within their camp, the Yorkist soldiers prepared to give battle.

In the Yorkist camp the day before the battle, someone pinned a note to Norfolk's tent: "Jockey of Norfolk, Be not so bold, Dickon thy master, is bought and sold."

Nonetheless, King Richard also had concerns. None too certain of the loyalty of his army or his nobles, he was particularly doubtful about Lord Thomas Stanley who had yet to commit his troops to either side. With a force of approximately 3,000 men, the Stanley contingent could make a considerable difference to the outcome of the battle.

While the brooding King looked down from his vantage, the Earl of Oxford, at the head of Henry's army, was arriving within arrow-range of the Yorkist vanguard commanded by the Duke of Norfolk. Detouring around the marsh at the foot of Ambion Hill, Oxford's ranks turned north, presenting their backs to Lord Stanley. If the Stanleys were ever to attack the Tudor army, now was the time to do it, hitting them in the rear while Norfolk's forces streamed down the hill in a hammer and anvil action. Stanley failed to respond. Realising that he was betrayed in that quarter, Richard looked towards Norfolk but the Duke stood firm. As the Tudor army turned eastward again, to face him, they were greeted by the deep goose-feathered moan of thousands of arrows in flight.

Now Norfolk advanced down the western face of the Ambion Hill, his front ranks a glittering, spiked hedge of bills, glaives, voulges, fauchards, bardiches, halberds and poleaxes. At the last,

only yards away from the enemy, the Yorkists sent up a great roar and leapt forward. Oxford's billmen screamed back at the top of their lungs to stiffen their own resolve for the coming struggle and the two sides slammed together making the air ring with the heavy strike of metal on metal. Thus began the grim struggle for the lower slopes of the hill.

Sweating in the armoured heat, men struggled for footing as the restless cross-current of battle shifted back and forth; opening and closing gaps, spilling and tumbling one line upon the other. While the battle 'continued thus hot on both sides betwixt the frontlines'[27] King Richard, watching from the crown of the hill, observed a body of horsemen riding across the heath towards the rear of Oxford's heavily engaged command. As they drew nearer, the forest of colourful standards and banners betrayed the party to be none other than that which accompanied Henry Tudor himself. 'Wherefore …', according to the Tudor chronicler Polydore Vergil, '… all inflamed with ire, [the King] strick his horse with the spurs and runneth against him'.[28]

In fact Richard's charge was not a furious impulse but a calculated decision. Beneath the fury of Norfolk's assault, Oxford had closed up his ranks, creating a gap between himself and the

marsy ground guarding his right flank. This presented Richard with two options. He could advance his mounted retinue into the gap to attack Oxford's now vulnerable right flank, or aim for a higher prize by charging through the gap to attack Henry's personal contingent beyond. Richard chose Henry.

As his orders were carried by the call of trumpets, the King reached up and slammed shut the visor on his crowned helmet. Around him the 1,500 mounted knights and men-at-arms of his personal retinue did the same. Here on the lush slopes of Ambion Hill in the warm August sunshine was all the panoply of English medieval warfare at its finest: the burnished steel, full plate armour; richly coloured tabards worked with armorial devices; heavy war swords in expensively tooled leather scabbards; deep-seated saddles on well accoutred mounts; and banners and flags galore. All of this mass of living, vibrant colour was about to be hurled down the slope in the last great cavalry charge of the medieval age.

Foot soldiers fought whoever their lords commanded: they knew where their loyalties lay. At Bosworth, neither commander could be sure his army would actually fight for him. Richard III had been reduced to taking hostages from some of his commanders.

At the other end of the battlefield, a hesitant Henry Tudor, guarded by a retinue of mounted knights and men-at-arms, had at last decided to lend some support to the battle which he hoped would win him the crown of England. Now, looking up, he saw the shining throng of Richard's mounted knights pour over the crest of the hill, rippling and flashing in the sun like a field of silver corn. At the very spear-point of this host, with his charger pointed directly at the Welsh dragon standard of Henry Tudor, rode the King himself. This fearful sight seems to have deprived Henry of all command initiative until it was too late for anything but a stand. Nonetheless, from desperation sprang a bold defence.

The momentum of the charge carried Richard right up to the knot of knights around Henry. Seeing the Tudor standard before him, the King struck such a furious blow that the standard-bearer instantly rolled dead from his saddle. As Henry's knights endeavoured to put themselves between him and the King, Richard next crossed swords with John Cheney, whom he battered from his saddle in his fury. Single-minded in his determination to deal Henry a mortal blow, the King had almost won within sword reach when the crush of the battle began to carry him away.

Nearby, Lord Stanley watched this desperate struggle. Realising that Richard would never forgive his failure to act earlier, while Henry would now be forever grateful for a timely intervention, he finally made his decision. With trumpets blaring, visors down and pennants streaming, Stanley attacked Richard's left flank. With this, King Richard's position became perilous. Many of the royal retinue were now down and fighting on foot amid the dead and

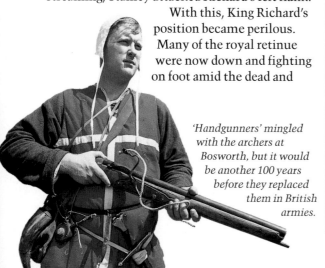

'Handgunners' mingled with the archers at Bosworth, but it would be another 100 years before they replaced them in British armies.

THE STANLEYS

There were three armies at the Battle of Bosworth; the Yorkists, the Tudors and the Stanleys. Lord Stanley, who had yet to decide which side he was on, took no part in the opening phase of the battle. However, with 3,000 men in the Stanley contingent, both Richard and Henry were anxious to command his support.

Lord Thomas Stanley was the second husband of Margaret Beaufort of the House of Lancaster. He was therefore closely linked to Henry Tudor by marriage (Henry being Margaret's son by her first marriage). However, at Bosworth he was more preoccupied with the fate of his own son, Lord George Strange, than that of his stepson. King Richard had taken the precaution of seizing Lord Strange as a hostage in surety for his father's support in battle.

Lord Stanley was on the horns of a dilemma. If he supported Richard and Henry won, there would be no place for the House of Stanley in the new order. On the other hand, if he failed to support Richard his son would be executed. As the fighting began, with Richard's vanguard streaming down the hill towards Oxford's division, Stanley had still to commit his force. His indecision almost cost him dear. The King, certain that he was betrayed, issued orders for Stanley's son to be executed immediately. Yet even in this, Richard was to be thwarted. The execution party, fearing retribution from the Stanleys more than the King, secretly released their hostage unharmed.

Indeed, fortune smiled on Stanley that day. Not only did his intervention late in the battle lead directly to Henry's victory; he further cemented his alliance with the new order by personally placing the crown upon his stepson's head.

dying. Close to Richard, his standard-bearer, Sir Percival Thirwell, screamed in agony as his legs were severed. Above the terrible din of battle, the Castilian knight Juan de Salazar could be heard shouting to the King, 'Sire, take steps to put your person in safety'.[29] But Richard knew 'for certain that day would either deliver him a pacified realm thenceforward or else take it away forever'.[30] Fighting like a madman, he roared defiance: 'God forbid I yield one step. This day I will die as king or win'.[31]

Even as the King uttered these words, the once

tight battle lines of his retinue were spreading like a stain into the marsh behind. The day was lost. In the saddle and on foot, knights, men-at-arms, billmen, bowmen and riderless horses were floundering in the stinking mire pursued by the triumphant forces of Henry Tudor.

Suddenly, amid the noise and terror and confusion of the rout, Richard was down. His horse, trapped in the marsh, '... could not retrieve itself'.[32] Tudor's Welsh billmen, splashing through the mud like hounds upon a stag at bay, fell upon him furiously with their polearms. Still Richard 'would not be taken'[33] and struck out with his battle axe. As many blows rained down upon him, the King of England '... bore himself like a gallent knight and acted with distinction as his own champion until his last breath, shouting oftentimes that he was betrayed, and crying 'Treason! Treason! Treason!'[34] His agonies were ended by a savage, denting blow to his helmet from a halberd which left him slumped in his saddle.

In a flash the billmen seized upon his senseless body, tearing without ceremony or mercy at the expensive armour and clothing adorning his limp frame. The crowned helmet was ripped off and, as his enemies fought over the spoils, the king's blood-spattered body was dumped in the dark, foul-smelling swamp.

The victorious Henry Tudor was crowned on the field by none other than Lord Stanley; who was doubtless relieved to hear the new King swear faithfully to remember the services of those who had fought for him. From this day forth, the young Welsh upstart and self-styled

Richard III's reserve of mounted knights headed directly for Henry Tudor, killing at least one Lancastrian knight in Henry's livery.

'Earl of Richmond' was King Henry VII of England.

Richard III was the last King of England to die in battle. Whatever judgements history has made upon his reign he 'fell in the field, struck by many mortal wounds, a bold and valiant prince'.[35]

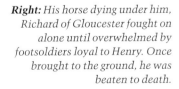

Left: Henry Tudor and Richard III both retained mounted reserves at Bosworth. Henry needed to escape if his plan failed: Richard intended to personally kill his opponent.

Right: His horse dying under him, Richard of Gloucester fought on alone until overwhelmed by footsoldiers loyal to Henry. Once brought to the ground, he was beaten to death.

STOKE
⫷ 16 June 1487 ⫸

After the death of Richard III, the foremost Yorkist pretender was the fifteen year old son of Edward IV's brother, the Duke of Clarence. The new Tudor King, Henry VII, imprisoned the young Earl in the Tower of London but a group of rebel Yorkists led by the Earl of Lincoln, set about training an impostor to take his place.

Their candidate was one Lambert Simnel, the son of a humble Oxford joiner. After a crash course in genealogy and courtly manners, Simnel was crowned King Edward VI in Dublin on 24 May 1487. In June an 8,000 strong invasion force landed in Lancashire comprised of lightly armed Irish around a hard core of 2,000 German mercenaries. Henry issued a summons of array and, with an army perhaps as large as 15,000, set off to confront the invaders. The two armies converged at East Stoke on 16 June 1487. Although the rebel army was nominally under the authority of the Earl of Lincoln, it was in actuality commanded by Martin Schwarz, leader of the German mercenaries. Schwarz was painfully aware of the shortcomings of his force. While his Germans were well equipped, the Irish levies which formed the bulk of his army wore

no body armour. He was also short of bowmen and heavily outnumbered. During the three mile march from Radcliffe, Henry VII allowed his vanguard, under the Earl of Oxford, to advance a fair distance ahead. Once again, as at Bosworth, it was Oxford who was destined to bear the brunt of the battle on behalf of the King. Fortunately, the vanguard contained the largest part of Henry's force.

For Oxford's men the prospect of a 'mass of barbarians ... arrayed on the brow of a hill ... lying in wait'[36] must have been a formidable one. But the discovery that the lightly clad Irish were vulnerable to arrow fire was very encouraging. Oxford's bowmen made the most of it. As the Irish levies charged down the hill they were shot 'full of arrows like hedgehogs'.[37] The close-quarter combat was a different affair. Schwarz's

Left: German mercenaries led by Martin Schwarz provided the backbone of the rebel army at Stoke. Relying on an imposter pretending to be a son of Edward IV, the rebellion was the Yorkists' last hope of dynastic victory.

Right: Henry Tudor's army prepared for battle, still uncertain as to the loyalty of their senior commanders. At any moment one of the great lords might have changed sides again.

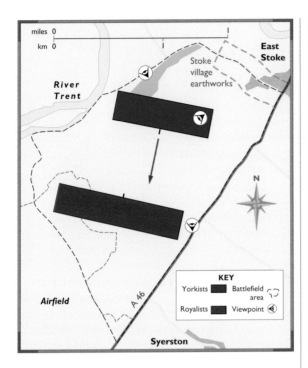

miles 0
km 0

East Stoke

Stoke village earthworks

River Trent

N

Airfield

A 46

KEY

Yorkists — Battlefield area

Royalists — Viewpoint

Syerston

With hastily raised armies comprised mostly of untrained levies, shrewd commanders salted their ranks with veterans; men who could pass on their skills. The Wars of the Roses employed many seasoned campaigners of the Hundred Years War in mainland Europe. In 1465 for example, Sir John Falstaff made a point of recruiting '... the older soldiers of [campaigns in] Normandy'. This demand for trained men sent wages up. Costs for a trained foot-soldier rose from 6d a day in 1459 to 10d by 1469, with the astronomic sum of 12d a day being demanded during 1471.

Among the indentured soldiers working for agreed rates of pay, there were also many foreign mercenaries. The most notable among these were Burgundian, French and Flemish soldiers employed for their specialist skills (notably Burgundian hand-gunners and artillery crews and Flemish/German pikemen).

'barbarians' fought with a ferocity born of desperation.

King Henry watched in horror, but did nothing to help, as Oxford's line began to buckle beneath the rebel assault. Although weight of numbers eventually told in the King's favour, Schwarz came very close to winning the day. In a battle lasting about three hours an estimated 4,000 rebels and 3,000 of the Tudor army were killed. Nobody was more relieved at the outcome than Henry, who had remained ready-mounted throughout for a quick getaway: '... joyus of his victory' he went immediately 'to give thanks to Our Lord for his good fortune'.[38]

Both Martin Schwarz and the Earl of Lincoln were cut down on the field. Lambert Simnel was spared and sent to work as a scullion in the King's kitchen. As for Henry himself, victory at Stoke strengthened his grip on the Crown and he never had to attend another battle. The battle of Stoke marked the last bloody full-stop of the Wars of the Roses.

Right and above: The German professionals fought hard before they were defeated. Henry Tudor would face further plots, but his spies betrayed them all. Stoke was the last chance for the Yorkists to stop the Tudor dynasty.

ANGLO-SCOTTISH WARFARE IN THE SIXTEENTH CENTURY

Henry VII died in 1509 to be succeeded by his son, the young Henry VIII. One of the first acts of the new English King was to antagonise his sister by refusing to hand over a legacy of jewels left to her by their father. This would hardly have been a matter of national importance if it were not for the fact that Henry's sister, Margaret Tudor, was the Queen of Scotland. Henry's father had taken pains to forge an alliance with James IV of Scotland in order to secure peace on his northern borders. For the price of a few baubles, his son foolishly placed this relationship in jeopardy.

Despite the fact that Henry VIII harboured territorial ambitions in France, the immature monarch had failed to appreciate the value of Scottish neutrality. In 1512 James, concerned that Henry's acquisitive eye might yet alight on Scotland, signed a mutual defence pact with Louis XII of France. The timing could not have been better for France nor more disastrous for Scotland. Henry invaded France early in 1513 and Louis activated the Franco-Scottish defence treaty; sending cash, arms and military instructors to Scotland to encourage James IV to honour his obligations.

James was a popular king, and to form his army Lowlanders, Highlanders, Borderers and men of the Western Isles (all habitually hostile to each other) put aside their differences and flocked to his banner. On 22 August 1513 the first truly united Scottish army, perhaps 35,000 strong, including 5,000 French professionals under the Comte d'Aussi; marched across the River Tweed into England.

The English were not caught unawares. Henry VIII had 'forgat not the old Prankes of the Scottes which is ever to invade England when the King is out'.[1] As a precaution he had left the northern levies in place and instructed the Lord Lieutenant of the North, the 70-year-old Earl of Surrey, to watch the border. Surrey quickly assembled an army to respond to the Scottish threat. Large contingents came from Yorkshire, Lancashire, Cheshire and Durham; lesser ones from Northumberland, Cumberland and Westmorland. On 8 September, with 26,000 men at his disposal, the elderly Earl (a veteran of Barnet and Bosworth on the Yorkist side) formally challenged the King of Scotland to battle on equal ground.

FLODDEN
⤞ 9 September 1513 ⤝

The Scots were deployed in a strong position on top of Flodden Hill. Unwilling to forego the advantages of this position, King James ignored the English challenge to battle, preferring to wait for the Earl of Surrey to attack.

When Surrey marched his men around to the north side of the feature however, it was a different matter. With the English now positioned between the Scots and Scotland, James abandoned his chosen ground. On the rain-sodden morning of 9 September he marched the Scottish army a mile across the top of the Flodden plateau to Branxton Hill on the northern side. It was mid-afternoon before the English were fully deployed for battle. Surrey himself took the left wing, while his two sons, Admiral Lord Thomas Howard and Edmund Howard, took the centre and right respectively. The small reserve of 3,000 was commanded by Lord Dacre,

It was said that King James intended to dine in London with his army on St. James' Day. With the bulk of the English army with Henry VIII in Flanders, it looked as if there was nothing to stop him. The defence of England was entrusted to a locally raised force of billmen.

The bill could be used to stab like a spear or to cut like an axe. The hook could unseat a horseman or impale a foot soldier's leg behind the knee.

Bringing the sacred banner of St. Cuthbert from Durham, the Earl of Surrey assembled his force at the old Percy stronghold of Alnwick.

Levies assembled from all over northern England and marched on to Newcastle from where Surrey issued his personal challenge to King James.

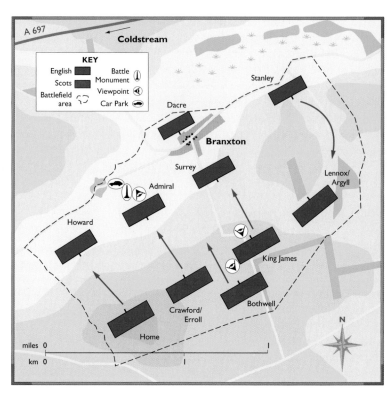

Warden of the Middle and West Marches. The only contingent yet to come up was that under the command of Lord Stanley. As at the battle of Bosworth in the preceding century, the Stanleys, though hindmost into the fray, were to play a crucial role.

The English had the better of the initial artillery duel. Concentrating his first salvos upon the Scottish guns themselves, William Brackenall, the English master gunner, 'shot fast and did great skaithe and slew [King James] principal gunners'.[2] He then turned his eighteen field guns upon the dense blocks of Scottish pikemen. After standing for an hour while round shot smashed into their formations, the Scottish left could endure no more. Abandoning King James' plan to force the English to attack uphill, Lord Home (the Chamberlain of Scotland) and the Earl of Huntly advanced their divisions 'down the hill in very good order, after the German fashion'.[3]

The bleak afternoon had worn into early dusk. The cold English soldiery, huddled at the foot of the hill, had already begun to think of making shelter and food for the night. Now, out of the lashing wind and rain, advancing in disciplined silence, came ranks of Borderers and Gordon Highlanders. The determination of this Scottish advance so shocked the front of Edmund Howard's brigade in that part of the field that they lost all will to stand and recoiled into their own rear ranks. The formation promptly fled, thus saving themselves from certain annihilation.

With his brigade in flight and his standard-bearer 'beaten and hewed in pieces', Edmund Howard suddenly found himself 'thrice stricken down …'[4] and fighting desperately for his life. He was only preserved by the timely arrival of Lord Dacre with 1,500 mounted Borderers from the English reserve. Eight score of this small force were killed extricating Edmund from peril, and many of Dacre's Borderers turned to looting the dead and played no further part in the battle.

Meanwhile King James, encouraged by the success of Lord Home, was himself tempted down from his invulnerable position. The offensive power of the Scottish infantry lay in fifteen foot pikes (supplied by the French). Deadly when correctly deployed en masse, the effectiveness of the pike depended on the ability of the troops to maintain formation and momentum. Unfortunately, the Scots were inexperienced in the use of such weapons. Although they removed their shoes in order to ensure a better grip on the muddy, rain-soaked slopes of Branxton Hill, the terrain proved rougher than anticipated. The English were deployed, not on level ground but on a slight rise. While not steep, it was enough to slow the momentum of the Scottish charge. James' pikemen failed to deliver the killing impact which might have won the day.

The English rallied and were heartened to discover that, at close-range, they could easily slice off the business end of the cumbersome Scottish pikes with their shorter bills and halberds. The Scots, left with nothing but the useless shafts, quickly abandoned them and resorted to more familiar weapons. It was too late. Though they '… fought sore and valiantly with their swords, … they could not resist the bills that lighted so thick and sore upon them'.[5]

As Lord Thomas Howard began to gain the upper hand over Crawford's brigade in the Scottish centre, the Earl of Huntly suggested to Lord Home that perhaps (having vanquished all opposition from Edmund Howard on the English left) they should intervene. Home dismissed him: 'He does well that does for himself; we have faught their vanguards and won the same; let the rest do their part as well as we'.[6] For his Lordship's countrymen, struggling valiantly on the blood-soaked Flodden moor, these words were effectively a death-sentence.

On the Scottish right however, King James surrounded by picked men from Lothian,

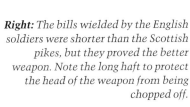

Left: Bills staked in the English camp as the army awaits news of the challenge. These formidable two-handed weapons would be pitched against the pikes of the Scots.

Right: The bills wielded by the English soldiers were shorter than the Scottish pikes, but they proved the better weapon. Note the long haft to protect the head of the weapon from being chopped off.

Linlithgow and Stirling, was driving back the forces of the Earl of Surrey. The King was of 'middle size and strong of a body … used to much exercise and of a slender diet'.[7] With his long red hair spilling from beneath his helmet, James laid into his enemies with a vengeance. Advancing 'from his company with many of his barons he struck with such force that he drove [the English ranks] back more than a long-bow shot [about 300 yards]',[8] reputedly slaying five Englishmen with his pike before it shattered in his hands. Undeterred, he slew five more with his sword. Then, hoping to exploit his success further, he called upon his reserves who 'with all the fury they could and in good order, got into motion and came bravely forward'.[9]

The only Scottish commanders now remaining on top of the Flodden plateau were the Earls of Lennox and Argyll, who had yet to commit their contingents of Highlanders and Islanders (Stuarts, Campbells, Macleans, Mackenzies and Macdonalds) to the fray. They were shortly to receive an unpleasant shock. To Lennox's right was a steep gully, along which the tardy English brigade commanded by Sir Edward Stanley was finally approaching the battlefield. The Scottish clansmen, preoccupied by events in the valley to their front, were oblivious to this danger.

Removing their shoes and scrabbling up the

THE EVOLUTION OF THE PIKES AND BILLS

The tactic of using concentrated formations of pole-arms to defeat cavalry had a long evolution in European warfare. The Flemish had defeated a superior cavalry force with just such a formation as early as 1302, at the battle of Cortrai. The Scots, seeking an advantage over the English, tested the long pike theory at the battle of Bannockburn in 1314; where they met with startling success. In the following year on mainland Europe, Swiss halberdiers achieved an astounding victory at Morgarten, killing 1,500 mounted Austrian knights in a matter of minutes. However while the Swiss went on to embrace the new system (achieving resounding victories at Laupen in 1339 and Sempach in 1386) the Scots were deterred from further experimentation by a devastating defeat at Halidon Hill in 1333. In consequence the longbow remained the dominant weapon in British warfare for almost 200 years.

By the sixteenth century, warfare on mainland Europe was dominated by the pike formations which the Swiss had by now perfected. It is therefore hardly surprising that the French contribution to the Franco-Scottish alliances existing at the time of Flodden (1513) and Pinkie (1547) included thousands of pikes. The Scots viewed the new system as an evolutionary step forward from their traditional schiltrons of spearmen. Unfortunately, effective use of the unwieldy pike required a considerable period of training.

Although French instructors accompanied the shipments of pikes to Scotland, extensive training time was a luxury which the Scots simply did not have. Hence both at Flodden and Pinkie the Scottish pikemen possessed considerably more enthusiasm than expertise; a significant factor in their failure on both occasions.

Left: Armed with pikes imported from France, the Scottish infantry formed up for battle in deep formations similar to those that brought victory at Bannockburn.

Below: Bills were fitted with a variety of heads, some with hooks as well as spikes.

Surrey's army had been assembled in great haste and marched from Newcastle with inadequate supplies. By the time of the battle, the army's beer supply was exhausted and food was running short in the camp.

steep side of the Flodden massif on their hands and knees, Stanley's men now launched a devastating flank attack. Unprepared and ill-armoured, the Highlanders could not withstand the sharp onslaught of the English bills and bows,

The English army marched around King James' position, cutting him off from Scotland and forcing a fight. James led his personal retinue directly against Surrey and was killed within yards of the English commander.

and fled. Sir Edward Stanley, somewhat to his own surprise, found himself in occupation of the top of Branxton Hill behind the main Scottish lines. In the dying light of the sinking sun, he charged down the slope and slammed into the rear of the King's contingent. By chance he arrived almost at the same time as Lord Dacre who had gathered together the remains of his reserve to charge James' exposed left flank.

With Surrey refusing to give another yard of ground before him and the forces of Lord Thomas Howard also beginning to press him on the right, the Scottish King was now 'constrained to fight in a round compass'.[10] It was to be a fight to the death: 'no prisoners were made, no quarter given'.[11] There could be no doubt as to the final outcome. By the end of the day no less than 9,000 Scots and 4,000 Englishmen would lie dead on Flodden Field.

As the sun went down the 'King of Scots was slain within a spear length of the ... Earl of Surrey'.[12] He had sold his life dearly. His body was later found to have been pierced by no less than five halberd blows and at least one arrow. With him, fighting doggedly to the last man, perished the flower of the Scottish nobility, including James' illegitimate son and 12 earls.

SOLWAY MOSS
❖ 24 November 1542 ❖

When James IV of Scotland was killed at Flodden, his only legitimate son became James V. He was seventeen months old. The power vacuum created by the long minority of the new King suited Henry VIII perfectly.

A leaderless Scottish court riven by rival factions posed no serious threat to England's northern borders. In retrospect it might have paid Henry to make some effort to befriend his young nephew. When James V finally reached maturity, he looked not to England for friends, but to his father's old allies the French. Eventually, exasperated by James' pro-French policy, Henry invited his nephew to a meeting in York. When James did not attend, Henry despatched 20,000 men under the Duke of Norfolk on a punitive expedition. Norfolk crossed the border, burned Roxburgh and Kelso, and then withdrew. James responded by raising a new army. In November 1542 this army crossed the River Esk and began burning the property of the Grahams; one of the principal Border families. In response Sir Thomas Wharton, the English deputy-warden of the March, led 3,000 men out of Carlisle.

A mere five miles north of Carlisle, between the Rivers Lyne and Esk, Wharton's small force came upon the Scottish army. Undeterred by the inequality in numbers, his men advanced bravely behind their six banners 'in good array upon foot with bows and bills'.[13]

Leaving off looting and burning the farms and homesteads of the English Borderers, the Scots dismounted and prepared for battle. However, the Scottish and English banners had barely reached 'within forty score' yards of each other when the Scots 'began easily to recoil'.[14] This sudden collapse of Scottish morale stemmed from two factors. Firstly, Wharton's confident advance had persuaded them that the English force must be the vanguard of a much larger army. Secondly, the Scottish force had no commander! James V had not seen fit to accompany his army into England, preferring to await news in safety back at Lochmaben. He had

Left: The Scottish border was beyond control of either Edinburgh or London for most of the sixteenth century. Border chieftains led their followers in a bitter cycle of raid and reprisal.

Right: English soldiers returned to the frontier in the 1540s, invading Scotland to burn Roxburgh and Kelso.

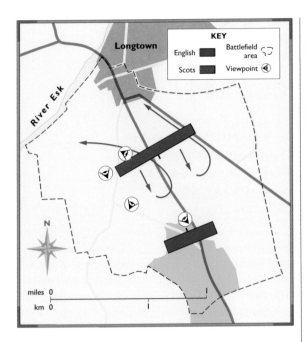

inexplicably failed to appoint a subordinate to serve in his stead. It was only when the army was apparently within minutes of a major battle that Sir James Sinclair of Pitcairns suddenly announced that he was in charge. Although he was one of the King's favourite courtiers the other commanders flatly refused to accede to his authority.

Leaderless, and with the dark shadow of Flodden lurking at the backs of their minds, the faltering Scottish army 'withdrew a soft pace homeward'.[15] Although their gunners did manage to fire a few salvos before all order broke down, the ensuing action barely deserves to be termed a battle. Hemmed in between the River Esk and the extensive marsh of Solway Moss, more Scots probably drowned attempting to escape over the treacherous bog than were felled by blows. At the end of the day Wharton's small force had captured around 200 Scottish nobles, 800 common soldiers and 24 guns.

King James took the news badly. Retreating to his bed in Falkirk Palace, he died a little over two weeks later aged only thirty. His daughter Mary, the new Queen of the Scots, was just six days old. Once again Scotland was condemned to a long minority.

RENAISSANCE MEDICAL ADVANCES

In the sixteenth century it was still common practise to treat gunshot wounds with boiling oil. However in 1530 a French surgeon named Ambrose Paré had an enlightening experience. Swamped by casualties after one battle, he was overcome by exhaustion and fell asleep before he could treat them all. When he awoke he was surprised to observe that among those patients whose gunshot wounds he had 'cured', a higher percentage had died than among those yet to receive the benefits of his attentions!

The same was true of amputees. Those who had their damaged limbs amputated and cauterised with a red-hot iron by the surgeon, suffered a higher mortality rate than those whose (uncauterised) amputations had been performed by a cannon ball!

Ambrose Paré vowed never again to subject such wounds to the fatal cures of the age. Instead he devised more effective systems of treatment (including the use of ligatures rather than cauterisation for amputees). Sadly the great medical experts of the day were unimpressed by these innovations. No less an authority than the Paris Faculty of Medicine concluded that '… ligature is far more dangerous than cauterization with red-hot irons … In truth, anyone who endures this butchery has every good cause to thank God that he is still alive after the operation'.

The victory at Solway Moss may have hastened James V's death, but it was avenged three years later when a strong force of English border raiders was defeated at Ancrum Moor. Hundreds of the raiders were taken prisoner.

PINKIE

⫷ 10 September 1547 ⫸

In 1543 Henry VIII arranged a marriage between
the infant Mary Queen of Scots and his six year
son Edward, the Prince of Wales. He was enraged
when the Scots repudiated the betrothal.

The resultant series of punitive expeditions
intended to restore the hand of Mary to the
young English Prince were known as the 'rough
wooing'. On Henry VIII's death in January 1547
his son became Edward VI. As the new King was
still only nine years old the 'rough wooing' was
resumed on his behalf by the new Protector of
the Realm, the Duke of Somerset. On 1
September 1547 Somerset crossed the border into
Scotland with 80 cannons, 8,000 foot and 4,000
cavalry (including a contingent of Spanish horse).
He was supported off the coast by the English
fleet, commanded by Lord Clinton.

In response to the English threat, the Earl of
Arran, Mary's Regent, summoned every Scottish
man between the ages of sixteen and sixty to
assemble at Edinburgh with one month's food.
Though woefully short of artillery and cavalry,
the resultant army of about 25,000 men was
deployed on high ground behind the River Esk.

*Artillery had become far more mobile since the Wars
of the Roses. Somerset's cannon inflicted terrible
losses on the deep formations of Scottish pikemen.*

To their right was a marsh and to their left the
sea. On the seaward side they had also erected an
earth bank to protect themselves from the
cannons of English ships. The Duke of Somerset
arrived to find himself outnumbered almost 2:1.
Reluctant to mount a frontal assault on the
formidable Scottish defences, he stalled for time.

On 9 September the Earl of Arran rashly
advanced his 1,500 cavalry in order to lure the
English to attack. Tragically for the Scots, this
bait worked only too well. In a relatively short
space of time the English horse, under Lord Grey,
effectively destroyed the Scottish cavalry as a
fighting force.

On the morning of 10 September 1547 the
English army began a slow advance, dragging
their heavy cannons over the rough ground
towards the river. The Scots responded by
abandoning their impregnable position in order
to launch an attack of their own. Somerset could
hardly believe his luck. On open ground his
strength in artillery and cavalry could be
deployed to the best advantage.

Three Scottish pike divisions led by the Earls
of Arran, Huntly and Angus crossed the river and
crowded in upon each other until they formed
one vast pike block. It was an imposing sight, but
the flanks of this formation were very
vulnerable. The Earl of Argyll's Highland
division, which should have comprised the left
wing, had been driven off by the guns of
Clinton's fleet offshore. On the other side the
battered remnants of the Scottish cavalry formed
a thin right wing.

As the English horse charged towards them,
the Scots adopted the defensive schiltron

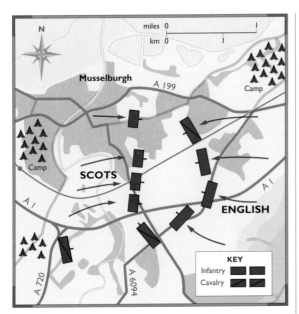

formation in which the mass of pike points bristled like '… the skin of an angry hedgehog'.[16] Grey's cavalry floundered into a ditch, struggled free and came gamely on to hurl themselves against the Scottish pikes. Not surprisingly the schiltron proved impervious. Providing the Scots kept close together, their pikemen were more than able to hold the English cavalry at bay. In the pandemonium that followed, men and horses were disembowelled and Grey himself was struck through the mouth by a pike point.

Then, at last, the English cannon began to pound, wreaking bloody havoc among the dense mass of the Scottish formations. Packed together like sardines, whole lanes of pikemen were gored and dismembered by flying round shot. While the Scots were still reeling beneath this onslaught, Pedro de Gamboa's contingent of Spanish cavalry sallied forth to demonstrate state-of-the-art European tactics; firing their arquebuses from the saddle. English arquebusers and archers rushed forward on foot to add a few volleys of their own. Finally, as sheets of rain began to sweep in from the sea, the persistent English cavalry rallied for another charge.

The Scots attempted an orderly withdrawal. However, with visibility reduced by smoke and rain, and shouted commands drowned out by the din of battle, panic swept the ranks and the army disintegrated and fled, with the English horse in triumphant pursuit.

Surprisingly, for all the blood spilled in the 'rough wooing', Somerset failed to consolidate his victory by taking possession of Mary Queen of Scots. The planned matrimonial union of England and Scotland never took place. It was not Mary, but her son James Stuart, who was one day destined to wear the English crown.

English soldiers faced the grim prospect of assaulting a larger army in a better position. Then, incredibly, the Scots advanced to the attack.

Many English skirmishers fought with muskets, although the archers reportedly inflicted more casualties.

The English cannon stopped the assault and broke up the Scottish formations. A final cavalry charge destroyed Arran's army.

SOLDIERING IN THE CIVIL WARS

That Charles I was a well-intentioned King is not disputed. Sadly, good intentions were no cure for the many ills of his mismanaged reign. Archbishop Laud described him at the time as '… a mild mannered and gracious prince who knew not how to be, or be made, great.'[1]

The corruption and incompetence which riddled his court continually set him at odds with Parliament. In 1629, despairing of endless talk of reform and restraints on royal power, he dissolved the third parliament of his reign and attempted to rule without it for the next eleven years. To do so, Charles resorted to devious means of raising revenue, reviving long-abandoned taxes. These increasing abuses of power were widely resented.

The King's religious reforms also caused widespread disaffection with the monarchy. In 1637 he imposed an Anglican Church settlement on the Presbyterian Church of Scotland which involved the introduction of a new prayer book. The Scots violently objected to any interference with their kirk, and when the book was first used, at St Giles Cathedral in Edinburgh, it caused a riot. The Scottish National Assembly of 1638 signed a covenant to reject the new prayer book and limit the power of the bishops. In response, the King resorted to that age-old habit of kings faced with an obstinate populace: war.

The Bishops' Wars: 1639–40

Behind their shiny drums and pristine plumes, the King's newly raised army marched for Scotland. While the officers sat in their finely accoutred saddles and dreamed of glory, those further down the pecking order shambled through the spring mud and dreamed mostly of food. Most of the soldiers tramping north were uncertain why they were being set upon the Scots. No such doubts plagued the newly raised, Scottish 'Army of Covenanters'. Under the leadership of Alexander Leslie, a veteran of other European wars, they were well-provisioned, well-drilled and highly motivated in defence of their land and faith.

On 2 June the Earl of Arundel, commander-in-chief of the English army, received word that the Scots were close by, at Kelso. The English army marched at dawn the next day. Over the sound of marching feet and the clatter of hooves, the Earls of Holland and Newcastle could be heard loudly disputing who should have the honour of going first in line. This issue apparently took precedence over basic march discipline: by late afternoon the English cavalry and infantry were so widely separated that they could neither hear nor see each other. It was at this point that Holland, commanding the cavalry, became aware of something disturbing on his otherwise cloudless horizon: the Covenanters' Army was closing in upon them in a large crescent formation.

Holland halted to observe this phenomenon and, deciding that it was not to his liking, sent a messenger across to the Scots to request that they withdraw. The messenger returned with the counter-proposal that the English should retire; a suggestion reinforced by the rattle of musketry. Sensing a battle in the making, Holland about-faced and led his squadrons in ignominious flight – pursued by nothing more deadly than Scottish laughter.

The first 'Bishops' War' was effectively over. Peace negotiations followed, with the 'Pacification of Berwick' signed on 19 June 1639. However, the King wanted obedience, not compromise. Even as he talked peace, he was plotting another war despite the refusal of Parliament to vote increased taxes to support him. Within a year the disbanded armies had been reassembled and marched once more to the beat of the drums. This time there were to be more casualties than English pride.

THE BATTLE OF NEWBURN FORD
❧ 28 August 1640 ❧

By August 1640 an army of 20,000 Scots had crossed the Tweed and were marching towards Newcastle-upon-Tyne. Rather than attack the city's strong, northern defences, the Scots' commander, Alexander Leslie, decided to cross the Tyne at Newburn Ford and attack from the south.

It fell to Lord Conway to block this advance. He arrived at Newburn Ford on 27 August with approximately 2,000 foot, 1,500 horse and four cannons, and set all hands to building barricades. Although Sir Jacob Astley brought him 2,000 reinforcements the next day, the English were still hopelessly outnumbered. According to Conway's own account, he would have retreated to Newcastle had he not '... at that instant received a letter from the Earl of Stafford commanding him to fight.'[2] With little time to organise his defences, Conway's fortifications

The English forces marched north, short of supplies and poorly motivated. The soldiers would have been surprised to learn how Parliament feared the creation of this new army.

were to prove ineffective. Captain Thomas Dymock later described how '[The Scottish] army appeared marching on the hills above the ford when we were drawing into our miserable works in the valley, where we lay so exposed to their battery, that their great shot was bowled in amongst our men, to their great loss …'[3]

DRUMS AND TRUMPETS

Shouted commands were often lost in the hue and cry of battle. To overcome this problem drums and trumpets were used. Essential infantry commands were communicated via the drums in eight prescribed beats (or 'points of war') while cavalry commands were sounded on the trumpets. Dragoons, who dismounted to fight, were essentially mounted infantry and were therefore commanded by drums rather than trumpets.

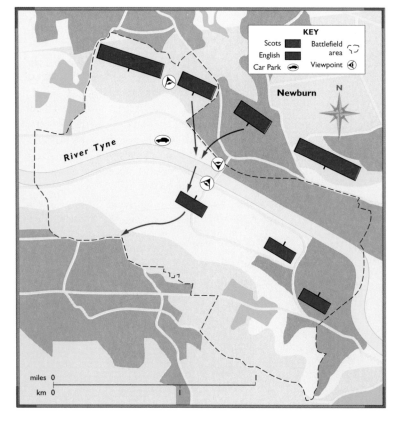

Conway stationed his cavalry behind the infantry, but their counter-attack was stopped dead by Scottish musket fire. The horsemen fled back towards Newcastle which surrendered to the Scots the next day.

THE FIRST CIVIL WAR 1642–46

The battle of Newburn Ford left the Scottish Covenanters' Army in occupation of northern England and demanding what amounted to 'Danegeld' before they would agree to leave. Desperate for funds, Charles was forced to summon his old bugbear – Parliament. The 'Long Parliament', which assembled on 3 November 1640, quickly secured passage of a bill prohibiting its dissolution by the King without its own consent. After this came other acts which banned non-parliamentary taxes and further diluted Royal power in favour of independent local government.

In October 1641 Ireland burst into rebellion and Charles requested funding for a new army, over which he would have sole control. There were many in Parliament who doubted the King's intentions, but the first to publicly voice his concerns was a little-known back-bench MP from Cambridgeshire – Oliver Cromwell. By the spring of 1642, this war of words had entered a grim new phase and Parliament issued the 'Militia Ordinance'. This ensured that they, rather than the King, would nominate military commanders and thus retain control of the new army. There were many who felt that this crossed the Rubicon between reform and revolution.

The divisions between the Crown and Parliament were soon to be mirrored by divisions in houses across the land. Bulstrode Whitlock lamented in Parliament that 'It is strange to note how we have insensibly slid into this beginning of a civil war by one accident after another, as the waves of the sea … and we scarce know how, but from paper combats … we are now come to the question of raising forces.'[4]

On 22 August 1642 the King raised his standard in Nottingham. England was at war with itself.

Alexander Leslie had installed a light cannon on top of Newburn Church, from where it played freely upon the English lines. The four English cannons returned fire with a noisy, but ineffective, bombardment. Under this exchange, the Scots began to cross the ford at around four o'clock that afternoon, advancing doggedly amid the spumes of water kicked up by the splash of English musket balls. Seeing this, the English, who had no heart for the fight, abandoned their best defence at the barricades. Putting up no more than a scattered resistance, they bolted. Thus the Second Bishops' War ended much like the first; almost before it had really begun.

MATCHLOCK MUSKETS

The most common type of musket in general use was the matchlock. This weapon relied on a lighted 'match' (strands of twisted tow impregnated with saltpetre). The match was held by a sprung lever known as the 'serpent'. When released by the trigger, the serpent snapped forward causing the match to ignite the fine powder in the 'priming pan', next to the 'touch hole' in the barrel. The flash in the pan set off the main charge, which had been rammed down the barrel. During the course of the war the matchlock was gradually superseded by the more reliable 'firelock' or 'flintlock'; so-called because it was fired, not by a lighted match, but by a flint chip sparking the powder-charged priming pan.

Most of the English losses occured after they abandoned their defences and were cut down by the pursuing Scots. With no army left, King Charles was forced to sue for peace.

POWICK BRIDGE

23 September 1642

The battle at Powick Bridge in Worcestershire was little more than a skirmish, with barely a thousand men a side, but it has earned its place in history as the first significant action of the Civil War.

Late on the afternoon of 23 September 1642 the King's nephew, Prince Rupert of the Rhine, stopped to rest beneath the shade of a tree in Wick Field, just north of the River Teme. He was riding to the relief of a Royalist treasure convoy in Worcester threatened by advancing Parliamentarian forces. As Rupert and his men rested their saddle-weary limbs, they became aware that the bustle of activity on the far side of the river was something more than the usual rural traffic. It was in fact 1000 Parliamentarian horse and dragoons under the command of Colonel John Fiennes.

The two sides were evenly matched. The Parliamentarians were better equipped than the Royalist troopers, but Fiennes had needlessly exhausted his men by keeping them in the saddle all night. Now, even as he and his officers argued whether to cross the River Teme or to wait until more certain of enemy dispositions, the van of his command was already strung out over the narrow span of Powick Bridge.

Rupert quickly realised that prompt action would carry the day. As the Parliamentarian horse emerged into Wick Field, Royalist dragoons greeted them with a ragged peppering of carbine shot. Then, having hurriedly marshalled his forces, the Prince launched a determined assault.

Colonel Sandy's troop had been first across the bridge and they were destined to bear the brunt of the charge. In the dreadful seconds before the impact they began to discharge their wheel-lock pistols into the body of oncoming Royalist horse but, once launched, the charge did not falter.

The whole action lasted no more than fifteen minutes, during which time the Parliamentarians were severely battered and 150 men were left dead upon the field. Prince Rupert himself received a sword-cut leading the charge,

CHARGE!

In seventeenth century cavalry actions various methods of mounted attack were used, although both sides preferred to maximise the disruptive value of cavalry as shock troops by plunging into the enemy lines; unless of course they were facing pikes. It was the action which preceded this final stage which varied. They might halt first, at close range, to deliver pistol fire; or rush headlong in, firing on the hoof. Alternatively they sometimes used the old fashioned, but effective, straight charge with drawn swords.

In the 'headlong' assault it was important to keep tight formation and not to fire until close to the enemy. The charge itself was saved for the final yards. Begun too early it would disrupt the formation and exhaust the horses, depleting the impact of the assault. Equally, if left too late, the charge was unable to gather the impetus upon which it relied for success.

but his decisive action carried the field and secured the Royalist treasure convoy. Fiennes was not destined to reach Worcester that afternoon. Beaten back across Powick Bridge his men retreated in disarray.

Left: *The cavalry of both sides were similarly equipped, with 'lobster' helmets and back and breastplates over buff coats.*

Right: *The Parlimentarian troopers had been riding through the night and little expected to run into Prince Rupert's Royalists (above).*

EDGEHILL
❧ 23 October 1642 ❧

In the autumn of 1642, King Charles marched on London. At Edgehill in Warwickshire he met the Parliamentarian forces led by the Earl of Essex. The scene was set for the first major battle of the war.

The 14,000 strong Royalist Army formed up on top of Edgehill. However, Essex, with an army of almost the same number, could not be enticed to attack up the steep ridge. Instead he fanned out in the fields below and waited for the King to redeploy on the lower slopes. When the Royalist army was ready the King rode along his lines to raise the morale of his men, who cheered loudly. The watching Parliamentarian gunners responded with a salvo of cannon balls, thus beginning an hour-long artillery duel. This was a nerve-racking introduction to battle for the raw troops on both sides, who were forced to stand in tight formation while round shot carved bloody furrows through their ranks. Finally, the Royalist trumpets sounded the 'Tuquet', signalling their cavalry to advance on both wings. Sir James Ramsey's Brigade on the Parliamentarian left wing watched Prince Rupert's Royalist dragoons advance towards them in tight formation. This

Above: Parliamentarian cavalry were no match for the Royalist horse at Edgehill, but two regiments managed to attack the Royalist infantry.

Right: The Royalists came down from Edgehill and, after an artillery duel, advanced to the attack. The King's cavalry were victorious, but then left the field in hot pursuit.

Below: Against soldiers massed six or eight ranks deep, a cannon ball could inflict murderous casualties. Fortunately for the infantry, the guns took a long time to reload and were relatively immobile.

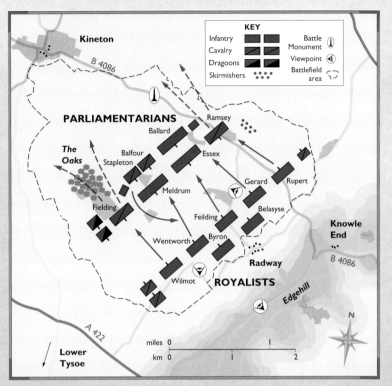

KEY

Infantry
Cavalry
Dragoons
Skirmishers

Battle Monument
Viewpoint
Battlefield area

Kineton

B 4086

PARLIAMENTARIANS

Ramsey
Ballard
The Oaks
Balfour
Stapleton
Essex
Meldrum
Gerard
Rupert
Fielding
Belasyse
Feilding
Wentworth
Byron
Knowle End
B 4086
Radway
Wilmot
ROYALISTS
Edgehill

A 422

Lower Tysoe

miles 0   1
km 0   1   2

N

A Parliamentarian infantry regiment prepares to meet the Royalist charge. Pikemen in the front ranks level their pikes and the musketeers prepare a well-aimed volley.

sobering sight prompted Sir Faithful Fortescue to make a last-minute decision to swap sides. Firing his pistol into the ground and tearing off the orange sash which indicated loyalty to Parliament, the faithless Sir Faithful dashed his troop forward, not to attack Prince Rupert but to join him!

The Parliamentarian left wing panicked. The remaining troopers of Ramsey's Brigade wheeled about and fled, bursting through the ranks of their own supporting foot soldiers. Seeing themselves abandoned, and only too aware of the thundering hooves of the Royalist cavalry about to break over them, the infantry also broke ranks. This was the worse thing that they could have done. As they threw down their weapons and ran for their lives, they were at the mercy of Rupert's cavaliers who duly butchered them in large numbers.

At the far end of the field, the parliamentarian right wing was also broken by a cavalry charge led by Henry Wilmot. However, this double

POWDER CHARGES

Musketeers wore twelve wooden bottles suspended from a bandolier across the shoulder. Each bottle contained the correct measure of powder for a single charge. Although this speeded up the loading of the matchlock there was an inherent risk that an unguarded spark, igniting the powder in one bottle, might set off a fatal chain reaction. The apostles were also a cumbersome method of carrying the charges and were prone to become tangled on the move. Furthermore, when used by several hundred men, the clattering of the wooden bottles made such a noise that it could be difficult to hear shouted orders. Later, charges contained in paper became increasingly popular. This method ensured that adequate wadding (often ignored by men in the heat of battle) was used, as the paper container was inevitably rammed down with the ball. The wadding gave the ball a firm fit in the barrel and hence a better velocity when fired. Some sources suggest that the use of paper charges could triple the rate of fire.

'Give Fire!' The regiment vanishes in its own smoke, sending several hundred lead musket balls into a densely-packed enemy formation perhaps only 50 paces away.

Many regiments did not charge straight into hand-to-hand combat. It took a great deal of courage to go the last few yards, and they paused, yelling abuse at the enemy

success was utterly wasted. Rather than remaining to support their foot soldiers and exploit their early gains, both wings of Royalist cavalry vanished from the field in uncontrolled pursuit of the Parliamentarian horse. In their excitement they had failed to notice that two further Parliamentarian horse regiments (Balfour's and Stapleton's) were sheltering unobtrusively behind Sir John Meldrum's Brigade of Foot. This error was to have grave consequences later in the day.

Now it was the turn of the infantry. Sir Jacob Astley, commanding the King's foot regiments, took a moment to say a quick prayer before ordering the general advance, 'O Lord! Thou knowest how busy I must be this day, if I forget thee, do not forget me!' Then he bellowed out the command which was to begin the real slaughter of the day: 'March on boys.'[5]

For those waiting to receive them it must have been a mesmeric sight to watch the King's infantry come rippling, rank upon rank, down the slope towards them. As they approached musket range, barked orders began to sound up and down the lines of Parliamentarian musketeers: 'Draw out your match. Blow your match. Cock your match. Try your match. Guard your pan…' With the drums of the enemy beating ever closer and the jangle of their equipage now

clearly audible, the musketeers concentrated upon the familiar drills on which their lives depended. The final 'Give fire' unleashed an explosion of sound. Flame flashed along the line from the pans and barrels of thousands of muskets, and the advancing Royalists were lost from sight in a cloud of smoke.

On the receiving end there was a shudder as the advancing line absorbed the shock of combat. Though many men now lay bleeding in the grass, the great majority marched grimly on behind their banners and flags, returning fire with a few loose volleys as they came. As the gap narrowed they prepared to charge the last few yards and the pikemen were commanded to 'charge' their pikes, levelling them at chest height to create a bristling hedge of steel. With no time for further volleys, the musketeers reversed their muskets ready for use as clubs.

In the face of this relentless Royalist advance, morale on the Parliamentarian right was crumbling: Lord Mandeville desperately attempted to stop his men from routing but '…though his Lordship beseeched them, yea cudgelled them …'[6] they broke ranks and ran off disrupting more regiments close by. All that was now left of the original Parliamentarian right flank was Sir John Meldrum's Brigade.

Meldrum, aware of the dangers of receiving a

charge whilst stationary, ordered a counvcharge. As the two armies impacted, the men in the rear ranks lent their weight to the general 'push of pike'; each side labouring to force the other to give ground. The leading ranks struggled for footing in a deadly and terrifying scrum. Above the splintering pikestaffs, the screams of the wounded, and the ringing of steel upon steel, the air throbbed with the roar of thousands of men locked in mortal combat. In the midst of this wild struggle Robert Devereaux, Earl of Essex, Lord General of the Parliamentarian army, fought like a common soldier with a pike in his hands.

It was now that the remaining two Parliamentarian cavalry regiments emerged to play their part. Without their own horse to protect them, the Royalists were vulnerable to enemy cavalry action and some of Richard Feilding's Brigade were put to flight. By this time the armies had drawn slightly apart, exhausted from the first great push. While the pikemen rested on their pikes, the opposing musketeers exchanged volleys. At close range, firing into ranks packed six to eight deep, it was hard to miss.

Essex, determined to win the infantry combat before the Royalist horse could return and tip the balance, ordered a second charge. With levelled pikes and reversed muskets the Parliamentarian foot regiments advanced once again over a field now littered with the broken and discarded detritus of battle. This time, while the Royalists of Sir Nicholas Byron's Brigade struggled to hold their own in the bitter push of pike, Essex's two cavalry regiments stormed into their exposed flank and rear.

As yet more Parliamentarian foot rushed forward in support, those packed tight against the Royalist line felt it begin to buckle and give ground. Encouraged, they pressed home their attack. With the will to fight beaten out of them, some of the Royalist infantry looked for ways of escape and began to run to the rear. This trickle

The Royalist infantry fell back, enabling their cannon to come back into action. Firing case shot — like gigantic shotguns — they stopped the Parlimentarian advance.

suddenly became a flood as two entire regiments of Byron's Brigade dissolved under the relentless pressure and streamed from the field.

The possibility of a decisive Royalist defeat hung in the balance. Thankfully for the King, both Wentworth's Brigade on the far left flank and Charles Gerrard's on the extreme right, retired in good order. This short pull back allowed the Royalist cannons a clear field of fire. Working in haste the gunners poured a deadly shower of case-shot at the advancing Parliamentarians, buying time for their infantry to form a new defensive line along the banks of a small brook. Without fresh reserves to consolidate his gains, or more cavalry to exploit them, the Earl of Essex had little choice but to preserve the Parliamentarian army and drew back.

Henry Wilmot now returned with some of the Royalist horse and Lord Falkland urged him to mount one last charge. Knowing that his horses were exhausted Wilmot refused to hazard it. 'My Lord' he replied, 'We have got the day, and let us live to enjoy the fruits ...'[7]

In the gathering gloom of evening, some three thousand men lay dead or wounded upon the field. With both sides reluctant to concede defeat Edgehill proved a bloody first round in what was destined to be a long Civil War.

THE PUSH OF PIKE

A charge of pike against pike could go several ways. The morale of either side might give out before contact, in which case they fell back. Alternatively, both sides might stand their ground within pike-reach, stabbing with the points of their pikes while fending off the lunges of their adversaries. The final, and most dramatic, possibility was when opposing pike blocks collided in the 'push of pike'; each driving headlong against the other in a brutal struggle to overwhelm the enemy.

In the push of pike there was no room to manoeuvre the pike shafts and most points were forced up over the heads of those who were wedged in the crush below. Nor was there adequate space for a pikeman to make use of his sword. In consequence, although a few men may be impaled in process, the push of pike usually involved surprisingly few fatalities. More casualties tended to occur when pike blocks became exhausted or disordered and abandoned the fight in favour of flight. It was then, presenting their defenceless backs to the enemy, that they exposed themselves to slaughter.

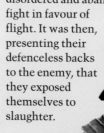

BRADDOCK DOWN

⤛ 19 January 1643 ⤜

In Cornwall Sir Ralph Hopton had raised an army of 16,000 men for the King. By January 1643 these Royalist volunteers were under threat from two converging Parliamentarian armies. Hopton decided to strike at Colonel Ruthin's 4000 Parliamentarians before they could combine with the army of the Earl of Stamford.

By noon on 19 January the armies of Hopton and Ruthin were drawn up '… within musket shot …' on either side of a small valley and '… saluted each other with bulitts'.[8] Initially neither side was willing to surrender the advantage of high ground, but Hopton finally lost patience. Realising that Ruthin's artillery had not yet come up, he sent secretly to the nearby house of Lord Mohun for two small cannon to reinforce his centre. Positioning these on top of a Bronze Age barrow, he ordered them to begin firing as the signal for a general advance.

Sir Bevil Grenville, a local Cornishman taking part in his first action, received his baptism of fire spearheading the Royalist assault:

'… following prayers in the head of every division I ledd my part [i.e. regiment] away, who followed me with so good courage, both down the one hill and up the other, that it strook a terror in [the enemy] while the seconds came up gallantly after me, and the wings of horse charged on both sides.'[9]

This uphill charge, made in the face of hostile fire, while laden with cumbersome pikes and muskets was no mean feat. Ruthin's Parliamentarians were shattered and they fled

Hopton's Cornishmen manhandle their cannon into action. The horses or oxen used to tow the guns were then taken to the rear, so it was rare for guns to move far during a battle.

A musketeer blows on his smouldering matchcord: keeping this alight and correctly trimmed was a fiddly task, difficult to perform under fire.

back towards Liskeard. In their flight they abandoned several brass guns and an iron saker (5 lb field gun) which were still being manhandled towards their position when the rout began. After Braddock Down, Parliament treated Royalist contingents from Cornwall with grudging respect.

The Parliamentarian forces marched back to Devon after this defeat, their leaders blaming each other.

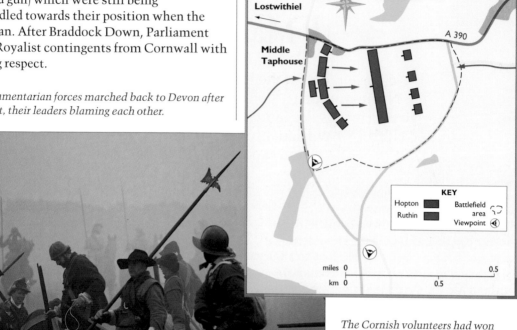

The Cornish volunteers had won their county for the King, but many were unwilling to cross the Tamar to take the fight to the enemy in Devon.

HOPTON HEATH

⊰⊱ 19 March 1643 ⊰⊱

Charles I despatched an army under the Earl of
Northampton to Staffordshire in March 1643. It
arrived just as Parliamentarian commanders Sir John
Gell and Sir William Brereton were planning to unite
and capture Stafford.

By the time Northampton had brought up his 1,200 men (mostly cavalry) it was already late afternoon. The 1,500 Parliamentarians, having had their choice of the ground, had deployed the main body of their foot on a warren of rabbit holes where horse could not charge without hazard. On their left wing, hedges and walls formed natural breastworks for their musketeers. In addition they had eight Drakes (5 lb field guns) and three larger guns set up on a hill well-protected by the terrain. The Royalists however, had 'Roaring Meg'; a twelve-foot long demi-cannon which fired a 29 lb ball.

As Northampton's dragoons advanced to skirmish with Gell's musketeers, the deadly voice of 'Roaring Meg', thundered through the winter gloom. According to an eyewitness, Meg's '... first shott killed six of their men and hurt four and the next made such a lane through them that they had little minde to close agayne.'[10]

For the next half hour the Royalist demi-cannon spat death and destruction as the gunners on both sides laboured over their smoking barrels. Although the Parliamentarian artillery

Left: The Royalists' heavy artillery opens fire. 'Roaring Meg' was one of several cannon to be given names: there were two others known as Gog and Magog, while 'Sweet Lips' was named after a Cavalier lady of easy virtue.

Right: 'Roaring Meg' fired a 29 lb iron cannon ball at a rate of about ten rounds an hour. Each shot required 25 lb of gunpowder.

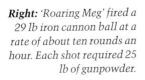

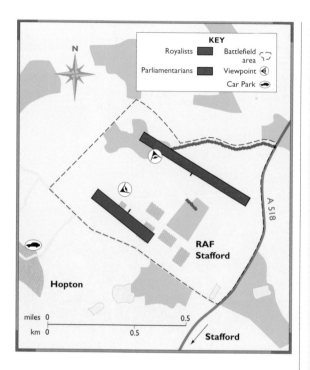

were more numerous, they were less effective; most of their shot flying harmlessly over the heads of the Royalists.

Encouraged by the success of his gunners, the Earl of Northampton personally led the first Royalist cavalry charge. This succeeded in driving back the Parliamentarian horse and capturing eight enemy cannons but failed to break Brereton's foot soldiers, who '... by the

With more Parliamentarian forces arriving, the Earl of Northampton led the Royalist horse in a desperate charge.

INFANTRY REGIMENTS

When the Civil War began there was no full-time standing army. Regiments were often expanded around the nucleus of one of the local 'Trained Bands'. While the London trained bands were reasonably professional, the provincial units were often reluctant to fight outside their local region, and they decreased in importance as more regiments were raised. Some new regiments were raised for the duration of the war while others served only for a few weeks or months subject to local needs. To begin with they were composed of volunteers but by 1643 it had become necessary to introduce conscription.

Each regiment incorporated both pikemen and musketeers, with a ratio of two to one in favour of pikes during the early part of the war. As the conflict progressed, the true potential of the musket as an offensive weapon was recognised and the pike/musket ratio reversed. By 1648 the musket was easily the most destructive weapon on the battlefield and a few foot regiments fielded no pikes at all. The musketeers, who were usually deployed on either side of a central block of pikes, inflicted damage at a distance by firing volleys. When threatened by cavalry they would rush to shelter behind the long reach of the pikes, while continuing to harass the enemy with random fire.

discharge of their first volley of shott did perform mighty greate execution.'[11] Among the casualties was Northampton himself. Surrounded when his

Drummers carried their drums on a sling, positioning them almost horizontally. Rich Colonels sometimes dressed their regimental musicians in elaborate uniforms.

Left: *Facing a cavalry attack, the musketeers withdrew behind the pikemen. The pikes were levelled outwards, ready to impale any horse than tried to close. The cavalry could try to shoot their way in with pistols, but they could be shot down in turn by the musketeers.*

Below far left: *The Royalist horse withdrew, leaving their commander dead behind them.*

Below left: *The Royalists rallied and tried a second time, breaking through the Parliamentarian line to win a surprise victory.*

horse was shot from under him, he refused to surrender to 'base rogues' and was killed by a halberd blow to his head. Meanwhile the dragoons on both sides were locked in a vicious engagement in which, according to Brereton 'they fought so long, and so fiercely, untill all their powder and bullet was spent. Afterwards they joyned, and fell to it pell-mell, one upon another, with the stocks of their musketts.'[12]

The Royalists rallied for a second charge and, as evening gathered in, the remainder of the Parliamentarian cavalry were driven back into their own stands of pikemen and fled. Although disordered by this experience, the pikemen stood their ground, striking with their pikes at the Royalist horse. With neither side able to wholly break the other, the battle was finally ended by the onset of darkness. The Parliamentarians quit the field under cover of night, sinking the rest of their artillery pieces into nearby pools to prevent them falling into the hands of the enemy.

Although Hopton Heath was a relatively small-scale encounter, the number of casualties, variously estimated between three to five hundred, was disproportionately high. It was a hard-fought engagement which could not really be called a victory for either side. Though the Royalists were left in possession of the field, they had lost the Earl.

REGIMENTAL STRENGTH

Ideally a full-strength regiment of foot was composed of around 1,200 men, subdivided into companies of 120 (each including company commander, lieutenant, ensign, two sergeants, three corporals and two drummers). However, there was wide variation and company sizes could range from 80 to as many as 200. There was also great diversity in the number of companies to a regiment. Some West Country regiments numbered only three, others as many as thirteen! Whatever the official strength of the army, the numbers actually employed in battle were often well below this figure due to the natural attrition of leave, sickness, desertion and casualties.

STRATTON
❧ 16 May 1643 ❧

In April 1643 Parliamentarian commanders in the
West Country discovered that Sir Ralph Hopton had
been ordered to advance his Cornish Royalists into
Somerset to join forces with Prince Maurice.
Determined to prevent this, the Earl of Stamford
deployed his army, with 13 cannons, in an
Iron-Age hill fort at Stratton and waited for
Hopton to arrive.

Desperate times require desperate
measures. Hopton's plan for the battle of
Stratton was both perilous and bold. As his army
of 2,400 foot and 500 horse was outnumbered
almost 2:1, he decided to try and take Stamford
by surprise.In the cold, dark hours before the
dawn of 16 May 1643 there was unusual activity
in the fields near Stratton. Perchance the nightly
activities of the hunting owls were disturbed by a
pike clattering into an unseen tree branch, or the
hissed curse of a man stumbling into a ditch, but
otherwise the Cornish Royalists passed
unobtrusively, hugging the shadows like an army
of ghosts.

Having taken the risk of dividing his army
into four columns of 600 men and 2 cannons
(keeping his horse in reserve) Hopton had moved
them up during the night for a dawn attack.
Aware that the enemy were '… all strongly
encamped and barracadoed upon the flatt topp of
a very high hill that had very steepe ascents to
them every way'[13]; he was relying on the

*Hopton's Cornishmen crept
around the enemy position
during the night, assembling
at dawn to attack from an
unexpected direction.*

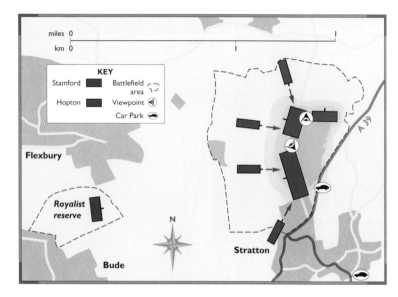

Below: The guns are brought into place to support the infantry attack.

Below middle: A prolonged musketry duel took place as the Cornishmen battered against the well-positioned Parliamentarian line.

Bottom: Parliamentarian gunners pounded the Royalist infantry at close range, but Hopton's men managed to fight their way to the top of the hill.

elements of surprise and concentration of force from four directions to offset numerical and topographical disadvantages.

Unfortunately, the Royalist advance guard was discovered by a vigilant sentry at the last possible moment. Consequently, when the attack went in at about 5.00 a.m., Stamford's Parliamentarian musketeers were already alerted. The battle began with both sides firing close volleys at each other and '... the Cornish foote pressing those four wayes up the Hill towards the Enemy and the Enimy [sic] as obstinately endeavouring to keep them downe.'[14]

Hopton's columns battled courageously against the formidable Parliamentarian defences with musket volleys and push of pike but, after eight dogged hours of effort, were unable to make headway. They were also beginning to run short of ammunition. It was at this moment, with the outcome of the battle in the balance, that the Parliamentarian pikemen levelled their pikes and surged down the hill. Led by Major General James Chudleigh, they slammed into the Royalist pike of Sir Bevil Grenville's regiment.

Grenville was bowled over in the rush, men in the leading ranks were speared and pikestaffs splintered. The slope of the hill helped propel the Parliamentarians deep into the Royalist formation. Amid that heaving throng, Chudleigh thought that he was gaining the upper hand until Sir John Berkeley's Royalist musketeers made a

The long line of pikes drop to horizontal, ready for another charge. The attack was carried out at a steady pace to avoid gaps appearing in the line.

Converging from both sides of the enemy position, Hopton's regiments drove their opponents off the brow of the hill.

desperate countercharge into the Parliamentarian pikes, laying about them and bludgeoning with the butt ends of their matchlocks.

Heartened by this, Grenville's pikemen were inspired to greater effort, and against the odds the Royalists began to push the Parliamentarians back up the hill. Hopton's four converging columns now drove forward with renewed vigour, '… growing nearer together as they ascended, the Enemy giving way and leaving the possession of some of their dead and some of their cannon …' At last, between three and four in the afternoon, the commanders of all four Royalist columns met '… in one ground neere the Topp of the Hill, where having joyfully embraced one another they pursued their victorie, and recovered the topp of the Hill, which the Enimy had acquyted …'[15]

Scenting victory, Hopton began to roll up the Parliamentarian line from the north. Once they were dislodged from the crown of the hill, the Royalist cavalry, hitherto kept in reserve, were also able to join the fray. Under this combined pressure Stamford's defence finally crumbled and his army fled the field. Three hundred Parliamentarians remained, dead, upon the hill and 1,700 were taken prisoner – including Major General James Chudleigh who, accused of treason by Stamford, promptly defected to the Royalist side.

Right: As the pike formations clashed, many pikes were driven into the air, others splintered on the ground. Anyone who lost their footing was doomed.

Below: The hand-to-hand fighting lasted several hours and left the Royalist infantry too exhausted to pursue when their opponents finally broke and ran.

TRAILING THE PIKE

That bible of the ranks, the much cursed drill book, recommended that only the '… tallest, biggest, and strongest should be ordered to carry pikes, that they may better endure the weight of their defensive arms.' The common soldier has a very practical turn of mind however and, soon after beginning his drills with those heavy, steel-tipped poles, realised that a shorter pike was easier to handle in the crush of battle. This fuelled a trend as the war progressed, for a reduction in the length of pikes to a more manageable size. Sir James Turner was moved to lament at the time that, while eighteen feet was the recommended length, '… few exceed fifteen feet; and if officers be not careful to prevent it, many a base soldier will cut some off the length of that, as I have often seen.'

This cumbersome weapon derived its battlefield power from deployment en masse. It was vital to keep formation and pikemen had to be well versed in the required drills. The pikes advanced steadily to the beat of drums, only increasing the momentum of the charge over the last few yards. Against other foot it was necessary to keep the pike held firmly horizontal while attempting to stab the point at the vulnerable faces or chests of the enemy. Directed against cavalry, the point was lunged with equal gusto at horse or rider. Unable to come within sword reach, the cavalry retaliated by discharging pistols into the close-packed ranks. A cavalry attack could be driven off by shots from the musketeers sheltering behind the pike points or by the steady march of the pikes themselves.

CHALGROVE
❧ 17 June 1643 ❧

The cavalry skirmish at Chalgrove earns a place in histories of the Civil War because it was there that the popular Parliamentarian commander John Hampden received a mortal injury when his pistol exploded in his hand.

Hampden had been a possible contender to replace the Earl of Essex as commander-in-chief of the Parliamentarian armies. His demise was to open the way for the man who was ultimately destined to assume the mantle of command; his first cousin, Oliver Cromwell. The other notable feature of this action was the quite remarkable behaviour of the Royalist commander, Prince Rupert. The battle took place when, after an abortive attempt to seize a Parliamentarian payroll, Prince Rupert was pursued towards Oxford. Ten miles south-east of the city the Prince ordered his infantry to hurry ahead while the cavalry remained behind to ambush their pursuers. This plan came to nothing when the Parliamentarian horse closed up unexpectedly rapidly and the two parties found themselves separated only by a large hedge. Never one to hesitate when action was required, the Prince dismissed recommendations to withdraw. Without waiting to see if his men would follow him, he '… set spurs to His Horse, and first of all (in the very face of the [enemy]) lept the hedge that parted [him] from the Rebells.' Taken by surprise 'The Captain, and the rest of His Troop of Life Guards (every man as they could) jumbled over after him.'[16] Then, as the Parliamentarian dragoons volleyed, Rupert formed up his troops and charged; routing his enemies in the short, sharp engagement which followed.

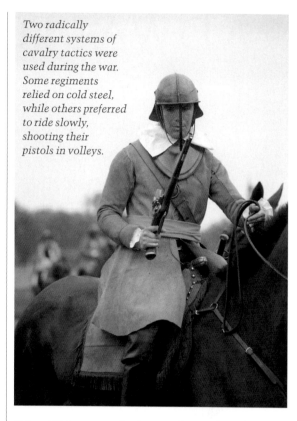

Two radically different systems of cavalry tactics were used during the war. Some regiments relied on cold steel, while others preferred to ride slowly, shooting their pistols in volleys.

Below: *With no anaesthetic, no understanding of infection and no idea of cleaning instruments between operations, medical staff could do little. John Hampden, one of the original parliamentary opposition leaders, died of his injuries.*

Left: *Pistols had large butts so that they could double as clubs. Since they took so long to reload, cavalrymen usually carried several into action: in the German wars where many commanders learned their trade, cuirassiers went into battle with as many as nine loaded pistols in their saddle holsters.*

ADWALTON MOOR
⟨⟨⟩ 30 June 1643 ⟨⟨⟩

Determined to prevent the 10,000 strong Royalist army commanded by the Earl of Newcastle from laying siege to Bradford Lord Ferdinando Fairfax led a Parliamentarian army of less than 4,000 men out, hoping to surprise him. Newcastle heard of Fairfax's approach and loaded the dice still further by deploying on the heights of Adwalton Moor.

Regardless of the odds, Fairfax enjoyed the first success of the day when his army drove back large numbers of Royalist skirmishers from the lanes and enclosed fields around Westgate Hill. In this terrain the Parliamentarians were less vulnerable to the Royalist cavalry. Rather than press on therefore, Fairfax chose to halt and establish a defensive line within the enclosures on the edge of the moor. This neutralised Newcastle's topographical advantage and forced the Royalists to attack. Seeking a way into the enclosures, Newcastle's men were funnelled towards a gap in the hedges where '… those that entered the pass found sharp entertainment, and those that were not yet entered, as hot welcome from the musketeers that flanked them in the hedges.'[17] However, having beaten back several assaults, the Parliamentarian left flank were emboldened to pursue the Royalists from the skirts of Adwalton Moor up onto the heights above.

Once clear of the enclosures, the shock of the Parliamentarian advance was absorbed by the greater number of Royalists, who counter-attacked. This was the critical moment in the battle. With their lines broken in the push of pike and outflanked by Royalist horse, the tide of battle turned irrevocably against the Parliamentarians. Their victorious advance became a bloody retreat.

Above: *The Parliamentarians hoped to take the Royalists by surprise, but even when it was obvious the plan had failed, Fairfax's commanders prepared to attack.*

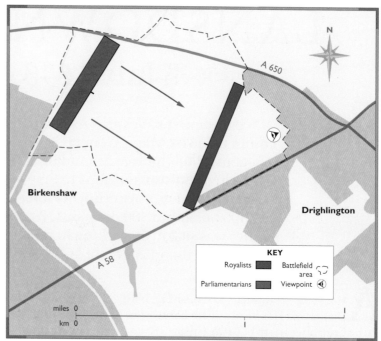

Birkenshaw

A 650

N

A 58

Drighlington

KEY

Royalists

Parliamentarians

Battlefield area

Viewpoint

miles 0

km 0

Left: *A musketeer takes careful aim, holding the smouldering matchcord in his left hand. There were appreciable delays between pulling the trigger, the match detonating the powder in the pan and the main charge actually igniting. Any hits achieved at over 100 yards were a matter of luck.*

Below: *Despite the numerical advantage, the battle swayed to and fro. Here a regiment prepares for another assault, the pikes are levelled and the musketeers reverse their muskets to use them as clubs.*

Far left: *Unable to break into the infantry formations, cavalry shoot pistols into the dense throng while musketeers return their fire.*

Left: *Royalist horse rally behind their own infantry, while a close range musketry duel continues. Eventually, the Royalist cavalry managed to attack their enemies in the flank.*

LANSDOWN HILL
⟫ 5 July 1643 ⟪

Parliament's Western Association forces,
commanded by Major General Sir William Waller,
controlled the area around Bath. The King
despatched additional troops to Sir Ralph Hopton in
the West Country, bolstering his forces to 4,000 foot,
2,000 horse and 300 dragoons. By comparison,
Waller was seriously lacking in infantry having no
more than 1,500 foot and 2,500 horse.

After some preliminary skirmishing, both Waller and Hopton made for Lansdown Hill, a few miles north of Bath. Waller arrived first and occupied the crest. Hopton then manoeuvred around to the steep north face and, unable to find a favourable line of attack, decided to break contact in order to conserve his limited ammunition. Although the Parliamentarians were outnumbered, the ground was greatly to their advantage and Waller decided to unleash his cavalry in the hope of converting the Royalist withdrawal into a rout. Sir Arthur Hesilrige's regiment of horse, supported by dragoons, charged down the steep slopes of Lansdown Hill to hit Hopton's retreating Cornishmen in the rear.

Left: Waller was outnumbered, but as a veteran of the German wars where he had served alongside his Royalist opponent, he selected his ground with skill. His infantry formed an unbroken line, their flanks protected by woods.

Below: From their position on top of a steep ridge, the Parliamentarians had a clear view of the approaching enemy.

The Royalist cavalry failed to charge home, but Hopton's five Cornish regiments battered their way into the Parliamentarian lines. The gallant Sir Bevil Grenville was killed at the head of his troops.

Captain Richard Atkyns, in the Royalist ranks, considered this '... the boldest thing that I ever saw the enemy do; for a party of less than 1,000 to charge an army of 6,000 horse, foot and cannon, in their own ground, at least a mile and a half from their [main] body.'[18] This audacious attack enjoyed initial success, disordering the Royalist horse which ploughed through the rear of their own retiring infantry in their haste to retreat. However the stoical Cornish foot regiments, the backbone of Hopton's force, rallied around their flags and held off the Parliamentarian assault until more Royalist horse, under the Earl of Carnarvon, charged to their relief. At the same time Sir Nicholas Slanning, rushing up with two or three hundred Royalist musketeers, fell upon the Parliamentarian dragoons still lurking in reserve.

The action rolled back and forth through the hedged fields as more troops from both sides joined the fray. Outnumbered and outflanked, the Parliamentarians gave ground and the Royalist army advanced back towards Lansdown Hill, enticed into the very battle which Hopton had earlier decided not to fight. The Royalists took breath at the base of the hill. The precipitous slope was crowned with the breastworks of Waller's army and above them, silhouetted against the summer sky, the Parliamentarian horse stood ready and waiting. Waller had made shrewd use of his ground and '... thus fortified ...' as one Royalist officer was later to recount, '... stood the fox gazing at us.'

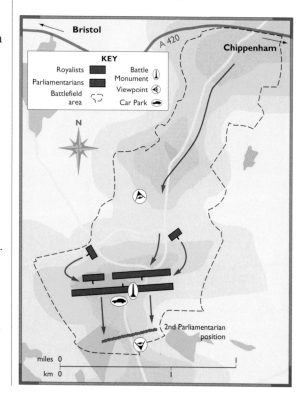

While the Royalist commanders deliberated, Waller's artillery battered the lines below. This so galled Hopton's doughty Cornishmen that they begged to be allowed to repeat their remarkable uphill storming of Braddock Down. At last, convinced that the morale of his army would carry them through, Hopton agreed. There now began a ferocious contest for possession of Lansdown Hill.

Deployed in an unusual formation, with the horse in the centre instead of on the flanks, the Royalist army was soon bowed into the steep slope. Although the central cavalry attack was quickly repulsed, the momentum of the advance was maintained by Sir Bevil Grenville's pikemen who bore on into the hail of enemy fire until they '... gain'd with much gallentry the brow of the hill receiving all [the enemy] small shott and cannon from their brest worke ...'[19] Holding firm upon ground which was as 'the eaves of a house for steepness ...' Grenville's stand of

pikemen preserved the Royalist army from total rout. Twice they withstood the charge of Sir Arthur Hesilrige's horse but under the third assault many fell; among them Sir Bevil Grenville himself, who fought with his men to the last.

By this time, according to Richard Atkyns, '... the air was so darkened by the smoke of the powder, that for a quarter of an hour together (I dare say) there was no light seen, but what the fire of the volleys of shot gave; and 'twas the greatest storm that ever I saw, in which I knew not whither to go, nor what to do, my horse had two or three musket balls in him presently, which made him tremble under me at that rate, and I could hardly with spurs keep him from lying down; but he did me the service to carry me off to a led horse, and then died ...'[20]

The fire was so intense that the bulk of the Royalist cavalry was forced to retire. Sir Nicholas Slanning survived a near miss when his horse was killed under him by a cannon shot. Hopton's men endured two more Parliamentarian charges and were beaten into disorder 'Yett at last they recovered the hill, and the enemy drew back about demi-culvern-shott, within a stone-wall, but there stoode in reasonable good order, and eache part played upon the other with their ordinance, but neither advanced being both soundly batter'd.'[21] Here, barely 400 yards apart, both sides stood their ground, cannon '... playing without ceasing till it was darke, legs and arms flying apace'.[22]

Above left: Headgear remained a matter of personal choice or what was available. A broadbrimmed hat was more comfortable than a helmet and the wearer could always place a steel skull cap underneath.

Left: Waller's gunners inflicted heavy losses on the Cornish, but the guns were taken.

Right: Waller's men withdrew several hundred yards, leading to a renewed musketry duel.

Pikemen ready to receive a charge: the front rank kneel with the base of their pikes wedged into the ground.

Although Waller had suffered relatively few casualties in comparison to the Royalists, who could count several hundred dead and wounded, it was crucial that he preserve his smaller force from further loss. At around one in the morning, he ordered a sudden, savage volley of musket fire. Then, as the Royalists leapt to their weapons the Parliamentarians crept away leaving 'all their light matches upon the wall and whole bodies of pikes standing upright in order within the wall as if men held them.'[23]

MISFIRING MUSKETS

By the mid-seventeenth century, the musket had long since replaced the bow on the British battlefield (with the exception of the odd idiosyncratic appearance). That said, the matchlock which dominated infantry firearms in the early part of the Civil War had a reputation for unreliability. Sir Thomas Kellie commented that it was not unusual for as many as four out of ten muskets not to fire. He attributed this to several factors, 'A musketeer may fail of his shot by sundry accidents, as by rolling out of the bullet, an badde matche, an matche not right cocked, by evill powder, or wet powder in his pan ...'

The only sure remedy to was to deploy the musket in large numbers. The most common method involved an almost continuous system of fire, with successive ranks firing and retiring to the rear to reload. Alternatively, ranks might combine their firepower in one thundering volley. This technique, which was thought to cause more destruction and fear among the enemy, was often used to precede a charge, or to break up an enemy assault. Timing was crucial. If the range was too great little damage was inflicted and insufficient time might be left to reload before an enemy charge impacted. Regular training in the requisite drills was the only solution.

ROUNDWAY DOWN

⤙ 13 July 1643 ⤚

The inconclusive battle at Lansdown Hill had failed
to resolve the power struggle in the West. Dispirited
and still short of ammunition, the Royalists
withdrew into Devizes, pursued by Sir William
Waller who had gathered reinforcements
from Bristol.

Before Waller could storm the town he
received news of the approach of a second
Royalist force. The King had despatched Lord
Wilmot and Sir John Byron to relieve Devizes
with 1,800 cavalry. As Wilmot's tired cavalry
approached Devizes, having ridden 40 miles from
Oxford, they found the Parliamentarians arrayed
on the southern slopes of Roundway Down.
Waller had deployed his more balanced force in
the conventional manner, with 3,000 foot in the
centre, supported by eight cannons, and flanked
by 2,000 horse.

After a brief skirmish between the advance
parties of each side in which Waller's Forlorn
Hope came off worst, Sir Arthur Hesilrige's
Parliamentarian cuirassiers moved forward to

Below and below right: Wilmot's troopers scattered the
Parliamentarian horse in a headlong charge. Some then
they fought in vain to break the infantry while others
chased Waller's cavalrymen over the cliff at the far end of
the battlefield.

support their retreating party of infantry. They
were met by Wilmot's own brigade.

Advancing on their large horses, carapaced
from head-to-toe in their armoured 'lobster
suits', the cuirassiers must have appeared a tough
prospect. However in foregoing the advantage of
terrain to meet Wilmot's expert, lighter cavalry
on even ground they had already made their fatal
mistake. Furthermore it was now impossible for
the Parliamentarian foot and artillery to fire in
support without hitting their own men. The
reaction of the practised Royalist horsemen was
swift and deadly. The young Royalist captain
Richard Atkyns recalled that '... the charge was
so sudden that I had hardly time to put on my
arms ... for though they were above twice our
numbers; they being six deep in close order and
we but three deep and open (by reason of our
sudden charge) ... no men ever charged better
than ours did that day ...'[24] Though Hesilrige did
rally, his second charge was to be his last. This
time, with Wilmot's horse seconded by Byron's

A Royalist cavalry trooper waits for the order to charge. Wilmot's brigade had left Oxford in the early hours of 11 July and now faced a larger army of both horse and foot.

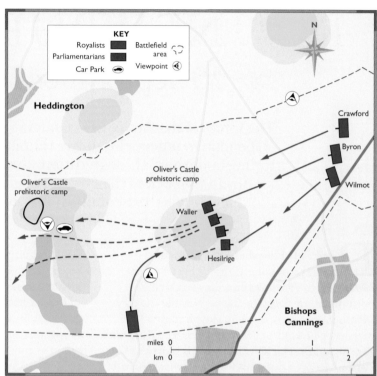

brigade, the Parliamentarian cuirassiers were broken and fled the field.

According to Sir John Byron, Waller now '… drew the rest of his army down the hill, and advanced with his own brigade of horse, with two pieces of cannon before it and two great bodies of foot on the left flank of it.'[25]

The Parliamentarian foot stood fast until Hopton's men counter-attacked from their entrenchments in Devizes. Then they broke, and Waller's army was destroyed. Two weeks later, Prince Rupert stormed Bristol and it looked as if the King might win the Civil War.

Marching uphill to meet this force, Sir John Byron's brigade, in the Royalist vanguard, rode head on into the Parliamentarian volleys. It was the iron discipline of Byron's men which was to win the day. Their orders were '… that not a man should discharge his pistol till the enemy had spent all his shot …' after which, as Byron later recalled '… we fell in with them, and gave them ours in their teeth …' In the hard fought action which followed, Waller's remaining cavalry were put to flight. With Byron's troopers hacking and slashing at their heels, they fled west. Neither side were aware of the dangerous 300 foot drop ahead, where Roundway Down ends abruptly at Oliver's Castle. Galloping for their lives, directly into the setting sun, many ploughed straight over, breaking both their own and their horses necks in that terrible fall.

Unaware that the broken bodies of their cavalry were lying in a bloody tangle of armour, flesh and bone at the foot of Oliver's Castle, the Parliamentarian infantry stood firm for another hour and a half. Only when Royalist reinforcements streamed out of Devizes to take them in the rear did the remainder of Waller's army finally disintegrate.

NEWBURY

⪡⪢ 20 September 1643 ⪡⪢

The forces of the Earl of Essex, having marched from London to relieve the siege of Gloucester, were toiling homeward through the autumn mud. But the Royalists blocked the London road, occupying Newbury on 19 September just a few hours before Essex arrived.

Deprived of the sheltered billets and stockpiled supplies awaiting them in Newbury, the Parliamentarians faced cold comfort in the damp meadows outside the town. While the two armies were evenly matched in size, with around 14,000 men each, the King had more cavalry. The King too had his worries. The consensus of opinion in the Royalist command was that Essex would escape under cover of darkness. But at dawn they were startled by the Parliamentarian artillery opening fire from the key position of Round Hill. The King had failed to take advantage of his head start to deploy first, and Essex had seized the opportunity to occupy the best ground. Now, as Lord Digby

Light cannon called 'Falconets' accompanied many infantry regiments. Weighing about 200 lb and firing 1.5 lb shot, they had a much higher rate of fire than the great guns of the artillery train.

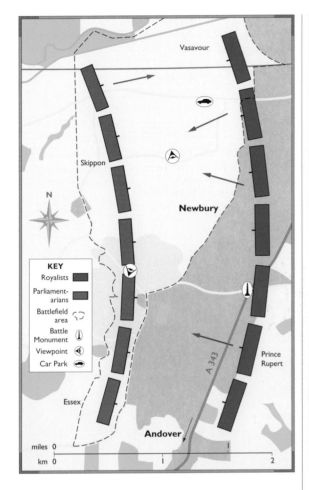

With most infantry companies carrying flags, Civil War regiments had up to a dozen banners floating above them. Carrying a standard was deemed a great honour, but standard bearers were always singled out by the enemy.

commented, '… unlesse we possest our selves of that hill, there was no holding of that field but the King must have retreated with his Army thence …'[26]

The vital task of taking the hill fell to the foot regiments of Sir Nicholas Byron's brigade, supported by his nephew John's cavalry. South of the hill, Enborne Heath was also to be hotly contested throughout the day. Here the bulk of the Royalist horse under Prince Rupert faced '… three bodies of Foot, both lined and flanked with strong bodies of Horse, and under favour of Cannon'.[27] Among Essex's foot were some of the London Trained Bands. Undoubtedly the most competent infantry on the field, they exacted a heavy toll on Rupert's cavalry despite taking terrible punishment from the Royalist cannon which, as Sergeant Henry Foster recalled, '… did some execution among us at the first and were

somewhat dreadful when men's bowels and brains flew in our faces'.[28]

The battle raged back and forth all day. On Round Hill every hedgerow or ditch was lined with Parliamentarian soldiers and was stoutly defended. The embattled Royalists advanced

'FRIENDLY FIRE'

In the midst of the noise, confusion and fear of battle mistakes were not uncommon. During the siege of Basing House in 1643 the Westminster Trained Bands accidentally shot seventy or eighty of their own men. According to a witness, the front rank was slow in getting out of the way once they had fired their volley '… and for want of intervals to turn away speedily the second and third ranks, fired upon their owne Front, and slew or wounded many of their owne men …'

under dense fire, obstructed by tall hedges and blinded by smoke. By heroic effort, Sir John Byron's horse briefly gained the crest of the hill, capturing one of the enemy guns, but they were unable to hold it. The Parliamentarians there had been reinforced by two regiments of the London Trained Bands.

This was in stark contrast to the behaviour of some of the Royalist foot. One group, finding themselves caught up in the savage artillery duel on the heath, 'found a hillocke … that sheltered them from the enimies Cannon', laid down behind it, '… and would not be drawne a foot from hence.'[29] Indeed this was not the finest hour of the Royalist infantry. Sir John Byron's judgement

Main picture: Royalist guns pound the Parliamentarian lines in a cannonade that lasted until there were but ten barrels of powder remaining.

Bottom left: The infantry fight it out in the centre where hedges and ditches prevented the cavalry from fighting effectively.

Bottom right: Both sides ran out of ammunition as night approached and the shooting slowly petered out.

This page bottom left: *Both sides lost heavily although the battle was inconclusive. Royalist losses included Lord Falkland and the young Earl of Caernarvon.*

Bottom right: *The next day, the Royalists withdrew to Oxford, leaving Essex free to fall back on London. The War would continue.*

was that '… had not our foot play'd the poultroons extremely that day, we in all probability had set a period to the war …'[130]

The tide of battle ebbed and flowed until darkness finally ended the engagement in a bloody stalemate. In a pitched battle of twelve hours duration, something in region of 3,500 men had died, the Royalists taking a slightly higher percentage of the loss. Unable to achieve a conclusive victory, nobody was more surprised the next morning than Essex to discover that the field was his. Having exhausted their ammunition the Royalists had pulled back in the night. Any hope of an early end to the war had been firmly put to rest.

WINCEBY
11 October 1643

The Earl of Manchester, marching north with Parliament's Eastern Association Army, received warning of the close proximity of Sir William Widdrington with almost 3,000 Royalist dragoons. Singing psalms as they marched, the Parliamentarians moved to intercept Widdrington at Winceby. By early afternoon on 11 October the two forces were drawn up facing each other on either side of a small valley.

The officer who was to lead the Parliamentarian vanguard that day was a talented colonel of horse by the name of Oliver Cromwell. In the best traditions of cavalry leadership he led by personal example. As the trumpets sounded across the hillside and the Parliamentarian advance gathered pace it was noted that he '… charged at some distance before his regiment …'[31]

Sir William Savill's Royalist dragoons retaliated with pistol shots. In the second volley Cromwell was seen to fall, his mount killed beneath him. Winded but essentially unhurt he struggled to his feet only to be bowled over in the Royalist countercharge. Amid the press of thrashing hooves and flashing blades Sir William Widdrington concluded that he must certainly have been slain. In fact Cromwell had somehow managed to mount another horse and remained in the thick of the action, urging his men on.

To this mêlée Sir Thomas Fairfax now added the weight of the Parliamentarian reserve with a second charge. Within half an hour the Royalist ranks had become a chaotic mob fleeing for their lives. Against light Parliamentarian losses Widdrington suffered several hundreds killed or taken prisoner. This victory cemented Cromwell's reputation as a leader of cavalry.

Cavalry advanced at a steady pace to avoid gaps appearing in the ranks. Only when the enemy was very close did they trot and finally canter.

Oliver Cromwell's Eastern Association horse proved themselves far superior to the northern Royalists at Winceby. At this stage, Cromwell was a respected but junior commander. His meteoric rise was just beginning.

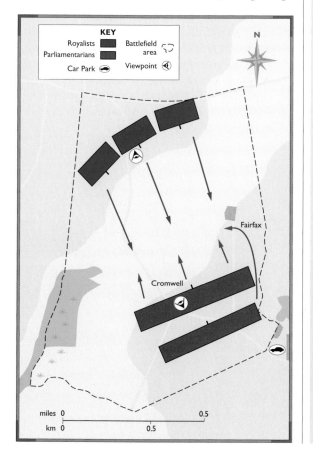

HORSE REGIMENTS

Regiments of cavalry or 'horse' were typically around five hundred strong, usually divided into six troops. At the beginning of the war, the Parliamentarians favoured the old style of deployment, six deep. Prince Rupert, General of the Royalist horse and a veteran of the German campaigns preferred a formation of only three ranks. The victory at Powick Bridge established his reputation as a cavalry commander and marked out the Royalist horse as superior to that of Parliament. In reality, on the battlefield the difference between the two sides was harder to judge; both achieved remarkable successes and sustained appalling reverses.

The presence of large bodies of horse invariably unnerved foot soldiers, creating a fear out of all proportion to the actual danger. In fact, providing they kept their heads and followed their drills, the infantry were quite capable of holding off a cavalry charge. At Marston Moor, Newcastle's Whitecoats fiercely resisted Cromwell's repeated cavalry charges and were overwhelmed only when they had exhausted their ammunition.

Horse were also deployed for the shock effect of their charge against other bodies of horse. To derive maximum benefit from this it was essential to retain full command and control after a successful charge had been delivered. All too often, swept up in the pursuit of routing opponents, the cavalry would be carried away far from the actual field of battle. While the dashing Prince Rupert commanded some of the most audacious charges of the war, he repeatedly failed to retain control over his command afterwards. Consequently his cavalry were rarely available to conduct a second charge. Victory rested not in winning the first charge, but in retaining sufficient control to deliver the last! This was the key to Cromwell's later emergence as the supreme exponent of horse during the Civil War.

NANTWICH
❧ 25 January 1644 ❧

Towards the end of 1643, a new 5,000-strong
Royalist army under the command of John Byron
(now Lord Byron) subdued all of Cheshire except for
Nantwich. Although it was late in the season for
campaigning, Sir Thomas Fairfax set off in
December 1643 with a Parliamentarian force of
2,500–3,000 foot, 1,800 horse and 500 dragoons
to relieve the town.

Hearing of Fairfax's approach, Byron
prepared to meet him by moving some of
his besieging force across the River Weaver to
Acton, situated on the road about a mile west of
Nantwich. The following day a sudden thaw
caused the river to burst its banks. The flood
swept away the bridge, leaving the Royalist army
divided: the Parliamentarian army appeared,
marching over the rise from Hurleston. Both
sides were ill-prepared. While Byron was forced
to make a detour of six miles in order to unify his
command, Fairfax also lost the opportunity for a

pre-emptive strike as he waited for his rearguard
to come up.

As the Royalists occupied the high ground at
Acton, Fairfax was not inclined to accept battle
on Byron's terms. Instead he decided to bypass
the enemy by marching across country; cutting a
passage through the hedgerows as he went. Byron
responded by wheeling his line to hit the tail of
the Parliamentarian column; forcing the last two
regiments to turn and fight a rearguard action.
Meanwhile the Royalist right wing pushed
forward to engage the Parliamentarian lead units.

Left: Two 'Falconet' cannon are prepared to fire while their regiment deploys. Musketeer and pike companies were often deployed alternately for mutual support.

Right: Byron's Royalist force had settled down to besiege Nantwich and was not prepared for a field battle.

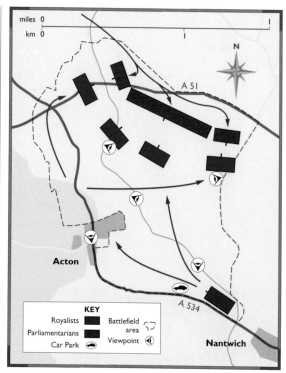

This manoeuvre dangerously overstretched the centre of the Royalist line where the cohesion of their infantry was broken up by the fields and hedgerows. It was here, as Fairfax's entire force now turned to face the developing Royalist flank attack (the front and rear of his column becoming his wings) that the fight was destined to be thickest. Regiments on both sides, disordered by the terrain, grappled for possession of individual fields. With visibility and movement so restricted by hedgerows, it was almost impossible to maintain proper command and control. Battle lines disintegrated into baying mobs of pikemen and musketeers who rushed upon the contested hedges only to be cut down by swords, spitted on pikes or bludgeoned by musket butts on the other side.

Lord Bryon and his cavalry became separated from his foot soldiers when the river flooded. The Parliamentarian infantry soon gained the upper hand.

In such terrain, the Royalist cavalry could do little to help their infantry. Although Byron's regiment on the western edge of the battlefield succeeded in extricating itself, the rest of his army was driven towards Acton churchyard, into the arms of Parliamentarian reinforcements from Nantwich garrison. There 1,500 Royalists surrendered. Two hundred more already lay dead on the field, heaped against the smashed hedges. The Royalist domination of Cheshire was over.

The Royalist infantry laid down their arms, at least half deciding to serve in the Parliamentarian army rather than languish as prisoners of war.

KEY

Infantry
Cavalry
Battlefield area
Viewpoint
Car Park

Hopton
Appleyard
ROYALISTS
Forth
Cheriton Wood

B 3046
N

Cheriton

Balfour

Hesilrige   Waller   **PARLIAMENTARIANS**

miles 0
km 0

A 272

CHERITON

⊰⊱ 29 March 1644 ⊰⊱

After a year of civil war neither side had been able to achieve total victory. To break the impasse, a new Royalist army was formed with the objective of securing all of Dorset, Wiltshire and Hampshire for the Crown. In command was Sir Ralph Hopton, who once again found himself facing his old adversary Sir William Waller.

When Waller marched his Parliamentarian army towards Winchester, Hopton set out to cut off his supply line. The advancing armies converged at the village of Alresford in Hampshire. The morning of 29 March 1644 found both sides deployed for battle but unable to see each other due to a heavy ground mist. Although the 6,000 Royalists occupied a ridge-top position, this advantage was offset by the numerical superiority enjoyed by the 10,000 strong Parliamentarian force.

As the rising sun began to burn off the mist, Hopton ordered Colonel Appleyard, with four divisions of musketeers, to capture Cheriton Wood in front of the Royalist left flank. Clutching their matchlocks tightly and blowing on their damp matches to keep them lit, the Royalist musketeers advanced into the trees. Hidden in the shadows, 800 men from the Parliamentarian City of London Brigade watched them come on; they had entered the wood earlier under cover of the mist. The two parties collided and firing erupted, banks of gun-smoke hanging on the still morning air. By a tragic coincidence each side shared the same battle cry, 'God with us', and had both that day chosen to identify themselves by a white token in their caps. In the middle of the woods and blinded by smoke, it was hard to be certain who was friend and who foe. With musket balls cracking through the branches, and twigs, bark and lead shot showering down, the sides edged closer. After the volleys came the brutal, close-quarter work with clubbed muskets and short swords.

Left: Marching with a pike took some practice. Drills were carried out slowly and steadily, with the emphasis on avoiding confusion rather than parade ground precision.

Right: Hopton's army was confident after its run of victories. Perhaps too confident, as the battle of Cheriton was to reveal.

HARD MEN

Under the pressures of combat it was not always possible to maintain proper drills. Powder not properly compressed by the ramrod resulted in low muzzle velocity. A ball from such a charge was unlikely to inflict lethal damage although it might still cause painful injuries.

Among the rank and file such injuries helped to preserve a superstitious belief in 'hard men' who could supposedly make themselves impervious to bullets by drinking special herbal potions. For the novice soldier, who put his faith in such tales, the vulnerability of flesh to close-range volleys must have come as an unpleasant shock.

Hopton despatched a messenger. His orders were for one division to retire and make a fresh assault against the vulnerable right flank of the Parliamentarians. Attacked from two directions, the Parliamentarians cracked. The Royalist musketeers now bludgeoned their way forward with renewed vigour and were able to secure the wood.

However, the day was far from over. As the Royalist command debated their next move, Hopton was appalled to see Colonel Sir Henry Bard, apparently on his own initiative, leading his cavalry regiment forward. From where Bard was positioned, the lie of the land prevented him from properly assessing the enemy force to his front. Unaware that destruction was lurking ahead in the form of Sir Arthur Hesilrige's Parliamentarian horse, he had decided to launch a charge.

As Bard's regiment was sliced to pieces by Hesilrige, more Royalist units rushed to the rescue, only to meet the same fate. Hopton, on the far flank, could only watch helplessly as the battle spiralled out of control. The day which had begun so well for the Royalists ended in confusion and defeat. Their new strategy for the West lay in wreckage upon the fields of Hampshire. After Cheriton, as the King's Secretary Sir Edward Walker observed, they were forced '… in the place of the offensive to make a defensive war'.

Above and left: Scarcely had the guns opened fire than a Royalist regiment attacked the Parliamentarian centre.

Above left and above: *Royalist regiments advanced without mutual support, and were defeated one by one.*

In a confused battle in which neither commander exercised much control, the Royalists suffered the most. The result was a serious defeat: Hampshire was lost and Hopton's army sadly weakened.

CROPREDY BRIDGE
⤜⤛ 29 June 1644 ⤜⤛

In early June, Parliament divided its forces, sending one army to Dorset to relieve the siege of Lyme and leaving a force under Sir William Waller to face the main Royalist army at Oxford. The King marched against Waller, whose forces were on the other side of the river Cherwell.

Looking down from the ridge of Bourton Hill to where the Cherwell lay glinting in the sun-filled meadows, Waller had a perfect view of the King's army. The forces were evenly balanced, both around 9,000 men, but the King had allowed his men to become dangerously strung out along the river. Ahead was Cropredy Bridge and about a mile to south of that lay the river-crossing at Slat Mill Ford. Between the two lay the King's straggling rearguard. Despatching Lieutenant-General John Middleton to cross Cropredy Bridge with two regiments of horse and nine companies of foot, Waller himself took 1,000 men across Slat Mill Ford hoping to catch the Royalist rear in a pincer movement.

Although Cropredy Bridge was held by a party of the King's dragoons, they were '… readily beat off …' by Middleton. Unfortunately, his cavalry then proceeded to repeat the original mistake of the Royalists. Racing ahead of their infantry, they '… too speedily pursued the enemy …

Below: Royalist soldiers were thankful the King did not order an attack on Waller's typically well-chosen position.

Right: The army prepared to return to Oxford, little thinking that Waller would launch an offensive of his own.

having no Foote within above halfe a mile …'[32]

As Middleton's dragoons collided with the main body of the Royalist force, the King became alerted to the perilous situation in which he had left his rearguard. He was fortunate in having two highly capable commanders at the tail of his army. At Slat Mill, the young Earl of

Northampton, still in his teens, reacted with a swift charge which drove Waller's force back across the Cherwell. Meanwhile at Cropredy bridge the Earl of Cleveland, having watched the Parliamentarian cavalry disappear into the haze, seized the opportunity to attack their unsupported infantry. Middleton's foot, thinking that '… the devil had come upon them in a cloud of dust'[33], beat a hasty retreat back to the bridge.

Although Waller had lost the initiative, the King was unwilling to risk forcing a passage over the Cherwell and the affray ended in a stalemate. Eventually, receiving intelligence of Parliamentarian reinforcements nearby, the Royalists slipped away under cover of darkness. While they had suffered few casualties, Waller had lost 700 men including many deserters.

KEY

Infantry	Battlefield area
Cavalry	
Car Park	Viewpoint

Charles I

Cropredy

Middleton

ROYALISTS

Cleveland

A 361

Astley

River Cherwell

PARLIAMENTARIANS

Oxford canal

Walker

Northampton

N

Banbury

miles 0
km 0

Top: The Parliamentarian attack was repulsed, with several regiments taking to their heels. Long simmering resentments led to mutinies and a large number of desertions.

Right: Waller's best men died defending Cropredy Bridge. The morale of the survivors sank so low, Waller's army was no longer an effective force.

MARSTON MOOR
2 July 1644

At the beginning of 1644, the King's problems were compounded by the return of an old adversary. The Scottish Covenanters' Army under Alexander Leslie, now Earl of Leven, had crossed the border in support of Parliament.

By the summer of 1644 the Royalist army of the Marquis of Newcastle was besieged in York by a 28,000 strong Allied force comprised of Leven's Scots, the Parliamentarian Eastern Association Army under the Earl of Manchester, and the local Yorkshire forces of Lord Fairfax and his son Thomas. The King, only able to muster a relieving force of 14,000 men, put his faith in

Prince Rupert to raise the siege and save the north of England for the Crown. Although heavily outnumbered, Rupert outwitted and outmanoeuvred the Allied army, lifting the siege with a forced march. The allies, under overall command of the Earl of Manchester, elected to withdraw, planning to intercept the Prince on his return south. However, Rupert decided to fall

The Parliamentarian and Scottish armies deployed for battle, acutely aware that Prince Rupert had never yet been defeated, but this time the Royalists were heavily outnumbered.

Civil War regiments had a large number of flags with separate standards for each of the ten companies. Each followed the same basic design with minor variations.

Above: *Parliamentarian musketeers deployed ahead of the main force as a skirmish line, or 'forlorn hope' as it was termed.*

Below: *Cromwell's Eastern Association cavalry formed up on the left flank. With only an hour or so of daylight remaining, Cromwell ordered his men forward.*

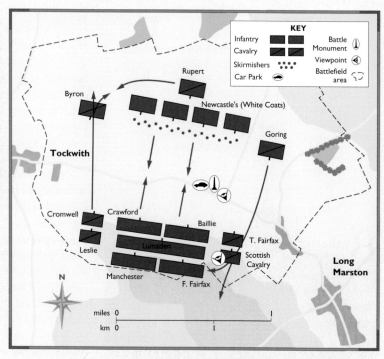

upon Manchester's rearguard and attempt to defeat it in isolation from the rest of the allied command. The success of this plan relied on two things: speed, and the addition of the Marquis of Newcastle's 4,000 strong York garrison to his own force. Accordingly, Rupert sent brief orders for the York troops to rendezvous with him at dawn the next morning. Had he known Newcastle better, he might have rendered his instructions more gracefully.

Piqued by the Prince's peremptory assumption of command, Newcastle saw no reason to interfere with the more immediate preoccupations of his men. Those not already celebrating the lifting of the long siege had streamed out of the city to search for plunder in the Allied siege works. Among the abandoned stores were 4,000 pairs of shoes; a valuable commodity for a seventeenth century army. While Rupert's forces waited, drawn up for

Each troop of horse carried its own standard, many bearing political slogans or the commander's family motto. Some Scottish cavalry were armed with lances, but the English relied on swords and pistols.

battle, the great shoe hunt served to delay the York garrison until late in the afternoon.

In the meantime Sir Thomas Fairfax, commanding Manchester's cavalry rearguard, had realised the danger and sent urgent messages for the Allied foot and artillery to rejoin him. Overhead, black thunderclaps heralded a summer storm, and the squall-soaked earth was soon churned to mud as the Allied soldiers tramped along the mile and a half long ridge of Marston Hill. Each unit, appearing in its place on the skyline, represented another blow to Rupert's plans.

The Prince's army were deployed defensively behind a long ditch on the edge of the moor. Even with the addition of Newcastle's 4,000 men, they would fall 10,000 short of the total Allied force. As rain swept across the open landscape, they cursed their ill-luck, knowing that damp powder would increase the risk of misfires once the battle began.

It was about 5 p.m. before the York troops

finally arrived. In the interim period a desultory exchange of artillery fire had begun. Now, with blood already soaking into the earth, a general quiet descended. Someone in the allied lines began to sing a psalm and the familiar words swelled along the line. As the allies hallowed the approaching conflict with prayer, many of Rupert's men were simply praying for the torment of waiting to end. The heavens conspired to grant their wish. At about 7.30 p.m. a mighty clap of thunder rent the air and the entire allied front began to roll down the corn covered slopes of Marston Hill towards the Royalist lines.

Both sides had deployed conventionally with cavalry on the wings, pikes and musketeers in the centre. Cromwell, on the allied left, was positioned directly opposite Prince Rupert's Life Guards. However the two greatest contemporary exponents of the cavalry charge were not destined to meet on the field that day. Rupert, assuming that the hour had grown too late for battle, had retired for supper and was caught unawares. It was therefore Lord John Byron who prepared to receive the charge of Cromwell's 'Ironsides'. Fearing to receive that ferocious tide of sabres while stationary, he launched a countercharge. The result was a violent collision of horse in which the Royalists were routed.

In the mêlée, Cromwell had received a sword stroke across the neck. Confident that his Ironsides had the better of the encounter, he delegated command to Lawrence Crawford and left the field to have his wound dressed. At this critical juncture Prince Rupert returned. A contemporary history records that, galloping up he '… met his own regiment turning their backs to the enemy which was a thing so strange and unusual he said "swounds, do you run, follow

HAND-TO-HAND COMBAT

English musketeers were reputedly more inclined to use their musket butts for hand-to-hand than their 'hangars' or swords. This was possibly because they had experienced little exposure to swords in normal civilian life; unlike the warlike clans of the Scottish Highlands for whom the sword was the weapon of choice.

me," so they facing about, he led them to a charge…'[34]

But fortune had deserted Rupert that day. Though he rallied his cavalry and led them back into the fray, it was to be their final attempt. David Leslie, charging forward with Cromwell's reserve of 800 Scottish horse, smashed their resistance. The Prince's horse was struck down beneath him. On foot, and separated from his Life Guard, he avoided capture by hiding in a bean field.

It was now that the superior discipline of Cromwell's Ironsides came into play. Rather than waste their gains in pursuit of a fleeing enemy, they rallied and reformed ranks. Cromwell was able to resume control of a concentrated and effective force.

On the opposite wing the Allies were not faring so well. Sir Thomas Fairfax's horse, unable to resist the Royalists led by Lord Goring, were beaten back with heavy losses. Lacking the restraint of the Ironsides, most of the Royalist cavalry either gave chase, or looted the Allied baggage train. Goring therefore had fewer horse left to support the heavily pressed Royalist infantry who were making a heroic effort in the centre of the line. There, according to one participant, '… the smoke of powder was so thick that we saw no light but what proceeded from the mouth of gunnes.'[35]

Nonetheless, against far superior numbers, the Royalist foot were winning; pushing forward yard by bloody yard against the Scottish regiments opposing them. Even the Allied command gave way to the general panic and abandoned the army to its fate. According to one chronicler, Lord Fairfax rode home and went to bed, while the Earl of Leven did not stop until he reached Leeds! Only the Earl of Manchester was to return to the field before the battle was over.

It was left to Sir Thomas Fairfax to redeem his family name. Just as all seemed lost, he saw a

Right: *The thunder of the guns was soon matched by thunder in the heavens, heralding an approaching storm.*

chance to reverse the course of the battle. Tearing off his Parliamentarian insignia, he worked his way through the Royalist army to Cromwell's undefeated Ironsides on the far side. Fairfax and Cromwell led the remaining Parliamentarian horse against the rear of the Royalist infantry, catching them in a hammer and anvil action against the Scottish regiments of the Earl of Lyndsey and Lord Maitland. The shattered remnants of the Royalist horse fled into the dusk abandoning their infantry to the slaughter. 'God made them as stubble to our swords'[36] Cromwell was to recall.

Only the best of Newcastle's infantry, the Whitecoats, endeavoured to make a stand against the Ironsides. They refused quarter and '... by mere valour for one whole hour kept the troops of horse from entering among them at near push

Main picture: *Newcastle's White Coat regiment ignored calls to surrender and made a desperate last stand that lasted far into the night.*

Below left: *Scottish infantry open fire on the Royalists.*

Below right: *Parliamentarian musketeers in action. After dusk the firing continued at point blank range.*

of pike; when the horse did enter they ... fought it out until there was not thirty of them living; whose hap it was to be beaten down upon the ground ... though they could not rise for their wounds, yet [they] were so desperate as to get either pike or sword ... and to gore the troopers' horses as they came over them or passed them by ...'[37]

It was only when all their ammunition was spent, that the valiant Whitecoats finally passed into history; every man falling '... in the same order and rank wherein he had fought.'[38] With their destruction the battle ended. In its wake an unusually large number of casualties littered the moonlit landscape. Something approaching 6,000 Royalists had been slain or taken. The losses of the opposing side were lighter; from the jaws of defeat the Allied army had snatched a most extraordinary victory.

Below left: Cavalry charged and counter-charged until the Royalist horse were driven from the field.

Below right: Scottish infantry pursue their beaten foe.

NASEBY
⇜ 14 June 1645 ⇝

Despite victory at Marston Moor, Parliament had
suffered enough reverses during 1644 to consider
reorganising its forces. The bulk of the
Parliamentarian forces were reconstituted
into a permanent standing army.

Command of this 'New Model Army' was given to Sir Thomas Fairfax who soon set about besieging the King's capital at Oxford. With only about 7,500 troops the King was outnumbered almost two to one. Notwithstanding, he decided upon the dangerous strategy of luring Fairfax away from Oxford by storming the Parliamentarian city of Leicester. Obligingly, Fairfax abandoned Oxford in order to pursue the King. By the morning of Saturday 14 June both armies were deployed on undulating ground between Market Harborough and Naseby. However, the low ridges which screened the

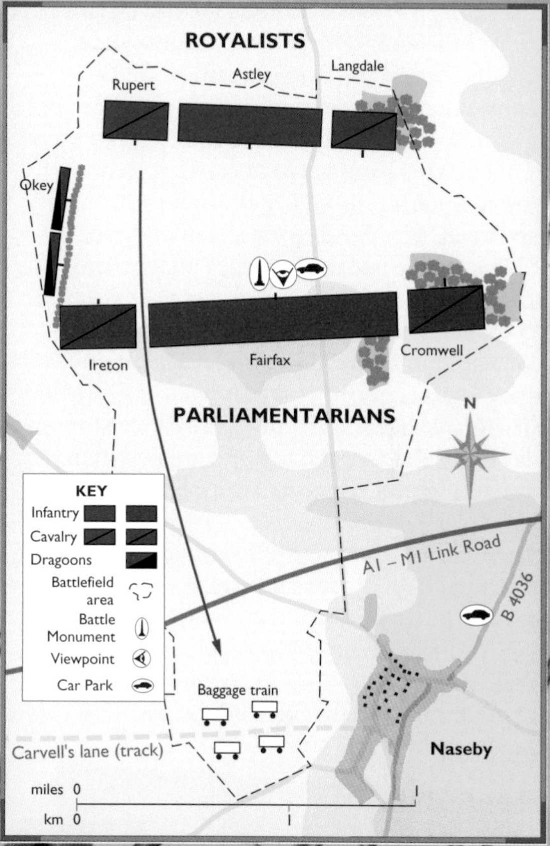

The King's veteran infantry regiments assemble for their last great battle. Outnumbered 2:1, they were to come tantalisingly close to victory.

ROYALISTS

Rupert Astley Langdale

Okey

Ireton Fairfax Cromwell

PARLIAMENTARIANS

N

A1 – M1 Link Road

B 4036

KEY

Infantry	
Cavalry	
Dragoons	
Battlefield area	
Battle Monument	
Viewpoint	
Car Park	

Baggage train

Carvell's lane (track)

Naseby

miles	0		1
km	0		1

King's dispositions also handicapped the Royalist view of the enemy. The King's Scoutmaster, Francis Ruse, was therefore sent to confirm reports that the enemy were nearby. When Ruse returned with '... a Lye in his Mouth, that he ... could neither discover or hear of the Rebels',[39] Prince Rupert refused to believe him and advanced to make his own reconnaissance.

The Prince had not marched above a mile when he caught sight of a body of enemy horse retiring hastily. These were not, as he surmised, the rearguard of the retreating Parliamentarian army, but a scouting party engaged on the same mission as himself. Aware that Fairfax's force was twice the size and better equipped than that of the King, the Prince had initially counselled withdrawal. Now however, 'flattered into an Opinion that [the enemy] were upon the retreat ...'[40] he sent an urgent message for the Royalist army to hurry forward.

Although the early part of June had been wet, it was a sparkling summer morning as the Royalists advanced in full order of battle across the sweep of Broad Moor.

If their attack was to succeed, it was essential that they maintain their lines and so they came on slowly, the cavalry reining in level with their foot. Initially the majority of the enemy force were hidden from view by the terrain. Only as the forlorn hopes of both parties exchanged musket fire, did Fairfax move the main body of his army up to the ridge-line above the advancing Royalists. It was not until they were within musket range that the King's men could perceive the enormity of the task before them.

Many had their doubts about the wisdom of the venture. Sir Edward Walker, the King's secretary at war, was to record that 'the Heat of Prince Rupert, and his Opinion [that the enemy] durst not stand him, engaged us before we had either turned our Cannon or chosen fit ground to fight on.'[41] Similarly Fairfax's newly appointed Lieutenant-General of Horse, Oliver Cromwell, looking down from his position upon the slopes of Mill Hill, could hardly believe his eyes. 'When I saw the enemy draw up and march in order towards us,' he wrote later 'and we a company of poor ignorant men ... I could not ... but smile out to God in praises in assurance of victory.'[42]

Typically, rather than remain where he could exert control over the whole field, Prince Rupert chose to personally lead the Royalist cavalry charge on the left wing. Ignoring the enfilading fire of Colonel Okey's dragoons lining the hedges on the western edge of Broad Moor, the Royalist cavalry stormed up the slope before them and struck like a whirlwind, smashing into Colonel John Ireton's Horse with devastating effect.

Although nothing can detract from the

Above left: The Royalist camp was quiet that morning, no-one knew the enemy were so close.

Left: Royalist pikemen 'trailing' their pikes. Only as they deployed for battle did the King's infantry realise quite how badly outnumbered they were.

Left: Prince Rupert led his Cavaliers in their traditional headlong charge. In a short sharp fight, he scattered Ireton's Parliamentarian cavalry.

Right: While the cavalry fought on the flanks, the infantry levelled their pikes and prepared to charge.

success of this remarkable uphill charge, Rupert, as so often, failed to exploit his gains. Instead of rallying his men for a second charge, he joined them in headlong pursuit far off the field of battle. In the confusion of the mêlée he had failed to notice that he had routed only part of the enemy. Sir Henry Ireton, together with some of his command who had survived the charge, were left at liberty to turn on the Royalist foot.

In the cavalry clash on the opposite wing the situation was reversed. Cromwell's Ironsides poured down the hill with their straight cavalry blades flashing in the bright sunlight. Although Sir Marmaduke Langdale's Royalist Horse 'made a very gallant resistance … firing at very close charge'[43] they were overthrown. While some fled the field others rallied behind the protection of the Royalist reserves.

In the centre of the field meanwhile, the Royalist foot advanced steadily behind their banners and drums with all the regularity of a parade. The New Model Army welcomed them with a volley of musket fire. Then screaming their battle cry 'God our Strength', they rolled over the lip of the ridge and spilled down the slope. The Royalists had time for only one volley in return before the bulk of the two forces were locked in physical contact. Naseby was a battle which was to be decided the old-fashioned way, not by firepower but by the shock of the charge, and the cutting work of sharp blades.

As the two armies collided, those pike shafts which did not strike home or splinter under the impetus of the charge were forced upwards, as if a clattering winter forest had suddenly sprung up in the June sunshine. With the Royalist pikemen

There was a brief exchange of musketry before the infantry lines clashed. Parliamentarian leaders soon saw some of their men slipping away to safety.

Veteran Parliamentarian officers knew that their famed New Model army contained a high proportion of conscripts.

Fairfax brought forward the Parliamentarian reserves to stop the remorseless advance of the King's infantry.

gaining ground, their Musketeers were no less forward. Crying aloud for 'Queen Mary' the veterans of Sir Jacob Astley's Royalist foot gave the New Model Army a hard lesson in what they could achieve 'with their swords, and the butt end of the Musquet'[44] The less experienced ranks of Fairfax's force were compelled, step by step, to fall back upon their reserves further up the slope. Fairfax threw his reserves into the fray. In order to boost their morale, he himself marched at their head.

Henry Ireton had also realised the desperate plight of the Parliamentarian infantry. As the advancing Royalist foot pressed close by the remnants of his horse, overlooked by Rupert's cavalry, he led a charge against their flank. This was supported by Colonel John Okey's 1,000 dragoons. Although the personal cost to Ireton of this piece of heroism was a pike point in the thigh and a head wound from a halberd, the renewed pressure on the Royalist front line in this quarter was telling. The combined efforts of Fairfax and Ireton enabled the New Model Army to hold their ground long enough for Cromwell to come to the rescue. Once again, as at Marston Moor, Cromwell's disciplined troopers had remained in the field to deliver a hammer blow to the Royalist foot.

Warned of the terrible punishment about to be

Fairfax's personal intervention at the head of the reserves stabilised the front line.

The infantry battle continued at point blank range, neither side willing to give way.

Musketeers of the New Model Army open fire. Staunchly Protestant, Cromwell's men took no prisoners from the King's largely Catholic Irish regiments.

visited on them by the drumming of hooves to their rear, some of the Royalists crowded forward to escape. This only added to the miseries of those in front, already hard up against the pikes of Fairfax's infantry. Nonetheless, at least one regiment of the King's veterans put up a stout resistance. Joshua Sprigge, Fairfax's chaplain, was moved to record that they stood firm '… with incredible courage and resolution, although we attempted them in flanks, front and rear, until such time as the general called up his own regiment of foot … which immediately fell in with them, with butt-end of muskets … and so broke them.'[45]

As his infantry collapsed, the King made a half-hearted attempt to lead the last remnants of Langdale's horse forward in a charge. He was prevented by the Earl of Carnwath, who, according to Sir Edward Walker, '… took the King's Horse by the bridle [and] turned him about, swearing at him and saying, Will you go upon your Death?'[46] Thus the last orderly stand of Royalist pikes on Naseby field fell to Sir Thomas Fairfax who personally cut down the ensign and seized the colours.

As Charles I fled towards Hereford, with some idea of raising new forces in Wales, the shattered army he left behind him surrendered.

Once again, Royalist cavalry were so scattered by their success they could not support the infantry.

Most of Charles I's infantry were killed or captured and many of their camp followers murdered in the pursuit.

LANGPORT
⤙⤙ 10 July 1645 ⤚⤚

Having won the north of England at Marston Moor
and the Midlands at Naseby, Sir Thomas Fairfax
began a campaign to crush the Royalist cause in the
West Country. The Royalist General George Goring
established a defensive position between Langport
and Sherborne but decided to withdraw to
Bridgwater. On 9 June he sent most of his guns
and baggage ahead. The following day Fairfax
fell upon him.

Although outnumbered 10,000 to 7,000, the Royalists were
deployed with 'a great Marsh'[47] between them and the
enemy. The only sure passage was the narrow ford of the Langport-
Somerton road. For as long as they could retain this, Fairfax's larger
numbers were irrelevant. Goring had posted two of his recently
raised Welsh foot regiments to defend it, flanked on either side by
his two remaining cannons.

Despite the strength of Goring's position, Fairfax did not
hesitate. Having battered the Royalist gun crews into silence with
his more numerous artillery, he thinned their foot back from the
hedgerows on the other side of the ford with the volleying of 1,500

A month after the King's main
army was destroyed, the west
country Royalists deployed for
their final battle. They were
outnumbered and outgunned.

Above: *This
sergeant is armed
with a halberd: a
two-handed
weapon derived
from the 16th
century bills. The
strip of cloth on his
arm is a field sign:
both sides had
regiments wearing
the same coloured
uniforms.*

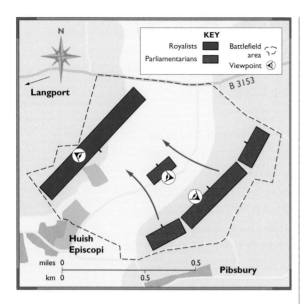

musketeers. Then, seizing his moment, he launched the Parliamentarian horse across the ford in one of the most courageous cavalry charges of the war. With Major Bethel at their head they galloped forward in a tight file four abreast, straight into the water which was 'deep and dirty and very narrow'.[48] Though still heavily outnumbered by the Royalist musketeers at the ford they went on '… with the greatest gallantry imaginable'.[49]

With Bethel seconded by more cavalry and a party of foot 'marching up furiously'[50] it was soon all over for Goring, who was obliged to retreat. Bridgwater fell soon after, isolating the remaining Royalist strongholds in Devon and Cornwall.

A gunner rams home the shot. Elizabethan experiments with breechloading cannon were not continued and Civil War guns were all loaded from the muzzle.

MONTROSE AND THE CIVIL WAR IN SCOTLAND

1645 was a bad year for the Royalist cause with defeat piling upon defeat. The only bright spot on the King's horizon was the unexpected success of the small Royalist contingent in Scotland, commanded by James Graham, the Marquis of Montrose.

Having begun his military career in the opposing camp (fighting for the Covenanters during the Bishop's War) Montrose had become disillusioned. The Covenanter's cause had been hijacked by ambitious lords such as the Earl of Argyll, who sought political power for themselves. What had begun as a campaign to redress Scotland's religious grievances, had become a rebellion against the constitutional authority of Charles I.

When the English Civil War intruded into Scottish affairs in 1643, Montrose decided to stand by his honour and fight with the King. It was a decision which was to cost him dear. By the autumn of 1644 he had been declared a traitor with a reward of £20,000 (Scots) on his head. For good measure the Scottish Committee of Estates also excommunicated him, stripped him of his title and defaced his coat of arms in Parliament.

Nonetheless, his victories, invariably against the odds, ensured that the name and reputation of Montrose would endure. Of his forces, General William Baillie of the Covenanters was to say, '… they were but a pack of naked runagates, not three horse among them, few either swords or musquetts.'[51] Yet by the end of February 1645, these 'naked runagates' had fought a string of successful actions against the Covenanters' Army; most notably at Tippermuir, Aberdeen and Inverlochy.

AULDEARN

⭐ 9 May 1645 ⭐

As the critical year of 1645 progressed, the Covenanters were determined to end any prospect of an army of Scottish Royalists lending support to the King. To this end they redoubled their efforts to hunt down that Highland fox, Montrose. The wet, foggy morning of 9 May found a Covenant army squelching up a track towards the small village of Auldearn where Montrose was encamped.

With 600 horse and 4,000 foot Sir John Urry hoped to reverse the Marquis' fortunes with a surprise dawn attack. As he advanced, some of his men discharged their muskets to clear them of damp powder (with a battle approaching no one wanted to risk a misfire). Further up the valley Montrose's alert sentries heard the muffled reports and raised the alarm. Thus warned, the Marquis decided to prepare a surprise of his own. The hamlet of Auldearn was built on the steep western slopes of a ridge running roughly north to south. Montrose who, with less than 1,500 foot and 250

It had taken several years for the Scottish Royalists to launch their revolt against the Covenanters. By 1645 the King's cause in England was now all but lost, but Montrose's tiny army kept defying the odds.

horse, had insufficient men to hold the entire ridge, decided to create a phantom army.

He deployed Alastair MacDonald, with just 500 Gordons and MacDonalds, as the 'bait'. Positioned on Castle Hill at the northern end of the ridge, this small force masqueraded as his 'right wing'. The centre of the ridge housed an even more illusory 'left wing'. This took the form of a few clansmen scattered among the cottages with orders to fire as fast possible and create the impression that the village was strongly held.

To sugar the trap, the great, golden standard of Charles II floated on the breezy slopes behind Alastair; as if marking the command post at the centre of Montrose's position. In reality the Marquis had kept the major part of his force concealed. Behind Castle Hill to the north, Lord George Gordon waited with 200 horse. To the south, hidden in a large hollow, were Montrose himself with about 800 foot, and Viscount Aboyne with 50 horse. The Marquis' plan was to wait until the Covenanters were heavily engaged against Alastair and then surprise them with a double flanking attack. The deciding factor would be whether or not Alastair's clansmen could hold on long enough against the odds.

By the time the Covenanters came within musket shot of Auldearn the morning mist had lifted. Sir John Urry saw the King's golden standard shining out against the slate grey skies and took the bait. His progress was slow at first.

Hampered by the boggy ground at the base of the ridge the Covenant regiments were unable to fan out in a proper deployment. Instead they were constrained to feed forward one behind the other.

Although Alastair's small contingent on the hill had been ordered to fight a static defensive action, the narrow frontage of their enemies presented the hot-blooded clansmen with a tempting opportunity. Furthermore, floundering through the mire, right at the vanguard of Urry's attack, the MacDonalds had spotted their bitterest enemies: the Campbells – with Sir Mungo Campbell of Lawers at their head. With Campbell insults added to the musket balls now flicking past their ears, the MacDonalds were goaded beyond endurance. Although outnumbered by about six to one, Alastair judged that he had to act or lose his command.

Montrose could only watch in disbelief as Alastair's standard streamed down the slope. He was powerless to intervene. To launch his flanking attack before all of the covenanting army had moved forward into the trap would imperil his entire force. The MacDonalds had been intended to stall for time and draw the enemy into position, not fight the battle alone!

The berserk charge foundered at the boggy

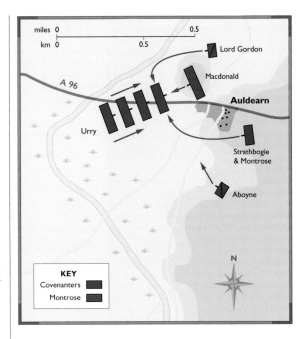

Montrose relied on MacDonalds's clansmen to hold off the bulk of the Covenanter army while he prepared a flank attack.

base of the slope where weight of numbers inevitably began to tell. Alastair himself was in the thick of the hand-to-hand fighting as his men were forced backwards. With the blade of his great broadsword broken, he looked desperately for support from Montrose. Seeing none to second him, he thought the day was lost; 'Wherefor he called to those that wer about him, "Ach, messoures," said he, "sall our enemies by this on dayes work be able to wreast out of our

Left: Covenanter fugitives were cut down, unable to outrun their pursuers in the chaos that followed their defeat.

Below: The Covenanter army was conventionally armed and equipped, like the regiments they had sent to England to bolster the Parliamentarian forces.

MONTROSE AND MACDONALD

Though the King's loyal Highlanders flocked to Montrose's banner, their traditions of clan warfare presented him with certain problems. Used to mounting raids of short duration, the need to remain in the field for a protracted campaign was alien to them. After battle they had the disquieting habit of retiring to their homes with the spoils. Hence the strength of Montrose's Highland army constantly fluctuated. The steady backbone of the force was provided by a large contingent of Irish MacDonalds, led by their chieftain Alastair MacDonald (or MacColla as he was often known).

Alastair MacDonald was a giant of a man, a mighty warrior who inspired devotion in the Highland and Irish clansmen. He was frequently able to overcome shortage of numbers by exploiting this Gaelic fervour in a massed infantry charge. With Alastair MacDonald at his right hand, Montrose was a force to be reckoned with.

Deserted by their cavalry, the Covenanter foot prepare to receive the charge of Montrose's highlanders.

handes all the glorie that we have formely gained … let us die bravely; let it never be thought that they have triumphed over our courage"'.[52] What Alastair was not able to see, due to the heavy banks of gun-smoke hanging about his position, was the arrival of Aboyne's 50 horsemen in a flurry of cutting blades.

Aboyne's sudden appearance also came as a surprise to Urry's right flank. A troop of Covenant horse were put to flight so quickly that they trampled through the Campbells in their haste to depart. The Campbells themselves responded with more gusto, unleashing such a volume of fire that Aboyne's troopers seemed 'to

A HOT TIP UNDER FIRE

In the village of Auldearn a handful of Montrose's musketeers were forced to masquerade as the left wing of an entire army. To keep up a rapid salvo of fire they used the old veterans' trick (not found in the drill book) of keeping a supply of musket balls in their mouths. This speeded up the loading process. Having charged the musket with powder and wadding, they simply spat a musket ball chaser down the barrel, thumped the butt hard on the ground to drive the ball home, and without delaying to ram it firm, primed the pan and fired.

assault a terrible cloud of thunder and lightening'.[53] Undaunted, Aboyne vanished into this lethal man-made storm cloud to deliver a thunderbolt of his own.

As he hit their disordered right flank the Campbells reeled back, disengaging from close contact with the MacDonalds and calling for the Covenant reserves to hurry forward. This was the moment Montrose had been waiting for. He sent a galloper across to Lord Gordon on the north side of the hill with the message 'MacDonald drives all before him. Is his clan to have all the honours this day?'[54]

Gordon responded instantly. Dispensing with any preliminary firing of carbines or pistols, his cavalry thundered into Urry's shocked left flank '… only with their swords to charge quhyt

Left: *Old enmities between clans made Auldearn a bitter fight indeed. Neither side expected any mercy if it lost.*

Right: *Black powder produces a great deal of fouling which makes the weapon progressively harder to reload. Barrels needed to be swabbed out even during a battle, using whatever fluid was available.*

throwgh ther enimies'.[55] At the same time Montrose unsheathed his hidden infantry reserves. Almost demented by the necessity to remain quiet and concealed all this while, the Strathbogie Gordon foot came swarming down the slope with blood-curdling cries of 'Strathbogie!'. Seeing this wild wave racing towards them, Urry's regular regiments prepared to fight for their lives. In vain: the savagery and speed of the charge which broke over them could not be resisted and '... the infantrie of the Royalists, keiping together ... did tear and cut

them in pieces, even in rankes and fyles, as they stood, so great was the execution'.[56]

In the face of overwhelming odds Montrose had achieved a remarkable victory. Although Urry himself survived, his army was annihilated. In particular the Campbells, MacLennans and MacKenzies suffered terrible losses. Sir Mungo Campbell, faithful to the honour of his clan and loyal to his troops, died with his regiment.

However, a second Covenanters' army commanded by General Baillie was already heading north to hunt down Montrose.

Formed lines of troops dissolve into a furious melee. One reason so many musketeers preferred to use their guns as clubs was that their government issue swords were of such poor quality they were easily bent.

ALFORD

⋙ 2 July 1645 ⋘

News of the Royalist débâcle at Naseby reached
Scotland in June 1645. Montrose, determined to
march his army to the King's assistance, despatched
Alastair MacDonald to recruit more troops.
Meanwhile the Marquis played cat and mouse
with General Baillie's Covenanter army in the
maze of Highland Glens.

*Montrose's men were King Charles I's
last hope. If they could hold on long
enough, there was a chance he could
bring over enough Irish soldiers to
form a new army.*

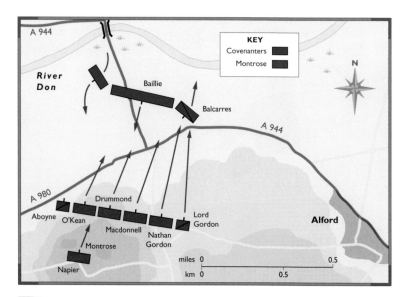

A musketeer pours the charge of powder down the barrel, then pushes down the musket ball and wadding. The load is then pushed down to the breech using a ramrod.

By now his reputation was such that Baillie was extremely cautious about accepting battle on ground of Montrose's choosing. However when Covenant scouts reported that Alastair MacDonald and several hundred of his formidable Irishmen were absent, Baillie finally picked up the gauntlet. On 2 July he came upon his enemy deployed on Gallowhill overlooking the village of Alford. Between the two forces lay the River Don which could only be crossed at that point by means of Mountgarrie Ford. The Royalist contingent appeared to be so small that Baillie assumed the bulk of the enemy had slipped away. Believing that he faced only Montrose's rearguard, he decided to commit himself to an attack. Once across the river it would be difficult to withdraw from contact as the narrows of Mountgarrie Ford would hamper a speedy retreat.

It was not until the Covenanters were plodding over the marshy ground on the far side of the river that they realised that they were in fact facing a force equal to their own; both sides numbering around 2,000. The bulk of Montrose's army had been concealed on the reverse slope of Gallowhill. Baillie had fallen foul of almost the same ploy which had been the undoing of Sir John Urry at Auldearn.

The Royalist attack was launched somewhat precipitously by young Lord Gordon, on Montrose's right wing. Outraged to see a herd of stolen Gordon cattle among Baillie's supply train, he unleashed his small body of cavalry in a furious charge. His single squadron of horse piled into the three cavalry squadrons of the Earl of Balcarres on Baillie's left. Though Balcarres rallied after the initial impact of the charge, Gordon was quickly seconded by a regiment of Irish foot, rushing forward with drawn swords to hack at the hamstrings of the Covenanter horses.

ARMS AND EQUIPMENT

While Montrose's Irish regulars were equipped in the conventional manner with pikes and muskets, some of his Highlanders still used the weapons of their forefathers: bows, two-handed claymore swords, long-handled lochaber axes and leather-covered targes (shields). His army was effectively a mobile guerilla force '… bold, hardy, and much inured to war'. Although they lacked cavalry, this deficiency was partially mitigated by the rough terrain over which they campaigned. In the steep wilderness of the highlands the clansmen could travel faster when not hampered by horses. According to one early observer they could 'march from twenty to four-and-twenty leagues without halting, as well by night as day'. Their arms, a plaid for warmth and a 'little bag of oatmeal' were all that they required to sustain themselves. Within their own highland regions they also enjoyed the advantages of detailed topographical knowledge and widespread support among the local population.

Musketeers were trained to fire by successive rank or to maintain a rolling fire, the ranks changing places to fire and reload in turn.

Unable to withstand the savagery of this assault Balcarres was routed from the field.

This pattern was repeated on the Royalist left where Viscount Aboyne (Gordon's younger brother) led the cavalry charge followed by more of the ferocious Irishmen. Montrose's Highland foot, charging in the centre, were no kinder than the Irish and though the Covenanters 'for some time fought on doggedly ... they were almost all of them cut down'.[57]

It had been more a blood bath than a battle. Though Baillie had narrowly escaped with his life, more than 1,600 Covenanters were slain. Against this the Royalists had suffered only a handful of losses. However there was to be no rejoicing in Montrose's camp that day, for among the dead was young Lord Gordon; felled by a shot through the back. It was a hard loss. In their grief, according to one witness, his fellow soldiers 'seemed more like a beaten army than victors in a battle ...'[58]

BITING THE BULLET

With no strict code of standardisation in their manufacture, lead musket balls varied in size and weight although they averaged twelve to the pound. If lighter they were a loose fit in the barrel which resulted in low muzzle velocity ('poor windage'). The opposite problem was encountered by Lord Orrey during a close fight in Ireland: '... few of the shot would fit the muskets, but were a size too large, whereby we had to have been worsted; for the soldiers were forced to gnaw off much of the lead, others cut their bullets; in which much was lost, the bullets flew less way and more uncertainly ...'

KILSYTH
❧ 15 August 1645 ❧

By August, Alastair MacDonald's recruiting campaign had added another 1,400 men to Montrose's ranks. However, the Royalists had by now lost the West Country, and Charles I was beset on all sides.

Under the circumstances, distant victories in Scotland were of little help. The King needed the Marquis in England. But between Montrose and England there was still General Baillie, with a new Covenant army of 6,000 foot and 800 horse. Receiving intelligence that Baillie was expecting more recruits from Glasgow,

With their enemies waiting for reinforcements from Glasgow, Montrose's troops assembled for battle at Kilsyth. The odds were unfavourable, but they were about to get worse.

Montrose positioned himself in the village of Kilsyth, cutting the Glasgow road. The Covenanters responded with a flank march to seize the Auchinrivoch ridges above Montrose's camp. Although this manoeuvre was masked by a lower ridge, Baillie and his officers betrayed their plans by riding over the crest in order to

Montrose's small troop of Gordon horse struggled in vain to stop the Covenanter advance on the right. Successive musket volleys shrouded the valley in smoke.

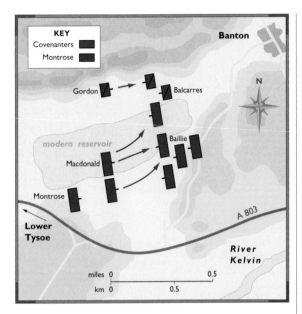

view the Royalist position. Correctly guessing their intentions, Montrose sent a body of foot racing to contest possession of Auchinrivoch and deployed the rest of his army along the valley. By moving quickly he hoped to surprise Baillie's vulnerable flank. However, as is often the way in war, nothing was to work out quite as planned for either commander.

Major John Haldane had been entrusted with the task of hurrying ahead of Baillie's column, with a force of lightly equipped musketeers, to secure Auchinrivoch before the rebels. Unfortunately, rough terrain caused him to swerve to the left, descending from the high ground much sooner than Baillie had intended. This diversion (quite against orders) brought him close to some stone cottages harbouring Montrose's left wing; a small unit of Maclean highlanders under Ewan MacLean of Treshnish. Seeing their enemies suddenly before them, the Macleans attacked (also without orders) and both sides began skirmishing for possession of the cottages.

General Baillie did what he could to restore matters by instructing Colonel Robert Home to speed on to the original objective. However, according to his own narrative he was soon appalled to observe that Home had 'left the way I put him in, and was gone at a trot, right west, in among the dykes and toward the enemy'.[59]

What Baillie was unable to see from his position was that Haldane was pinned down and in imminent danger of being overrun. The enemy to his front were rapidly being reinforced by Glengarry's men and a contingent of Irish under none other than the formidable Alastair MacDonald. Home, with Baillie's strongest regiment under his command, felt compelled to disregard orders and go to Haldane's aid. To make matters worse, the better part of Baillie's army ploughed blindly on behind. Only the Earl of Balcarres continued to lead his horse on a lonely ride around the top of the valley in an attempt to win possession of the Auchinrivoch ridges.

Montrose, observing the bulge in his line caused by the Macleans' precipitous attack, ordered his Ogilvy and Gordon horse forward to charge the Covenanters' right wing. This charge cut the enemy line in two and the Marquis followed up with a general advance. The valley now echoed to a heated exchange of fire in the centre of the field.

At the same time Balcarres' attempt to reach Auchinrivoch was stopped short by Captain-Adjutant Gordon, who came crashing heroically through the bracken with a small party of Royalist horse. A vicious engagement ensued in which the Gordons were greatly outnumbered. Looking up the valley from the opposite end of the battlefield, Viscount Aboyne noticed that his Gordon kinsmen were seriously imperilled by

THE DEATH OF MONTROSE

Within a month of his victory at Kilsyth, Montrose was to meet his nemesis in the form of Alexander Leslie, the Earl of Leven. Leslie, that shrewd veteran of Marston Moor and the Bishops' Wars, was to hunt the Highland fox from his last bolt-hole at Philiphaugh on 13 September 1645. Though the Marquis escaped with his life, his army was routed. The King's last beacon of hope in the north had been extinguished.

Having fled Scotland in 1646, Montrose returned in 1650 to fight for the young Charles II. He landed near John o'Groats on 12 April only to be defeated later that month at Carbisdale. Captured shortly afterwards, he was finally hanged by the Covenanters in Edinburgh on Tuesday 21 May 1650.

The Covenanters had murdered some of Montrose's Irish camp followers before the battle. MacDonald's men took vengeance at Kilsyth.

this rash action and proceeded to go to their aid. To accomplish this he led his Life Guard in a remarkable charge up the centre of the valley, right between the volleying lines of Highlanders and Covenanters. Recoiling from Homes' Red Regiment and Balcarres' lancers on the way,

Better armed and equipped, the Covenanters did not expect to lose at Kilsyth. The Duke of Argyll temporarily fled to England after Montrose's victory, but he would return to destroy Montrose.

Aboyne arrived in time to rally the Gordon horse. Nonetheless, it was not until Montrose committed the remainder of his cavalry to the action, that Balcarres was finally routed.

Freed from the threat to their left flank from the direction of Auchinrivoch, Montrose's foot were now sufficiently encouraged to brave the volleys of Haldane's command and 'lept over the dyke, and ... fell on and broke these regiments'. Looking around desperately for reinforcements, Baillie and Haldane 'galloped through the inclosures to [find] the reserve' but, according to Baillie's account, before he '... could come at them, they were in flight'.[60]

The Covenanting army, with Montrose chopping up its flank, was beaten into a bloody retreat. The Irish, who had not forgotten the ruthless slaughter of some of their camp-followers by Covenanters a few days before, were merciless in cutting down stragglers. Thus, against all odds, this haphazard battle resulted in a complete and devastating victory for the Royalists. It was Montrose's finest hour.

ROWTON HEATH
24 September 1645

By the autumn of 1645 the King's prospects in England looked bleak. Two months after the defeat of Goring's army at Langport, Prince Rupert was obliged to surrender the port of Bristol, crucial to Royalist supply lines.

The Prince's stock had fallen considerably since Marston Moor. Now, beguiled by the whispers of Rupert's enemies, Charles I reacted with cold-hearted resolve. The King's greatest soldier was dismissed in disgrace under the dark and unjustified suspicion of treachery. There were none left in England who could replace him. Charles' final hope was that he could resurrect an army around the core of 4,000 Royalist cavalry which had escaped destruction at Naseby. Having failed to raise a new army in Wales, he marched north to link his fortunes with Montrose in Scotland. It was to be his last throw of the dice. Unfortunately, having set off on 18 September, he was fatally distracted from his purpose by the plight of the Royalist garrison at Chester.

The result was the confused and scattered battle which took place two miles south-east of Chester on Rowton Heath. Sir Marmaduke Langdale, commanding the Royalist horse, had hoped to take the Parliamentarian besiegers of Chester by surprise. Instead he himself was surprised by a second Parliamentarian force arriving under General Sydenham Poyntz. He decided to deal with Poyntz first.

With both forces composed entirely of cavalry, the ensuing battle was short but fierce. Langdale despatched Colonel Geoffrey Shakerley to cross the River Dee and summon help from the King, who had entered Chester with his Life Guard.

Many Royalist cavalry made their escape from Naseby, but an infantry force could not be improvised.

Officers were distinguished by their individual dress rather than by variations in a standard uniform.

The enterprising Shakerley, eschewing the nine mile detour to Holt Bridge, 'got a wooden tub and a batting staff for an oar, put a servant into the tub with him and in this desperate manner swam over the river, his horse swimming by him'.[61] By this means he reached the King a mere quarter of an hour after leaving Langdale. However Poyntz had also summoned help and a small body of Parliamentarian musketeers, despatched from the force of Colonel Michael Jones besieging Chester, were the first to arrive.

Poyntz now advanced with his horse in the centre and his musketeers on the wings and 'a little before five o'clock … [both sides] joyned in a terrible storm, firing in the faces of one another, hacking and slashing with swords … as if everyone was resolved there to breathe their last'.[62]

By the time the Royalist reinforcements under Lord Lichfield sallied out of Chester it was already too late to save the day. The King did not ride with them into the buzzing bullets and flashing blades but watched from the relative safety of Chester's city walls. With the destruction of his cavalry went his last real vestige of hope. As he saw the forces of his enemies prevailing Charles was heard to lament 'O Lord, O Lord what have I done that I should cause my people to deal with me thus'.[63]

The King's standard is cheered as it is raised for what proved to be a hopeless fight.

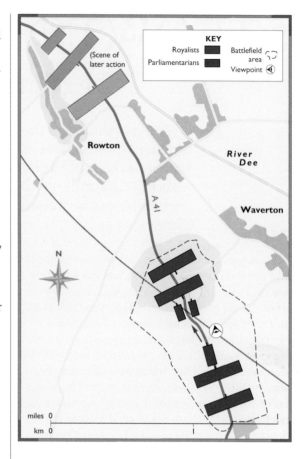

Parliamentarian soldiers give their thanks to God. Religious fervour in the ranks was already making the established leadership frightened of the New Model Army.

STOW-ON-THE-WOLD
21 March 1646

Only a week after the King's defeat at Rowton,
Montrose's army was defeated at Philiphaugh.
Unable to believe the news, the King dismissed it as
fabrication and continued to march north. Only
when Montrose's own despatch reached him, did
Charles accept that there was nowhere left to run to.

It was left to that veteran campaigner Sir Jacob Astley to play out the Royalist epilogue. Although he was by now sixty-six, he was by all accounts 'an honest, brave, plain man, and as fit for the office … of major-general of foot, as Christendom yields'.[64] The King appointed him lieutenant-general of all the royalist forces in the west and the Marches and tasked him with the unenviable job of raising a new army. There was a poetic symmetry in Astley being the King's last champion. It had been he who, in 1642 at the very beginning of the war, had marched the Royalist army down the slopes of Edgehill.

By March 1646, Astley had somehow scraped together 3,000 'hungry and penniless'[65] men from garrisons in Shropshire, Staffordshire and Worcestershire. With this miserable force, more than half of whom were raw recruits, he set out towards the King's

Oxford refuge. On the Wolds of Gloucestershire he was intercepted by Sir William Brereton.

Before dawn rose on 21 March, both armies were drawn up and ready. Astley had occupied the high ground. As the first watery light of morning smudged the horizon, the drums of the Parliamentarian foot began to beat. Flanked by their horse, they came gamely up the slope, their lines echoing to shouts of 'God be our guide'.

The Royalist line responded no less vigorously with their battle-cry, 'Patrick and St. George'. In this manner, with volleys thundering from both sides, the two armies came to blows. The Royalists had the better of the first exchange, forcing the Parliamentarian left wing to a disorderly retreat. However, they were unable to withstand Brereton's fierce attack with horse and foot on the right.

As their cavalry routed from the field, the

Charles I tried to form a new army by concentrating the garrisons of his surviving strongholds. Before they could all assemble, Parliament intercepted the main force at Stow.

Royalist infantry fled up the hill into Stow-on-the-Wold where many 'gentlemen and Officers of Quality' finally met their end trapped in the market square. Astley was among those captured alive and Brereton accorded the old war dog the respect due his rank and age. A drum was rolled out for the Royalist general to sit upon.

The handful of cannon remaining to the King were captured at Stow.

Accepting that the Civil War was over, he remarked to the enemy officers 'Gentlemen, ye may now sit and play (for you have done all your Worke) if you fall not out among yourselves!'.[66] His words were to prove strangely prophetic. By the following year the gentlemen of Parliament had indeed fallen out among themselves.

Only a handful of Royalists escaped death or capture. Some returned to their garrisons to await a siege, others quietly dispersed to their homes.

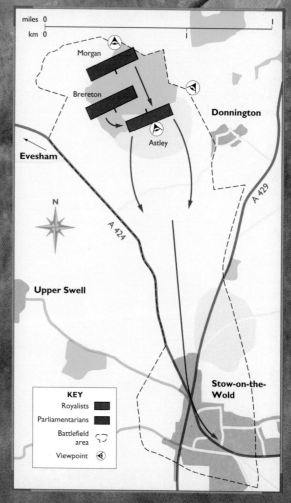

KEY

Royalists	
Parliamentarians	
Battlefield area	
Viewpoint	

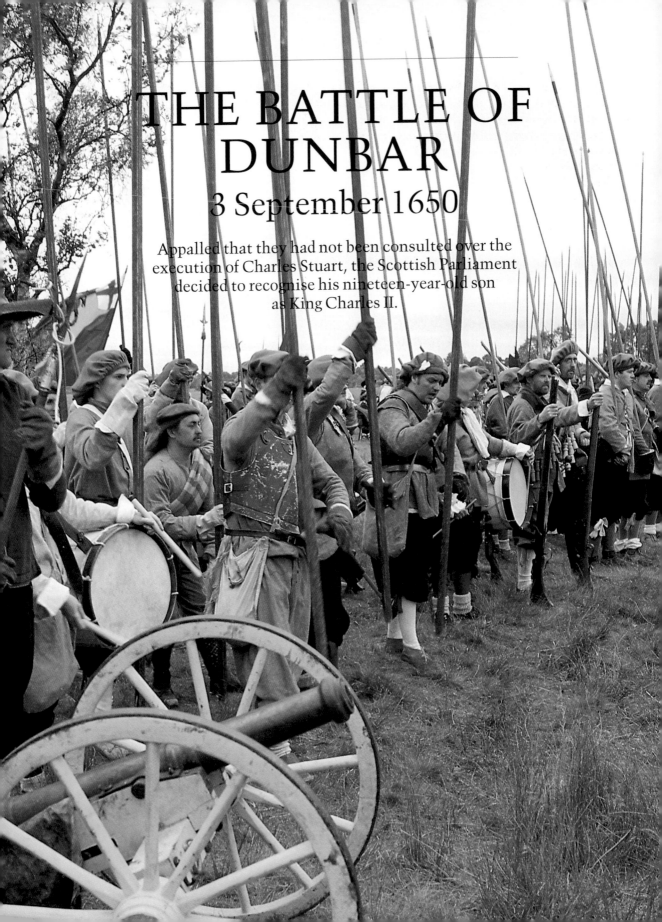

THE BATTLE OF DUNBAR

3 September 1650

Appalled that they had not been consulted over the
execution of Charles Stuart, the Scottish Parliament
decided to recognise his nineteen-year-old son
as King Charles II.

This triggered alarm bells in the English Council of State. With another war against Scotland now inevitable, Parliament decided to launch a pre-emptive strike. Fairfax declined the command, so it was left to Cromwell to lead the expedition which crossed the Scottish frontier on the 22 July 1650. His force was comprised of eight horse regiments and nine regiments of foot; some 16,000 men.

On 6 August, within a mile of Edinburgh, his progress was barred by David Leslie with an army of 22,000 men. Outnumbered, and outmanoeuvred, Cromwell was forced to fall back on Dunbar where he was blockaded by the Scots.

Leslie's strategy was based on his awareness of the fact that, while he possessed superior numbers, his troops were not of the same quality as the veterans of the New Model Army. His

Left: The former allies at Marston Moor were now on opposite sides. Scotland recognised Charles II as King and prepared to fight Cromwell's New Model Army.

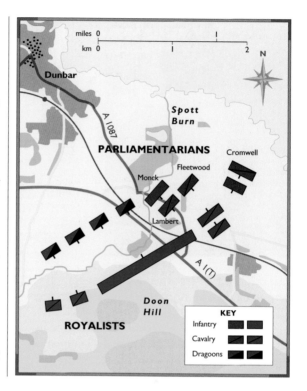

THE SECOND & THIRD CIVIL WARS
1648–51

In January 1647, Charles Stuart, King of England, Scotland and Ireland, was delivered into the hands of his enemies; generating much dissent over how best to deal with him. By the summer, Parliament had fallen out with its own creation, the New Model Army. The Army refused to disband until its overdue wages were paid, and its leaders, Fairfax and Cromwell, were at risk of arrest. The matter was only resolved when the New Model Army marched on London.

While his captors were thus preoccupied, Charles was secretly negotiating with those erstwhile allies of the Parliamentarians, the Scottish Covenanters. Having escaped from Hampton Court to the Isle of White in the winter of 1647, he signed a secret agreement with the Scots. In exchange for their support in returning him to the throne, he agreed to

impose Presbyterianism on England and confirm the Covenant in Parliament. He had come a long way since subjecting the Scots to two Bishops' Wars in a futile attempt to impose the English prayer book on them!

On 8 July 1648, a Scottish Army crossed the border into England heralding the beginning of the Second Civil War. By 18 August they had been defeated by the New Model Army at the battle of Preston. Determined to end the matter once and for all, Cromwell ruthlessly pursued the remaining fragments of the Royalist/Scottish force, hunting the survivors across the border into Scotland.

The last casualty of this brief war was the King himself. Having proved that he could not be trusted, he was brought to trial in London. There, on 30 January 1649, he finally kept his appointment with the executioner's axe.

Left: Cromwell's army was cut off from England and short of everything except hostile Scots. Fortunately for Cromwell, Leslie was persuaded to attack, giving the English a chance of victory.

Right: Experienced soldiers kept their matchcord dry during the overnight storm. In the morning the cord smouldered nicely, ready for action.

intention was to remain outside Dunbar, on the impregnable Lammermuir Hills, and starve Cromwell into submission.

By September Cromwell's army, ravaged by sickness, was down to 11,000 men. Trapped between the mountains and the sea, short of supplies and with winter coming on, he had good reason to be worried. He wrote gloomily to Sir Arthur Hesilrige that the New Model Army would require 'a miracle' in order to escape. Then the unexpected happened. The ministers of the Scottish Kirk, convinced they 'had got God on their side',[67] compelled Leslie to abandon the blockade and launch an all out attack.

At around 4 p.m. on the 2 September, Cromwell was surveying the enemy lines when he 'discerned through his glass an extraordinary movement in the Scottish camp'. This cheered him up immensely. 'They are coming down' he exclaimed, 'the Lord hath delivered them into our hands.'[68] That same night, in the utter darkness of a rainstorm which had blown in off the sea, he prepared a surprise attack. Cannons and dragoons were deployed to engage the Scottish left, while the bulk of the army filed across the deep Brox Burn ravine towards Leslie's right wing.

The English vanguard went in before sunrise, spearheaded by General Lambert's cavalry and seconded by General Monck with three infantry regiments. Although they were successfully contained by the Scottish horse, thundering down with their lancers in the front ranks, it was

to no avail. Almost before the Scots could draw breath, Cromwell had put the second part of his plan into action. On the previous day he had noticed that Leslie's right wing was so cramped for space between the mountains behind and the ravine in front, that they 'had not great ground to traverse their regiments … [or] wheel about'.[69] Seizing upon this weakness, he now led his own cavalry regiment of Ironsides, together with a regiment of foot, in a crushing flank attack. Although some of the Scottish infantry put up a tenacious resistance, many were disordered by their own horse, which routed through their lines. Even as their embattled ranks began to crumble, the Presbyterian ministers among them continued to preach; assuring the Scots that God would grant them success, '… till the English were upon them; and some of their preachers were knocked in the head whilst they were promising victory.'[70]

As Cromwell pushed forward, the morning sun suddenly broke through the clouds to bounce off a silvery sea. Inspired by this omen he cried out 'Now let God arise, and his enemies shall be scattered'. Without ceasing the busy rhythm of their blades, his regiments pressed their flank attack steadily home, rolling up the Scottish right until at last Cromwell's voice boomed out again: 'I profess they run!'. Then as the last pockets of Scottish infantry 'threw down their arms and fled',[71] he halted his men and sang the seventeenth psalm.

The worst of the fighting was over in about an

Left: Pikemen wore their steel armour over buff coats that helped to absorb blows.

Right: The English infantry waited as Cromwell's veteran cavalry drove the Scottish horse from the field.

hour. While the speed and lethal effectiveness of the English flank attack had preserved Cromwell's army almost intact, 3,000 Scots were listed killed and 10,000 captured.

As Leslie's soldiers tasted the bitter ashes of defeat, one Scottish preacher was to lament that Cromwell was worse than the Devil: 'For the scripture said, Resist the Devil and he will flie from you – but resist Oliver and he will flie in your face.'[72]

Right: Discarded equipment marked the path of the Scottish retreat.

Below: The front rank of musketeers kneels to shoot, while the next rank prepares to deliver a volley.

WORCESTER
⤜❦⤚ 3 September 1651 ⤜❦⤚

In the summer of 1651, Charles II and David Leslie marched south towards London. Closely shadowed by Cromwell with a massive force of 30,000 men, they decided to take refuge in Worcester. The King's supporters numbered just 12,000.

Having destroyed the bridges over the River Severn to the north and south of Worcester, King Charles hoped to channel Cromwell into a costly frontal attack on Worcester's strong eastern fortifications. However, Cromwell hit on the audacious plan of dropping pontoon bridges in the very face of the enemy. This enabled part of his force, under Lieutenant-General Charles Fleetwood, to launch an unexpected attack from the south-west.

Despite the originality of this plan, Fleetwood's advance was stalled by the fierce resistance of the Royalist and Highland troops west of the Severn. Anxious to maintain the momentum of the attack, Cromwell personally led three brigades of reinforcements across the pontoon bridge; thus weakening his right flank in order to strengthen his left.

This movement was observed by the young King, watching from the tower of Worcester Cathedral. Charles dashed down the tower steps,

rallied what forces he could and 'made a very bold sally … with great bodies of horse and foot'[73] out of Worcester's eastern Sidbury Gate. By the time that Cromwell had rushed back over his pontoon, his right flank was on the brink of defeat.

For the next three hours the area to the east of Worcester was fiercely contested as the Parliamentarians battled to win back lost ground. Despite the valour of the Scottish foot, 'fighting with the butt-ends of their muskets when their ammunition was spent', the King's forces were gradually edged back. Had Leslie come to the King's assistance with his cavalry, the city might yet have been saved, but he had sunk into a deep depression and could only ride up and down 'as one amazed'.[74]

As Cromwell's general advance came on, with drums beating behind battle-torn banners, the King's lines finally disintegrated into a panic-stricken mob streaming back towards the city's Sidbury Gate. By the time Charles rode up, this

Left: Charles II persuaded the Scots to advance into England, claiming that a massive Royalist rising would take place. The army marched, but there was little support for another Civil War.

Right: Musketeers adjust their matchcord ready to open fire. The first volley, loaded carefully, was usually the most effective.

Left: Charles II was as brave as his father on the field of battle and led his troops out of Worcester, splitting Cromwell's army.

Right: For the last time, the armies of King and Parliament faced each other on the field of battle. After Charles' defeat, England was to be ruled by Cromwell and his army.

passage had become blocked by an overturned ammunition cart and the King was forced to dismount and enter the city on foot. Within the walls of Worcester he mounted a fresh horse and tried to rally his forces; 'I had rather you would shoot me,' he declared 'than keep me alive to see the sad consequences of this fatal day.'[75] His efforts were in vain, '... [the troops] were so confused that neither threats nor entreaty could persuade them to charge with His Majesty.'[76]

Meanwhile on the Parliamentarian left flank, Fleetwood's attack had begun to gain momentum, forcing more of the Royalist troops back into Worcester. With darkness falling, the

battle became a vicious street-fight. The Royalists, caught like rats in a trap, battled desperately for avenues of escape. In their frenzy, according to one survivor, men trampled 'one upon another, much readier to cut each other's throat than to defend [themselves] against the enemy.'[77]

With all hope of victory gone, the King was finally persuaded to flee. Though he had lost both his army and his Kingdom, it had not been for want of personal courage. A witness was later to comment: 'What became of His Majesty afterwards I know not, but God preserve him for certainly a more gallant prince was never born.'[78] Although the final death-toll is hard to estimate, it is clear that the Royalist army had virtually ceased to exist. One of the inhabitants of Worcester wrote that '... the number of slain is certainly great ... the dead bodies lay in the way from Powick bridge to the town. Many lie killed in the houses, in the College and Church, on the Green, and in the cloisters and quite through Sidbury and about a mile that way.'[79]

Appropriately the last battle of the Civil Wars had taken place where the first war began. It had been nine long years since Prince Rupert's first victorious charge across the Worcester water meadows at Powick Bridge. Now the wheel had turned full circle and Cromwell's army had marched across those same meadows to win the final victory. Afterwards his chaplain, Hugh Peter, advised the weary Parliamentarian foot soldiers, 'When your wives and children shall ask where you have been, and what news: say you have been at Worcester, where England's sorrows began, and where they are happily ended.'[81]

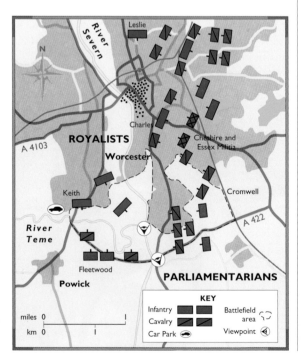

KEY

Infantry	▮ ▮
Cavalry	◪ ◪
Car Park	🅿

Battlefield area	〜
Viewpoint	◀

SOLDIERING IN THE STUART UPRISINGS

Charles II was restored to the throne in 1660, two years after the death of Oliver Cromwell. Astoundingly he regained the crown, not by force of arms, but by the invitation of Parliament. Unlike his father, he was a cool and pragmatic man who manoeuvred his way through political difficulties with skilled charm. That he employed the same technique with his mistresses is attested to by his acknowledgment of no less than seventeen illegitimate children. In April 1679 Samuel Pepys referred in his diary to 'Mr Crofts, the King's bastard, a most pretty sparke of about 15 years old'.[1] In fact 'Mr Crofts' (later better known as the Duke of Monmouth) was the King's eldest natural son. Unfortunately, the royal marriage bed had failed to produce any legitimate offspring. The recognised Royal heir was Charles' openly Catholic brother, James, Duke of York. At a time when Parliament was electrified by fears of a 'Popish Plot' to seize power and reinstate the Catholic Church, this was rather awkward. Not surprisingly, the 'pretty' and, more importantly, Protestant Duke of Monmouth became the focus of a political movement to remove the Duke of York from the succession.

By October 1679, according to Pepys, it was being 'whispered at court that young "Crofts" is lawful son to the King, the King being married to his mother'[2]. During the course of his reign Charles II was to issue no less than three declarations denying Monmouth's legitimacy, but the rumour persisted. Ultimately the intrigues revolving around Monmouth became so dangerously treasonous that the young Duke prudently removed himself to exile in Holland.

Charles II was a man of his time who believed that kings ruled by 'divine right'. To disinherit his unpopular Catholic brother would contravene that right. When the Oxford Parliament of 1681 asked him to guarantee the Protestant succession by making Monmouth his heir his reply was unequivocal. Within a week he had dissolved Parliament. In consequence when he died in 1685, Charles II's legacy was a succession crisis which smouldered for sixty years; periodically igniting into open rebellion.

Trouble first raised its head less than a year after the coronation of the devoutly Catholic James II. Predictably, that trouble bore the name Monmouth.

SEDGEMOOR
⋙ 6 July 1685 ⋘

Claiming that he was the true Stuart heir and that James II was a Popish usurper, the Duke of Monmouth set sail for England in June 1685 to incite a 'Protestant' uprising. Landing in the West Country he received a warm welcome.

On 20 June, before magistrates brought at sword-point to witness the event, the Duke declared himself King of England, Scotland and Ireland. As there were now two King James IIs, the new King was to be known, at least temporarily, as 'King Monmouth'. The original James II responded by despatching the Earl of Feversham to the West Country with a Royalist force of 2,500 men. Faced with a real army, the enthusiasm of Monmouth's following of untrained country yeomen began to wane. By the time they faced Feversham in battle their numbers had dwindled from 7,000 to 3,000 men. On 5 July, having learned that 'King Monmouth's' rebel forces were at Bridgwater, Feversham camped nearby at Westonzoyland. In one last, desperate bid for power Monmouth decided to risk all on that most hazardous of manoeuvres: a surprise night attack.

As the lights of Bridgwater faded from sight, Monmouth's men embarked on their night march with grim resolve. Stealth was essential to their plan. Each man was under strict orders to kill the man next to him if he spoke or made a sound. With the hooves of their horses muffled in rags and the wheels of their four gun carriages greased into silence, the mute rebels hugged the shadows like a phantom army.

While Feversham's officers and cavalry were billeted in Westonzoyland, his main encampment was on nearby Sedgemoor. The guns and primary defences of this camp faced west towards Bridgwater, from whence the Royalists anticipated any attack would come. Westonzoyland was to the south of them and they were protected from the north and east by deep drainage dykes (known locally as rhynes) and the treacherous ground of Sedgemoor itself.

Left: Volunteers flocked to Monmouth's standard, but there were only enough weapons for the fortunate few.

Right: The army of Charles II proved loyal to his Catholic brother, for the time being. The rebels had nothing to match Feversham's artillery.

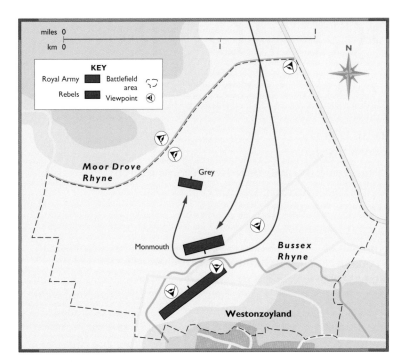

Lord Grey's cavalry might have made a better showing if the ground had been favourable, but his hastily-assembled force became hopelessly confused during the night approach march and contributed little to the battle.

As an added precaution cavalry picquets from the King's Horse Guards and Sir Frances Compton's Regiment patrolled in all directions.

Aware that the Royalist guns had been placed to cover the Bridgwater road, Monmouth's plan was to march across the moor at night and attack unexpectedly from the northwest. His poorly armed peasantry would be required to find their way over the difficult moorland in darkness and silence, avoiding the Royalist picquets and keeping together in order to deliver an effective concentration of force at the other end. Finally they would be forced to cross the Bussex Rhyne right under the noses of the Royalists encamped on the other side. It was a strategy which would have tested far more experienced troops.

At Peasey Farm on the edge of Sedgemoor they were forced to leave behind one of their four precious cannons, as a wheel persisted in squeaking. Worse still, the moon was lost behind a thickening cloak of fog. Ahead in the impenetrable gloom lay the ancient peat moor; an arcane landscape of swirling ground mist and deep black pools. To the superstitious minds of Monmouth's followers it was an unnerving prospect.

With their fears magnified by the mist, the night-blinded rebels were soon reduced to feeling their way. In this manner they advanced, 'much incumbered, and retarded, by the narrowness of the lanes'[3] into the dank environs of the deeper moor. Twice, during the course of that night, Sir Frances Compton's cavalry picquets were to pass within a stone's throw of the silent line of soldiers. Twice they failed to spot them, standing like statues in the impenetrable shadows.

MIDNIGHT BATTLE

Monmouth's plan began to unravel after midnight. As the rebels filed across the Langmoor Rhyne, a lone picquet from Compton's regiment became aware of the ghostly shuffle of thousands of feet. Firing his pistol, he rode hell-for-leather, first to warn Compton and then to the Royalist camp behind the Bussex Rhyne. There he bellowed no less than twenty times 'Beat your drums, the enemy is come. For the Lord's sake, beat your drums'[4].

In danger of losing the advantage of surprise, Monmouth ordered Lord Grey to ride ahead with the cavalry, cross the Bussex Rhyne (via the Upper Plungeon bridge) and attack the enemy's right flank. Meanwhile he would hurry the infantry forward to '... finish what the horse had begun, before the King's horse or cannon could get in order'[5] In their rush to obey, Lord Grey's cavalry charged off into the mist without a thought for their poor local guide Benjamin Godfrey, who rather optimistically chased after them on foot. As he was the only one who knew the exact location of the Upper Plungeon, it would have been prudent to wait for him.

Lord Grey's cavalry collided with Compton's patrol, also racing back towards the Royalist camp. In the brief, chaotic skirmish which followed the rebel horse were scattered; many vanishing into the misty night never to return. The rest became divided. By the time Grey found the elusive Bussex Rhyne, some 300 of his remaining force had fallen behind. To make matters worse his Lordship had no idea of the whereabouts of the Upper Plungeon crossing. Haphazardly turning right he began a fruitless search; oblivious to the fact that he was now traversing the frontage of the Royalist camp on the other side of the rhyne.

Lining the opposite bank were Feversham's dishevelled soldiers, still struggling into their uniforms. As they became aware of the strange, shadowy figures looming out of the mist, they challenged the riders to identify which side they were for. Realising too late their horrendous mistake, the rebels replied ambiguously that they were for 'The King'. Not satisfied with this reply, Captain Berkley of the 1st Guards asked 'What King?' and received the surprising answer 'Monmouth ... God with us'. Shouting back 'Take this with you'[6], Berkley commanded the

BOTCHED EXECUTION

Had Monmouth behaved with as much self-possession during the battle of Sedgemoor as he did at his execution, things might have gone differently. On the scaffold he '... carried himself with great sedateness of mind ... and told them he was not afraid of death and called for the axe and ran his thumb over the edge and believed it was sharp, praying the executioner not to mangle him as he did Lord Russell, but the rogue served him much worse, for striking two blows at him, he lay'd done the axe and was feine to take it up again and gave him three more before he could sever the head from his body'.

'THE BLOODY ASSIZES'

The battle of Sedgemoor was followed by the arbitrary detention of any man in the area who could not account for his movements during the rebellion. About 1500 people were arrested. A series of show trials followed, in which those accused of treason were brutally treated by the judiciary; not least by Judge Jeffreys' infamous Bloody Assizes. Very few were found innocent or pardoned. On the whole the lucky ones were those sold into bonded slavery in Barbados. The majority were hanged.

Henry Pittman, a Quaker doctor found himself sold to Robert Bishop, a harsh and sadistic plantation owner. Determined to escape, he and some companions stole a small open boat and took to the sea. They landed on the deserted island of Tortuga and survived on turtles and birds eggs until rescued by English privateers. Pittman eventually made his way back to England via New York only to discover that his name was included in a General Pardon issued after James II was deposed.

The good doctor's account of his adventures, 'A Relation of the Great Sufferings of Henry Pitman', eventually formed part of the inspiration for Daniel Defoe's famous novel, Robinson Crusoe. Interestingly Defoe had also been a member of Monmouth's army, but had managed to evade capture. Had he come before Judge Jeffreys, he too might have experienced Crusoe-like adventures at first hand!

Guards to open fire. Unable to withstand the successive volleys which now greeted them all along the rhyne, Grey's cavalry reeled back towards their own infantry. This terrified Monmouth's foot soldiers who, 'supposing them to be enemy coming from the left wing of the King's army', fired at them 'with some execution'[7].

In the meantime the missing 300 rebel horse finally blundered up to the rhyne and, turning the opposite way from Grey, stumbled upon the elusive Upper Plungeon crossing. Sadly for them the bridge had already been located by Compton's patrol who, as much from surprised fear as gallantry, now violently assaulted them with pistols and swords. Forced to fall back, the last of the rebel horse also collided with Monmouth's infantry.

Surviving this additional fright, the rebel

infantry pressed on steering themselves by a strange pink glow in the mist ahead. Only when they drew 'within about eighty paces'[8] did they realise, with some shock, that this glow was caused by the lit matches of enemy musketeers in Dumbarton's Regiment (the only Royalist regiment at Sedgemoor still using the old matchlocks). Already emotionally drained by the difficulties and perils of the march, the rebels were now subjected to the very real dangers of a close volley. With the firefight escalating along their lines, they lost momentum and their courage began to fail. Monmouth had expected too much of raw troops. Though they stood and bore 'very considerable execution'[9] from the guns of their enemies, not one regiment could now be induced by any means to advance another step.

Meanwhile the Royalist defence consolidated and Feversham's cavalry ventured over the Upper Plungeon to skirmish with the rebel left. This was enough to persuade Monmouth that his dream had faltered within a 'halfe musket shot'[10] of his objective. Before his enemies could encompass him, the would-be king 'put off his arms, and taking one hundred guineas from his servant, left his foot still fighting, and went away'[11].

By sunrise all effective resistance was over. As soon as it was light, Feversham's infantry swarmed over the Bussex Rhyne and scattered the remaining rebels. Through most of that long day Monmouth's supporters were tirelessly pursued and 'creeping into hedges and cornfields were started and shot like game by the King's soldiers'[12]. About 1,000 rebels lost their lives at Sedgemoor, while Royalist casualties numbered less than 200.

When Monmouth was captured nine days later, he had already despaired of life. In his pocket book he had written a prayer: 'I ask not of thee any longer the things of this world; neither Power nor Honours, nor Riches, nor Pleasures. No, my God, dispose of them to whom thou pleasest, so that you give me mercy.'[13]

However things stood between Monmouth and his maker, the ill-starred Duke was to meet no mercy at the hands of King James II. On 15th July 1685 he was beheaded on Tower Hill.

THE JACOBITE UPRISINGS

James II's reign was destined to be turbulent and brief. By 1688 many of the Protestant hierarchy were exasperated by his zealous advancement of Catholicism. However there was still hope that they might weather the storm. Aged 55, the King had only two daughters, Mary and Anne, both the offspring of his first, Protestant marriage. Mary, who was next in line of succession was married to a Protestant Dutch Prince, William of Orange.

The timely birth of a son and heir to James' second, Catholic, wife was the final straw. A clandestine gathering of English lords sent an invitation to William of Orange imploring him to invade England, take the crown with his wife, and rid the country of its troublesome Catholic king once and for all. William complied and seized the crown from his father-in-law in November 1688.

In 1689 after a meeting of the Scottish Parliament, William and Mary were also offered the crown of Scotland. At the same time the commander of James II's remaining forces in Scotland, Viscount Dundee, was declared a renegade. He responded by raising the Standard of King James at Dundee Law in April 1689, effectively marking the beginning of the first Jacobite rising. By 18 May Highland chiefs, attracted as much by the prospect of plunder as by the Jacobite cause, were already assembling at Glenroy. Lowland Scotland remained quietly neutral.

KILLIECRANKIE
❧ 27 July 1689 ❧

The task of containing the Jacobite revolt fell to
General Hugh Mackay of Scourie. In July 1689 he set
off with a Scottish Government army of 5,000 men
to confront Viscount Dundee.

*The famous 'Claidaemh mor' (Claymore) was a
two-handed sword up to 6 ft long and dating
from the 14th-16th century. The name was
eventually transferred to single-handed
basket-hilted swords, and Killiecrankie
was probably the last occasion the
original sword was swung in anger.*

On 27 July Mackay's army negotiated the Killiecrankie Pass between the slopes of Creag Eallaich and Creag on Eirionnach to find Dundee waiting, with 2,500 Jacobite foot and one troop of horse, on the other side. Turning his army to the right, Mackay advanced up the slope of Creag Eallaich hoping to win possession of the high ground. However Dundee was quicker off the mark. Even as Mackay's army scrambled up the first ridge, the Highlanders had already taken possession of the higher Orchill ridge beyond it. Finding himself on 'ground fair enough to receive the enemy, but not to attack them'[14] Mackay ordered his infantry into half-battalions (advancing the rear three ranks of each battalion into the first three ranks to extend his frontage). Although this manoeuvre increased his immediate firepower, it left his slender battalions perilously vulnerable to the shock of a Highland charge.

Dundee watched this manoeuvring and matched it by extending his own line; not by thinning the depth of his formations, but by increasing the gaps between them. With both sides thus deployed, events reached a hiatus. Mackay was unwilling to assail Dundee's formidable position and Dundee had grave doubts about his ability to defeat a better equipped enemy twice his size. For two hours the Highlanders shouted insults (punctuated with

Viscount Dundee's army was overwhelmingly recruited from the Highlands. Lowland Scotland remained opposed to the Stuarts.

long-range sniping) and dared Mackay to come and get them.

At approximately 8 pm, with only an hour or so of daylight left, Dundee decided to attack. Mackay's unwillingness to advance and the derisory results of his short artillery barrage (a total of just nine shots) had emboldened the Jacobite clansmen. Priming their muskets and throwing aside their plaids, the Highlanders began their advance; firing sporadically as soon as they were within musket range. Below, on the receiving end, sergeants cautioned the extended Government lines to wait for the order to fire.

The hills of Killiecrankie echoed with thunder when Mackay's men finally demonstrated the killing power of a good, disciplined volley. Almost seven hundred dead and dying Highlanders collapsed into the heather. But it was not enough. Mackay had staked all on crippling the Highland charge with his initial firepower. His gamble was about to fail.

Surrounded by their kith and kin, with their

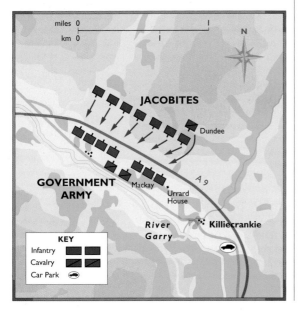

ancient battle cries ringing in their ears, the remaining Jacobites raced the final yards; taking less than thirty seconds to impact with the centre of Mackay's line. The regiments of Lord Kenmore and George Ramsey, who bore the brunt of the rush, had no time to reload for a second volley. Even as they struggled to insert their newly-introduced 'plug bayonets' they were being massacred by Highland blades: 'soldiers were cut down through the skull and neck, to the very breasts; others had skulls cut off above the ears … some had both their bodies and cross belts cut through at one blow; pikes and small swords were cut like willows'[15].

Although Mackay attempted to save the situation by charging his cavalry towards the Jacobite left, they were worsted by Dundee's single troop of horse. Severely shaken, the government cavalry fled through the ranks of their own infantry, beginning a general rout. Only Mackay's right flank held firm; consisting of the regiments of the Earl of Leven, Colonel Hastings and Mackay himself. These embattled survivors were saved by the marksmanship of Leven's regiment.

As Viscount Dundee galloped across to encourage his men to finish the job, a steady volley from Leven's musketeers threw him from his horse. A musket ball had passed beneath the rim of his iron breastplate into his stomach. With their commander down, Dundee's aides reeled to a halt and attempted to retrieve him from the blood-speckled heather. Leven's men calmly reloaded. Before the Viscount could be carried away a second volley was fired, killing two more Highlanders and forcing the others to abandon the attempt. Though soundly beaten, the battered remnants of Mackay's army miraculously found themselves in possession of the field and able to make an orderly retreat.

The Government survivors who limped into Stirling thirty-six hours later constituted little more than a quarter of the original 5,000-strong force. On the opposing side, the Jacobites had suffered in the region of 1,200 casualties as well as the loss of their commander. Viscount Dundee had received his final death wound from a looter as he lay mortally wounded on the battlefield.

With the death of Dundee the heart went out of the Jacobite army. Though there were minor clashes at Dunkeld in 1689 and Cromdale in 1690, the first Jacobite rebellion failed to gather momentum and the army eventually drifted apart.

SEVENTEENTH CENTURY FIELD MEDICINE

Although medicine had made progress by the 17th century, it still had a long way to go. As king, William III could rely on the very best of medical advice, including the liberal application of powdered crab's eyes to his boils. Despite the King's faith in such prescriptions he had an enlightened approach to military medicine. He improved the medical facilities available to his soldiers, with a 'Marching Hospital' to accompany them on campaign.

Army surgeons were now available to treat the mundane complaints of everyday life. Sir John Pringle (Physician-General to the Forces in 1744) had a sure cure for throat infections: a mixture of mustard, vinegar, mel rofraum and barley water. This spicy gargle, together with a good laxative, blistering and bleeding were, according to Pringle, 'all the medicines I find necessary'. The Physician-General's faith in a little judicious bleeding was perfectly in line with the medical philosophy of the age. For inflammatory conditions he recommended draining 12–13oz of blood as a sound starter. In his opinion many deaths could be prevented by 'the timely use of the lancet'.

An efficacious alternative was 'bleeding by leeches'; for which treatment 'two or more [leeches were] … applied to the eye and the wounds allowed to ooze till they stop of themselves'. Though Pringle was confident that, given such treatment, 'soldiers will seldom complain of a cough … or inflammatory symptoms', many patients doubtless preferred to suffer their cough in silence, rather than subject themselves to the cure!

Pringle was by no means an old reactionary clinging to the medical practices of the past. On the contrary, he was a genuinely forward-thinking surgeon with the best interests of his patients at heart. If for nothing else, he should be hailed by all serving soldiers for one thing alone: it was Pringle who first recommended that every soldier's tent should have a blanket!

SHERIFFMUIR

⋘ 13 November 1715 ⋙

None of Queen Anne's children survived childhood. When she died in 1714, Parliament ensured the succession of James I's great grandson, the Elector of Hanover. He may have been a German-speaking prince, but he was a Protestant. Parliamentary opposition was crushed, but in little over a year the 'Restoration Standard' was raised at Castleton Braemar in support of Prince James Frances Edward Stuart, son of the deposed James II.

On 10 November 1715 James Erkine, Earl of Mar, led an army of 6,000 men south to link up with Jacobite forces in England. The task of opposing Mar fell to the Duke of Argyll, who blocked the route south near Dublane on 12 November. With most of the British army on campaign in Flanders, Argyll could field only 3,500 soldiers.

On the bitterly cold morning of 13 November 1715 the two armies approached each other over the winter dark heather of Sherriffmuir. As the moor lay on undulating ground neither commander enjoyed a good overview of the field. Their forces were significantly misaligned, with the right wing of each outflanking the left wing of the opposing side. By all accounts, Mar was psychologically unprepared to command his men in battle and failed to take adequate control of his enthusiastic followers. In consequence a most unusual battle ensued.

On the Jacobite right flank, 'The order to attack being given, the two thousand Highlanders … ran towards the enemy in a disorderly manner, always firing some dropping shots …' When the enemy responded with 'a general salvo' the Highlanders took protective measures; 'throwing themselves flat on their bellies'[16] so that the buzzing musket balls passed overhead with little effect. As the only man on horseback among all his prostrated men, the unfortunate Captain of the Clanranald clan presented rather an obvious target. He was blasted out of his saddle by the enemy volley and dead before he hit the heather.

Far left: *Highlanders flocked to Mar's standard, ready to fight for the son of James II.*

Left: *Basket-hilted swords were the primary weapon of the Highlanders. If they had muskets, the Highland tactic was to fire one volley just before the charge.*

The right wing of the Highland army surges forward to attack the Duke of Argyll and his men.

Left: Argyll's forces included several regiments of dragoons which charged the Jacobite left and stopped it in its tracks.

Right: Body armour had all but vanished by 1715, the breastplate shrinking to a 'gorget' worn on the top of the chest by officers.

With the ill omen of their dead captain before them the Clanranalds hesitated. Glengarry broke the evil spell by dashing forward with his broadsword twirling above his head screaming 'Revenge! Revenge! Today for Revenge and tomorrow for mourning'[17] Throwing 'away their fugies [muskets] and, drawing their swords'[18], the Clanranalds surged after him, howling for blood. Within 'four minutes time from receiving the order to attack', the Highland charge burst onto Argyll's left wing. Government forces on the left were unable to withstand the shock. '… pierced … everywhere with an incredible vigour and rapidity'[19], they were driven entirely from the field. One survivor of this attack later complained that the Jacobites at Sheriffmuir demonstrated a 'merciless and most savage nature'[20].

At this critical point, the Highlanders allowed themselves to be distracted by a small party of Argyll's horse. Had Mar but taken control of his excited forces, victory might have been his.

Left: Mar's soldiers had enough muskets to sustain a violent firefight with Argyll's soldiers before they began their charge.

Right: Scottish pistols, or 'dags' were often made with all-metal stocks. You could beat someone to a pulp without fear of damaging the pistol.

HIGHLAND COSTUME

As early as 1582 George Buchanan stated that it was the Scottish habit 'to wear marled cloaths, specially that have long stripes of diverse colours, sundry-ways divided … but for the most part now they are brown, most near to the color of the [heather], to the effect when they lie among [heather] the bright colours of their plaids shall not betray them'.

The plaid was a cloth of several yards in length, usually fixed on the right shoulder (so as to leave the right arm free) and tied about the body so that it covered the thighs. When the Highlander was obliged to spend nights in the open, his long plaid served him as a blanket. In battle however he often threw it off, charging unencumbered in just his shirt.

Typically a clansman carried little about his person other than his plaid and his weapons. According to William Sacheverell writing in the late seventeenth century, '[their plaids are] loose and flowing … their thighs are bare with brawny muscles … what is covered is only adapted to necessity – a thin brogue on the foot, a short buskin [puttee] of various colours on the legg, tied above the calf with a striped pair of garters. What should be concealed is hid with a large shot-pouch, on each side of which hangs a pistol and dagger, as if they found it necessary to keep these parts well-guarded. A round target [shield] on their backs, a blew bonnet on their heads, in one hand a broadsword and a musket in the other; perhaps no nation goes better armed…'.

In the bitter wake of Culloden this traditional form of Highland dress was prohibited, on pain of death, by the 1747 Act of Proscription. Ironically it was retained as the uniform of the various Highland Regiments serving the Hanoverian monarch.

Instead, with the battle hanging in the balance, he cast his eyes across the field and 'rode off, without pretending to give orders'. This catastrophic indecisiveness was to prove a mortal blow to the rebellion.

Although the Jacobite right wing had utterly

Most Highlanders fought with sword and shield. Their shields were light enough to be used offensively, punching the opponent's musket to one side before delivering the fatal blow with the broadsword.

routed Argyll's left, circumstances were exactly reversed on the other side of the field. There the Highlanders had 'arrived in such confusion that it was impossible to form them according to the line of battle projected [and] every one posted himself as he found ground'[21]. Hence the Jacobite left resembled an uncontrolled mob rather than an army. Worse still, the marshy ground which might have protected their flank had frozen solid overnight, enabling Argyll's dragoons to charge across it.

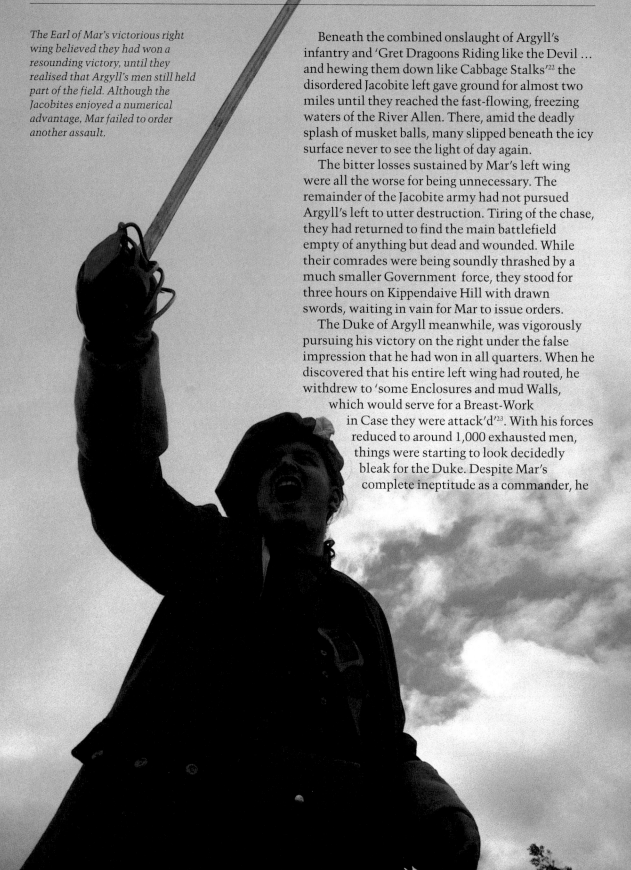

The Earl of Mar's victorious right wing believed they had won a resounding victory, until they realised that Argyll's men still held part of the field. Although the Jacobites enjoyed a numerical advantage, Mar failed to order another assault.

Beneath the combined onslaught of Argyll's infantry and 'Gret Dragoons Riding like the Devil … and hewing them down like Cabbage Stalks'[22] the disordered Jacobite left gave ground for almost two miles until they reached the fast-flowing, freezing waters of the River Allen. There, amid the deadly splash of musket balls, many slipped beneath the icy surface never to see the light of day again.

The bitter losses sustained by Mar's left wing were all the worse for being unnecessary. The remainder of the Jacobite army had not pursued Argyll's left to utter destruction. Tiring of the chase, they had returned to find the main battlefield empty of anything but dead and wounded. While their comrades were being soundly thrashed by a much smaller Government force, they stood for three hours on Kippendaive Hill with drawn swords, waiting in vain for Mar to issue orders.

The Duke of Argyll meanwhile, was vigorously pursuing his victory on the right under the false impression that he had won in all quarters. When he discovered that his entire left wing had routed, he withdrew to 'some Enclosures and mud Walls, which would serve for a Breast-Work in Case they were attack'd'[23]. With his forces reduced to around 1,000 exhausted men, things were starting to look decidedly bleak for the Duke. Despite Mar's complete ineptitude as a commander, he

The first bayonets fitted directly into the musket barrel, preventing the weapon from being fired. Since it took timt to fit, the 'plug' bayonet caused the Hanoverian foot to cease fire just as the Highlanders charged.

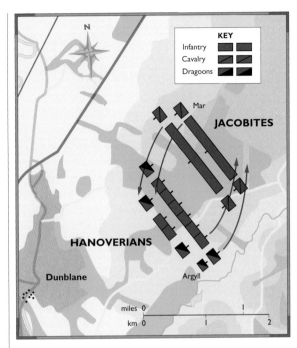

now possessed all the advantages. He held the high ground, his remaining force were well-rested and, with 4,000 men still at his disposal, he possessed a huge numerical advantage. At around 4pm he finally made his decision and Argyll's battle-weary, smoke-begrimed soldiers watched in dismay as the Highland army began to fan through the heather towards them.

What happened next was entirely unexpected. Within 500 yards of Argyll's forces, the Jacobite advance ground to a halt. The Highlanders began to draw back. Once out of musket range, Mar's

forces dispersed ending the battle. Although the Jacobites had suffered only 230 casualties against almost 700 inflicted upon Argyll, the Highlanders had all lost faith in their leaders. After Sheriffmuir the 1715 rebellion was over, and even the arrival of James himself in December could not rekindle the flames of rebellion.

In the gathering gloom, the Hanoverian survivors awaited an attack that never came. Mar eventually retreated, dooming the uprising before James had even set foot in Scotland.

THE 1745 JACOBITE UPRISING

After the failed rising of 1715 another generation was to pass before circumstances once again appeared to favour the Jacobite cause. By the early 1740s a new Hanoverian King, George II, was in conflict with France (the War of Austrian Succession). The House of Stuart therefore hoped for some assistance from Louis XV. This time Jacobite hopes were pinned on a 25 year old Stuart prince, destined to become known to his Scottish adherents as 'Bonnie Prince Charlie'.

In July 1745 a small invasion force set sail from France only to fall foul of the Royal Navy. Although the Prince's ship escaped, a second vessel carrying troops, swords and muskets was forced to turn back. It was an inauspicious beginning for the rekindled Jacobite dream. When Charles finally set foot in Scotland on 3 August, without the promised French army, the response of the clans was less than wholehearted. The two great chieftains of Skye, Norman MacLeod and Sir Alexander of Sleat, bluntly advised him to return to France.

Undeterred the Prince began to drum up support. On 19 August 1745 the royal standard of the Stuarts was raised again at Glenfinnan, officially beginning a new Jacobite Rebellion. Although several clans refused to rise, by September Charles had occupied Edinburgh with 2,500 men. The Government forces moved swiftly to crush the uprising.

By 1745 the British army had established a fine reputation in European wars. Officers and men were confident of defeating the small Jacobite force that rose to support Prince Charles Stuart.

General Cope's force included six battalion guns, but only their commander, Colonel Whiteford remained to fire them. His gunners (volunteer seamen and three old soldiers from Edinburgh) fled in terror when the Highlanders charged.

PRESTONPANS
21 September 1745

In the summer of 1745 almost the entire strength of the the British Army was fighting in Europe. Only 2,300 men were available to Sir John Cope, commanding the regiments stationed in Scotland. Having failed to intercept the Jacobites as they marched on Edinburgh, he headed for Aberdeen, intending to reach the city by sea.

The Government forces landed at Dunbar. The Jacobites marched out of Edinburgh to meet him and on 20 September the opposing armies sighted each other near Prestonpans. Cope deployed his lines facing south with the sea behind him, and a dyke and marsh in front. In his opinion: 'There [was] not in the whole of the ground between Edinburgh and Dunbar, a better spot for both Horse and Foot to act upon'[24]. The Highlanders were less enchanted with the spot; the marshy ground made it almost impossible for the two armies to come to grips. As night fell they manoeuvred eastward towards the enemy left flank. Cope turned his lines to conform to the Jacobite movement until the opposing sides lost sight of each other in the darkness.

On the mist-shrouded autumn morning of 21 September 1745, the red-coated British soldiers of King George II, were at the ready by dawn. When the Jacobite army, charged out of the gloom with 'a hideous shout'[25] they were met by a volley. On the English right wing Cope's six artillery pieces opened up with a 'straggling fire'[26]. But although the Highland lines gave 'a great shake' as the cannon balls ploughed gory furrows through their ranks, their charge slammed home

When Cope's army took the field, his officers expected an easy victory. Their families were lucky they stayed in Aberdeen.

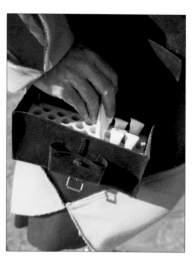

Left: *Only the lucky few Highlanders had muskets. Weapons had been confiscated after 1715 and the promised weapons from France never arrived.*

Right: *Paper cartridges (containing one bullet and a charge of powder) enabled soldiers to fire their muskets much more rapidly.*

with 'a swiftness not to be conceived'[27].

There was no time for a second musket volley. Cope's gunners fled; their panic infecting Gardiner's Dragoons standing to their left. Colonel Gardiner, badly wounded by musket shot, found himself almost deserted as his men began to bolt from the field. Attempting to make them stand he cried out 'Fight on, my lads and fear nothing'[28] but as there was already more fear in them than fight, they kept going. For his pains Gardiner was dragged from his saddle and struck a mortal blow to the head.

On the Government left wing, Hamilton's

Dragoons fared little better. Once among their lines, the Highlanders slashed and stabbed, butchering as many men as they could. At close quarters the outnumbered dragoons stood little chance against the whirling blades of the sharp Scottish broadswords. Unable to withstand this savage onslaught for long, they soon followed Gardiner's regiment, leaving the infantry without cavalry support. General Cope made frantic efforts to stop the rout. Over the din of battle he could be heard screaming 'For shame, Gentlemen, behave like Britons, give them another fire and you'll make them run'[29], but it

The plug bayonets of 1715 had largely been replaced by socket bayonets that did not stop the soldier firing his musket when it was fitted.

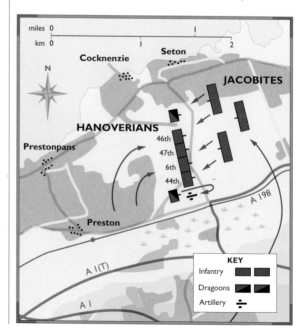

Many of Cope's soldiers were new recruits drawn from the Lowlands. Cope promised them they could pillage Edinburgh and Leith after they had won, to punish the city for welcoming Prince Charles.

was to no avail. With the infantry now fighting hand-to-hand all along the line, the battlefield was 'a scene of horror [on which] noses, hands and legs were promiscuously strewed'[30].

Captain Blake, fighting among the infantry, was felled by a claymore which neatly sliced off a piece of his skull. On the Jacobite side, Malcolm MacGregor, commanding officer of Perth's Highlanders, was hit by five musket balls. Propped up on his arms he called out to his men 'My lads, I am not dead, and, by God, I shall see any man of you who does not do his duty'[31]. Sensing that their first rush had carried the day,

his clansmen needed little encouragement.

Within minutes of battle being engaged, the battered remnants of Cope's army were streaming from the field with the Highlanders in murderous pursuit. One eyewitness commented that 'Never did deer run faster before hounds than these poor betrayed men ran before the rabble. Disciplined they were, but had no head and no confidence in their leaders'[32].

According to General Wightman, who was present, the battle of Prestonpans was no more than a 'scuffle … I say scuffle for a battle it was not, which lasted four minutes and no longer'[33].

Cope's infantry delivered a crashing volley into the Highland centre. The Jacobites replied with their meagre stock of firearms, then drew their swords and charged.

THE HIGHLAND CHARGE

The muscular agility of men raised among the rough slopes of the Highlands was consistently underestimated by their Lowland foes. In consequence the Highlanders were often foremost in taking possession of the high ground before a battle. Their subsequent downhill charge would then be launched without warning; maximising the shock to the opposing side. When circumstances prevented this strategy, both sides might engage in an exchange of fire.

Such exchanges were galling work for the tartan-clad clansmen. Standing in lines like sheep waiting for slaughter formed no part of the Celtic vision of war. Once cannon-fire began to spatter the life out of their crowded lines, their commanders could barely contain them. With the wind snapping at their banners and the curling notes of their pipers stirring their hearts, the clansmen began to seethe with blood-lust. Throwing off their plaids to free their sword arms, they demanded the order to advance. When it came, the Highland line surged forward like a racing torrent, gathering momentum as it went.

The red-coated regiments on the opposing side could only stand like pebbles on a beach, waiting for the smothering tide. The mouth of every soldier was bitter with the taste of black powder, spilled from the paper cartridges which they tore open with their teeth. Though their practised hands went through the drills, pouring the charge down the barrel and stuffing the ball and wadding in after, it was hard to tear their eyes from the rushing enemy. Raising their primed muskets to their shoulders, each man surely prayed for the next volley to drop every tartan-clad target before he need feel the cold kiss of a Highland blade.

The clans fuelled their courage and terrorised their opponents by howling wild war cries. Speed was now the key: the faster they ran, the fewer volleys they had to endure. Bending low to escape the lethal hail of shot, they bounded across the heather like a pack of hungry wolves.

As the clansmen burst through the hot, white cloud of the final volley, the silent Redcoats turned side-on, meeting them with their bayonet-tipped muskets held firm; one hand gripping the butt to ensure that every thrust drove home. The Highlanders fell with furious violence on all they saw. In this grim abattoir the air was thick with the pungent aroma of heather, black powder, and the all-pervasive, sickly-sweet, smell of violent death. Bloody broadswords twirled high and struck home with a distinctive metallic ring. Bayonets bent beneath the weight of those impaled upon them. The ground underfoot was carpeted by the dead and the writhing wounded. In such hot disputes no quarter was given.

During the Jacobite Rebellions the Highlanders fought troops who acted in ordered units; obeying commands in unison. By contrast the Scottish clansmen were individuals; fighting for personal honour and martial glory. However, despite their lack of discipline they lost only one major engagement (Culloden).

As the Highlanders surged towards them, the infantry raised their bayonets to receive the charge. Seconds before impact, the line wavered and fled.

Cope's army had been virtually obliterated. In addition to those slaughtered during the rout, the Jacobites had captured eighty British officers and more than a thousand men. On the Jacobite side, casualties probably numbered less than fifty. Defeat came as a rude shock to London. Pro-Government pamphleteers, like the novelist Henry Fielding printed blood-curdling tales of Highland atrocities as England prepared for invasion.

Colonel Gardiner (13th Foot) and a few NCOs fought on alone, but they were soon cut down. Prince Charles was piped through Edinburgh the next day to the tune of 'The King Shall Enjoy his Own Again.'

FALKIRK II
❧ 17 January 1746 ❧

By the end of 1745 a new British Army commander
had arrived in Edinburgh, Lieutenant-General Henry
Hawley. The Jacobite army had returned to Scotland
after its abortive invasion of England, and laid siege
to Stirling Castle, near Falkirk. By 16 January 1746,
Hawley had marched to Falkirk and was
poised to attack.

With just over 8,000 men the Government
forces slightly outnumbered the
Jacobites. General Hawley was a stern
disciplinarian who held a poor opinion of the
Highland army, of which he said dismissively
'There is nothing so easy to resist'[34]. He also held
firm opinions on the best manner of dealing with
the reckless Highland charge: 'The sure way to
demolish them is at three ranks deep – to fire by
ranks, rear rank first, and even that rank not to
fire till they are within ten or twelve paces …'[35].

On 17th January 1746, British Army scouts
reported that the Highlanders were massing on
Falkirk moor. Considering his eagerness to put
his military theories to the test, Hawley's arrival
on the battlefield was surprisingly tardy.
Seemingly distracted by the blandishments of
Countess Kilmarnock ('a woman of splendid
person[36]' and suspiciously Jacobite connections),
it was 2pm before he ordered his troops to deploy
on the moor.

This delay enabled the Jacobite army to take
possession of the high ground. Furthermore their
strategy was quite unexpected. In obedience to

By 1746 the
majority of Scots
bearing arms
were fighting for
George II against
Prince Charles.
Hawley's force
included
Highlanders, the
Royal Scots, and
volunteers from
Glasgow.

Hawley belatedly sent 3 regiments of dragoons (7th, 10th and 14th) to seize the high ground, but by the time the horsemen arrived, the Highlanders were established on the summit.

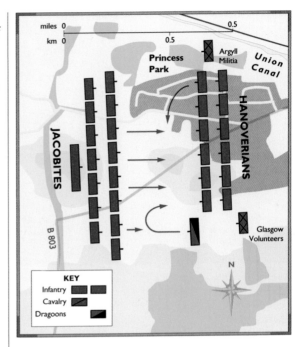

meticulous instructions from Lord George Murray, the Highlanders did not launch one of their wild, massed charges. Instead, having positioned themselves on the hill, they waited for the enemy to attack. Though surprised, Hawley took no warning from this uncharacteristic change of tactics. Disdainfully he commanded the 700 dragoons on his left flank to advance up the hill.

Lord Murray had done his job well. With astounding discipline the Highlanders waited until the enemy horse were within easy pistol

shot (about ten yards) before firing their ragged volley. At least eighty dragoons were blasted from their saddles, cutting such a swathe through their dense ranks that according to one observer it was possible to see 'daylight through them in several places[37]'. With their morale

Eleven British line regiments formed the core of Hawley's army. Three other armies had narrowly failed to intercept Prince Charles' force during its foray into England. Hawley believed he was about to end the uprising once and for all.

The armies drew up within a few hundred yards, the Highlanders yelling defiance and preparing to charge.

Prince Charles Stuart knew this was his only chance to secure the crown. No European government was going to recognise him as King after the death of his father.

Some Highlanders had spikes fitted to the bosses of their shields, enabling them to stab with either hand.

dashed by this shocking turn of events most of the cavalry immediately fled back downhill; bursting through the ranks of their own infantry in their desperation to escape.

Only a few of Ligonier's Dragoons remained to press home the attack. According to one Jacobite witness, they were to be savagely mauled in the 'extraordinary combat' which followed: 'The Highlanders, stretched on the ground, thrust their dirks into the bellies of the horses ... seized the riders by their clothes, dragged them down, and stabbed them with their dirks ...'[38].

Only as the survivors of this brutal assault ran for their lives, did the triumphant clansmen finally forget Lord Murray's instructions to stay put. Charging off the brow of the hill behind the terrified dragoons, they fell upon the ranks of enemy infantry beyond. The Redcoats managed only a few weak volleys before the Jacobites were among them, busy with their broadswords.

Sir Robert Munro, commanding officer of Hawley's 37th Regiment, was among the casualties. His fate was later described by his son: '... after being deserted, he was attacked by six of Locheal's Regiment, and for some time defended himself with his half-pike. Two of the

Left: Flintlock pistols were carried as secondary weapons by officers on both sides.

Right: Hawley's infantry watched in horror as the dragoons were driven off by the Highlanders. Then the whole Jacobite army charged.

LEADERSHIP OF THE JACOBITE ARMY

The most significant figure among those who rallied to the Jacobite cause was Lord George Murray, who joined the Prince at Perth. Brother to the Duke of Atholl, Murray was a respected and wealthy landowner with much influence. Moreover, as a veteran of other European wars (including the previous Jacobite uprising) Murray was by far the most competent of the Prince's advisors. Sadly while the Highlanders appreciated his canny advice, Charles preferred to listen to the courtiers and Irish Officers who had accompanied him from France. The schisms and intrigues which bedeviled the Jacobite army were the direct result of the Prince's failure to establish a firm command-and-control structure. He needlessly complicated matters by trying to please both sides of his divided camp. Thus Lord George Murray and James Drummond (Duke of Perth) were appointed to joint command of the Jacobite forces, with supreme command rotating between them. This weakened the position of both men while doing nothing to appease the French/Irish contingent who thought that they should have supreme command.

six, I'm informed he killed; a seventh, coming up, fired a pistol into my father's groin, upon which falling, the highlander with his sword gave him two strokes to the face, one over the eyes and another on the mouth, which instantly ended a brave man'[39].

Faced with such punishment it was not long before the Redcoat infantry turned tail and tumbled down the hill after their cavalry. Within half an hour of the onset of battle, having suffered in the region of 280 killed or missing against fifty Jacobites casualties, the entire Government army had retreated from Falkirk Moor. Hawley was forced to abandon both his supper and the enticing Countess Kilmarnock to the attentions of 'Bonnie Prince Charlie'.

The second battle of Falkirk was over in less than 30 minutes. Few redcoats stood to face the Highland charge, and the handful of soldiers that resisted were cut down. Hawley tried to rally his men, but they had scattered all over the moor. In his fury, the defeated general broke his sword against the market-cross in Falkirk!

CULLODEN

❧ 16 April 1746 ❧

After his defeat at Falkirk General Hawley was
replaced by William, Duke of Cumberland, the
second son of George II, known affectionately to the
troops as 'Sweet William'. In the meantime Prince
Charles Edward Stuart had assumed direct control of
the Highland army. For the final battle, a
Hanoverian prince and a Stuart prince were to
personally face each other in the field.

On April 1746, against the advice of his clan chiefs, Charles deployed 5,000 men for a set-piece battle on Drummossie Moor close to the Culloden Park estate. However his opponent appeared to be in no hurry to engage in action. While the unfortunate Highlanders stood ready in their ranks all day with neither food or shelter, the opposing, 9,000-strong, Government army enjoyed a day of rest. It was after all Cumberland's twenty-fifth birthday.

Changing his plans, Charles decided to opt for a night-march and dawn attack. This was to prove disastrous. Losing their way, the Scots became widely dispersed and blundered into boggy ground. Eventually the Duke of Perth, in command of the advance-guard, decided that the plan was doomed and ordered an about-turn. By the time Charles discovered that the front of his army was retreating it was too late to reverse the order. Arriving back at their starting point only hours before the most important battle of their campaign, the Jacobite army had been reduced to an exhausted, hungry and dispirited force.

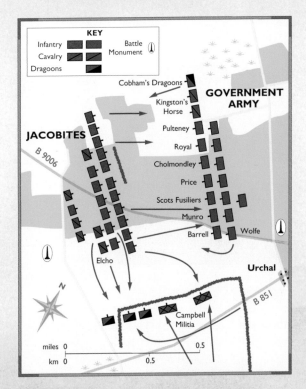

KEY

Infantry
Cavalry
Dragoons

Battle Monument

GOVERNMENT ARMY

Cobham's Dragoons
Kingston's Horse
Pulteney
Royal
Cholmondley
Price
Scots Fusiliers
Munro
Barrell
Wolfe

JACOBITES

B 9006

Elcho

Urchal

B 851

Campbell Militia

miles 0   0.5
km 0   0.5

N

Left: With a larger and far better equipped army than the Jacobites could muster, the Duke of Cumberland was confident of victory. Wealthy Scottish families loyal to King George were welcome spectators.

Right: Like most eighteenth century armies, the British forces were accompanied into the field by a large number of women and some children. 'Following the drum' often involved great privation, but as many soldiers effectively enlisted for life, it was the only way families could stay together.

On the morning of 16 April 1746, the Prince's advisors urged him to reconsider the wisdom of his plan. Charles' reply betrayed his own doubts: 'God damn it! Are my orders still disobeyed? Fight where you will gentlemen, the day is not ours'[40]. However he was determined to make a stand: it was his last chance to gain the crown.

As Cumberland's Redcoats arrived, deploying in disciplined silence '… like a deep sullen river'[41], Lord Elcho edged closer to Lord George Murray and asked what he thought of their prospects. 'We are putting an end to a bad affair'[42] was Murray's grim conclusion. To complete the misery of the Highlanders it now began to rain; an icy north-easterly gale lashing straight into their faces.

THE BAGPIPE

The origins of the bagpipe are buried in the mists of time. There is a strong possibility that the pipes are part of a cultural tradition inherited from the Celts in the wake of their European expansion. The general concept is certainly not unique to Scotland (various forms of Celtic pipes survive elsewhere in Europe). However it was in the glens of Scotland that the greatest of all pipes was perfected: the Piob-mhòr (the Great Highland Pipe), commonly known today as the 'bagpipe'.

The contribution made by the bagpipe to Scottish military history should not be underestimated. Untold numbers of Scots have felt their blood stirred for battle by its martial airs. The army fielded by the Duke of Cumberland at Culloden in 1746, contained the Highland Regiments of Munro, Campbell and Sutherland. Watching their pipers march past, the mystified Duke asked, 'What are these men going to do with such bundles of sticks? I can supply them with better instruments of war'. A Scottish officer assured him, 'Your Royal Highness cannot do so. These are the Bagpipes, the Highlanders music in peace and war. Wanting these, all other instruments are of no avail'.

After Cumberland had learned, at Culloden, to respect the rousing power of the mighty war pipe, the Courts of Justice declared the mere playing of the instrument to be a treasonous act. At his 1746 trial in York, piper James Reid's defence was that he had carried no weapon in the rebellion. The judge decided otherwise, declaring that as a Highland Regiment never marched without a piper, the bagpipe was indeed a weapon. In consequence poor Reid was condemned to swing to a different tune upon the gallows.

Although the Jacobites captured some government weapons in their earlier victories, the arms and ammunition from France promised by Charles Stuart never arrived. Most of his soldiers would rely on cold steel.

The battle began around 1pm with a cannonade. Concentrating initially upon the Jacobite guns, Cumberland's more numerous artillery 'made a great slaughterhouse of the rebel batteries'[43]. In the fury of this bombardment a man standing only yards away from Prince Charles was sliced in two by a cannon ball. This was too close for comfort. Leaving the royal standard bearer in his perilous position ('lest the sight of my standard going off, might induce others to follow'[44]), the Prince allowed himself to be ushered further to the rear.

There were no such options for the Highlanders who stood waiting while 'grapeshot made open lanes through them, the men dropping down by wholesale'[45]. For more than twenty minutes the clans endured the dreadful slaughter of Cumberland's guns while their Prince hesitated to order the advance. Finally, Lord George Murray's Atholl brigade on the Jacobite right wing could bear no more. Charging straight into the massed redcoat volleys they vanished into the thick gun smoke drifting across Drummossie Moor. With this act the ill-fated Highland attack was unleashed.

Shrieking their battle cry of 'Claymore', the Jacobite centre now surged forward only to stall in the rain-soaked, boggy ground in the midst of the battlefield. The Clan Chattens, at the forefront of this charge, were mown down in great numbers by steady musket volleys. Those behind them veered over to the right; increasing

the mayhem on that flank which was hemmed in against the stone wall of the Leanach farm enclosure. Hidden behind the wall, Cumberland had positioned a detachment of Wolfe's Redcoats and Campbell Highlanders (serving on the Government side). In consequence the Jacobite right wing ran a murderous gauntlet of flanking fire. Nonetheless the clansmen, knowing that victory depended on closing with the Redcoats, stormed onwards through the frightful hail of bullets.

Cumberland had instructed his men to keep up 'a continued close fire'[46]. He was later to recall how 'The Royals and Pulteney's [Regiment]

THE BROWN BESS

By 1689 the old matchlock musket of the Civil Wars was being phased out, replaced by the more reliable Land Pattern flintlock. The most enduring of any firearm issued to British forces, the Land Pattern musket (and its later variants) was affectionately known to the troops who used it as the 'Brown Bess'. It was a good, solid weapon, weighing almost 11 pounds and capable of firing two rounds a minute. Using prepackaged paper cartridges (with ball and powder together) it was claimed that a well-trained soldier could fire as many as five rounds a minute.

However though the musket ball, properly loaded, could carry over 700 yards, its effective range was less than 100 yards. At greater distances they became increasingly inaccurate. In 1804 Colonel George Hanger stated that 'a soldier must be very unfortunate indeed who shall be wounded by a common musket at 150 yards, provided his antagonist aims at him'. Such limitations served to ensure that the volley remained the most efficient method of using the musket in battle. With a few modifications (including a reduction in calibre from .85 to around .76) the Brown Bess remained in general service until well beyond the Napoleonic wars of the early nineteenth century.

hardly took their firelocks from their shoulders'[46]. According to another British officer 'the King's men discharged a complete running fire that dropped [the Scots] down as they came on'[47]. Even this was not enough to stop the heroic charge of the Highland right wing which slammed right into Barrel's Regiment and part of Munro's.

Lord Robert Kerr, armed with a spontoon, impaled the first Highlander to dash up. Preoccupied with this gory work he failed to notice that the rest of his line had been driven back. While struggling to recover his spontoon he was cut down, 'his head being cleft from crown to collar-bone'. As Barrel's regiment buckled in shock, some 500 clansmen burst through 'in a cloud[48]' to the second line, hacking and slicing with their broadswords. In response the Redcoats frantically stabbed and clubbed with their bayonets and musket-butts.

The British infantry regiments had adopted a new method of close-quarter fighting for this campaign. Rather than tackling the enemy head on, each Redcoat was to stab at the man to his right; the upraised sword-arms of the Scots rendering them vulnerable to bayonet-thrusts from that side. One British soldier said 'it was dreadful to see the enemies' swords circling in the air … And to see the officers of the army, some cutting with their swords, others pushing with spontoons, the sergeants running their halberds into throats of their opponents, the men

Top left: The British infantry regiments were supported by light cannon firing case shot. Acting like giant shotguns, they inflicted terrible losses on the charging clans.

Middle left: Charles Stuart left his army without orders, leaving the clans to face a deadly artillery bombardment which they could not reply to. Many men instinctively raised their shields, but they could not stop a bullet.

Left: Volley after volley crashed out from the Redcoat line, but the nothing could stop the Highland right wing. Surging through the smoke, they drove back Munro's regiment and killed Lord Robert Kerr.

ramming their fixed bayonets up to the sockets'[49]. Although hopelessly outnumbered, the doomed Highlanders fought on with ferocious courage. After the battle 'there was not one bayonet in [Barrel's] Regiment which was not bloodied or bent'[50].

Meanwhile on the Jacobite left flank, which was a greater distance from the Redcoats, the attack had faltered. For some reason the clan MacDonald, who claimed the honour of fighting on the right, had been positioned on the left. Resentfully they now refused to advance. Though Keppoch and his brother charged forward alone to encourage them, both men fell to the ground riddled with shot. As Clanranald persuaded his clansmen to charge he too was hit, and their charge also faltered. Unable to advance, unwilling to retreat and short of muskets, the Highland left wing vented their frustrated rage by the only means available. According to Cumberland's post-battle report they 'threw stones for at least a minute before their total rout began.'[51]

At last the clan chiefs took matters into their own hands and ordered the charge. Yelling defiance, they started across the moor.

Cumberland's pre-battle training paid off: in the savage hand-to-hand fight that followed, the Redcoats used their bayonets to terrible effect.

By this time 500 English dragoons, pouring through breaches in the Leanach walls, had engaged Prince Charles' small cavalry force. Outnumbered five to one, the poorly mounted Jacobite horsemen suffered grave losses protecting their Royal master. When one of their officers galloped up with the warning 'all is going to pot', Charles replied with a show of bravado, 'They won't take me alive'[52]. However he advanced not an inch to rally his men for one last charge. As he allowed himself to be led away to safety, ultimately to return to exile, the Prince was exposed to one last broadside. This was delivered by Lord Elcho, who screamed bitterly after him 'Run, you cowardly Italian!'[53]. The disillusioned Chevalier Johnstone was later to comment: 'There are occasions when a general ought to expose his person, and not remain beyond the reach of a few musketry, and surely there never was a more pressing occasion for disregarding a few shots than the one in question, as the gain or loss of the battle depended on it'[54].

When their Prince deserted them, the spirit of the badly mauled Highlanders finally broke. The Duke of Cumberland now ordered his men forward, but the Redcoats could 'hardly march for dead bodies'[55]. Wounded Highlanders were stabbed with bayonets or shot on the spot as the soldiers obeyed the Duke's command to show no mercy. According to young Will Aiken, who had fought on the right flank, 'it was a Ghastly Sight to see some Dead some tumbling and wallowing in their Blood others not quite dead Crying for mercy we followed and slew them for three miles till the Dragoons were quite glutted with Gore'[56].

The last pitched battle ever fought on British soil was over in less than an hour. When the mopping up was finished more than 1000 Highlanders and 360 British soldiers lay dead and 'Sweet William' Cumberland had earned a new nick-name: The 'Butcher'. Though loyal Jacobite survivors headed northwards to regroup, hopes for a renewed guerrilla war were dashed when their Prince informed them that he was bound for France. It was to be every man for himself. The long rebellion was over at last and 'Bonnie Prince Charlie' sailed away into the pages of history never to return. The Jacobite dream had been buried forever on the rain-soaked, blood-drenched heather of Drummossie moor.

On the left flank, the clans were stopped in their tracks by volley fire. Without enough firearms to fight back properly, they wavered and fell back.

With victory secured, Cumberland ordered a general advance, the soldiers carrying out his orders to give no quarter. Wounded Jacobites were bayoneted where they lay.

GLOSSARY

arquebus A smoothbore musket, also called the hachbut ('hook gun') because of the curved stock. Developed in the late 15th century, they were a major step forward from earlier 'hand guns' because they could be aimed from the shoulder.

bardiche A variant of the bill (q.v.) which had a single large axe-blade that curved to a point at the top, and so could still be used to deliver a stab as well as a chopping blow.

berserk (berserker) From the Icelandic *berserkr*, a Viking warrior who working himself into a frenzy before battle, then launched himself at the enemy in an (often suicidal) attack. Careless of their own lives, they were greatly feared by their opponents.

bill A spear, typically 7ft long which also had a large axe-blade fitted. Used with both hands, a soldier could stab or chop his opponent. Some had hooks fitted as well, useful for dragging men from horses, or pulling men off their feet by slashing behind their knees.

case-shot A variable number of small shot, typically 1-in in diameter, fired from a cannon instead of a single, much larger cannon ball. The cannon became, in effect, a giant shotgun.

couch, vb,. To position a lance under arm, enabling a mounted knight to impart the full weight of man and horse to his spearpoint.

cuirassier A horseman wearing body armour (from the 15th–19th centuries)

demi-cannon A 3-ton cannon firing a 27–29lb cannon ball.

demi-culverin-shott A 9lb cannon ball from a demi-culverin.

fauchard A variant on the bill (q.v.) which had a large axe-head with several projecting spikes added for good measure.

flintlock A type of musket in which pulling the trigger releases a hammer striking sparks from a flint to ignite gunpowder in a priming pan. The flame from the pan passes through a hole into the breech, igniting the main charge. Also called a 'firelock' during the 17th

century, when this (more expensive) weapon began to replace matchlocks (q.v.).

fyrd The peasant militia of the Anglo-Saxon kingdom which was sometimes called out to support the professional soldiers of the major nobles.

glaives A broad-bladed spear, a variant on the bill (q.v.)

halberd A development of the bill (q.v.) in which the axe-head, spearpoint and rearward facing spike were all enlarged. With various changes to the shape and size of the blade, this remained in service until well into the 18th century, carried by junior officers and NCOs.

hauberk A long coat of mail, often sleeveless (from Old French *hauberc* and Old English *healsbeorg*)

hobilar A 14th century name for an infantryman who campaigned on horseback although he dismounted to fight. Hobilars were typically raiders, attacking villages and exploiting their mobility to avoid battle with regular forces – a regular feature of the Hundred Years War.

housecarls The household warriors of Danish, and later, Anglo-Saxon kings and great nobles. They formed the bulk of the English army at Hastings.

Marches The border areas between England and Scotland and England and Wales, characterised by raiding and feuding throughout the 13th–16th centuries.

match A length of smouldering cord, used to fire matchlock muskets (q.v.).

matchlock A musket fired by use of the match (see above).

men-at-arms Professional soldiers equipped like knights.

picquets Small detachments of troops posted to give early warning of an enemy attack

pike A spear used with both hands, typically 12–15 ft long

pikestaff The wooden pole on which the metal head of the pike was attached

polearms Generic term for two-handed

cutting/thrusting weapons used from the 14th century e.g. bills, halberds, glaives, spontoons (q.v.) etc.

poleaxes Two-handed axes

schiltron A tightly-packed formation of Scottish pikemen, used from the late 13th to mid 16th centuries. The Scottish schiltrons were an important development in medieval warfare. At Falkirk (1297) they were the first infantry formations to withstand a charge of mounted knights since the battle of Hastings.

spontoon Another development of the bill, this time more spear than axe, it remained in use by officers and NCOs during the Civil Wars and lasted until the mid-18th century.

summons of array The administrative procedure whereby an English medieval king summoned an army from the great nobles, major cities and English counties. Often used as a tax-generating mechanism while the real army was constituted by professional warriors. The system survived, albeit as an anachronism, to be revived by Charles I in 1642.

surcoat A sleeveless garment worn over armour, displaying the coat of arms of a knight or his retainers.

thegn In Anglo-Saxon England, a member of an aristocratic class whose status was heriditary and who held land from the king or another great nobleman in return for military and other services. In Scotland, a person of rank, often chief of a clan, holding land from the king.

tow Hemp or flax fibres

voulges Another variant of the bill (q.v.)

wheel-lock pistols Pistols in which the spark to ignite the powder came not from a flintlock (q.v.) but from the release of a spring-driven serrated wheel which sparked against a flint. It was less liable to misfire than a flintlock, especially when fired from horseback and became the primary weapon of some continental cuirassiers (q.v.) in the 16th-17th centuries: emulated by some Civil War regiments e.g. the Parliamentarian 'Lobsters'.

RE-ENACTMENT SOCIETIES

Conquest
John Cole
61 King Edward's Grove
Teddington
Middlesex TW11 9LZ
Tel: 0181-977-1768

Wolfbane Historical Society
High Wickham
Buckinghamshire

Wolfshead Bowmen
Heath Pye
Rosemary
15 Tus Combe Way
Willington
Eastborne
Sussex BN20 9JA
(A5 SAE appreciated)
Tel: 01323-503666

**Staffordshire Household
1450–1500**
Bills & Bows 1500–1600
Graham Smith
248 Wetmore Road
Burton-on-Trent
Stafford DE14 1RB
Tel: 01283-517-871
(A5 SAE appreciated)

Fairfax Battalia (ECWS)
Ian Barret
2 Hartley St
Merridale
Wolverhampton
Staffordshire WV3 9QS
Tel: 01902-711873
(A5 SAE appreciated)

Medieval Tournament
Michael Loades
Crogo Mains Farm House
Corsock
by Castle Douglas
Scotland DG7 3DR
Tel: 01644-440256
(A5 SAE appreciated)

The Vikings (N.F.P.S.)
Commercial Special Events
Coordinator/Bookings:
Paul Lydiate
119 Market Street
Broadly
Whitworth
Rochdale
Lancashire OL12 8SE
Tel: 01706-344-773
e-mail: p.lydiate @ zeumail.co.uk

Membership: Sandra Orchard
2 Stanford Road
Shefford
Beds SG17 5DS
Tel: 01462-812208

The Troop
(Multi-period cavalry)
Alan Larsen
28 Heatherdale Road
Camberley
Surrey GU15 2LY
Tel: 01276-66867
(A5 SAE appreciated)

**National Association of
Reenactment Societies**
Public Relations Officer
Victoria Dyke
49 Stagsden
Orton Goldhay
Peterborough
Cambs PE2 5RW
(A5 SAE appreciated)
Tel: 01753-521187

The Sealed Knot Society
Public Relations Officer
136 Beechcroft Rd
Wallheath
Kingswinfry
West Midlands DY6 OHU
Tel: 01384-295-939
(A5 SAE appreciated)

**Kings Army & Roundhead
Association (English Civil War
Society)**
Public Relations Officer
70 Hillgate Howden
Northumberside DN14 7ST
Tel: 01430-430695
(A5 SAE appreciated)

**Marquess of Winchester's
Regiment**
Ian & Mary MacDonald-Watson
Thorntons House
Bowridge Hill
Gillingham
Dorset SP8 5QS
Tel: 01747-825693
(A5 SAE appreciated)

**Bosworth Battlefield Visitor
Centre**
Sutton Cheney
Market Bosworth
Leicestershire CV13 OAD
(A5 SAE appreciated)
Tel: 01455-290-429

Regia Anglorum
J K Siddorn
9 Durleigh Close
Headley Park
Bristol BS13 7NQ
(A5 SAE appreciated)
Tel: 0117-964-6818
Internet Home Page:
http'//www/ftech.net.~.regia.htm

Corridors of Time (Historical Presentations Ltd)
Alan Jeffrey
11 Mulberry Court
Pagham
Bognor Regis
West Sussex PO21 4TP
(A5 SAE appreciated)
Tel/fax: 01243-262-291

Plantagenet Society
John Roberts
Jasmine House
Bromsberrow Heath
Ledbury
Herefordshire HR8 1NX
Tel: 01531-650329
(A5 SAE appreciated)

Companions of the Black Bear
Dave Cubbage
60 Upper Park Street
Cheltenham
Gloucestershires GL2 9LN
(A5 SAE appreciated)
Tel: 01452-730630

Chapter of St Bartholomew
(1460s Burgundians)
68 Minerva Street
Bulwell
Nottingham NG6 8GR
(A5 SAE appreciated)

Ordre of the Black Prince
John & Carol Buttifint
Thatch Cottage
140 Canterbury Road
Lydden
Dover
Kent CT14 9LT
(A5 SAE appreciated)

The Ragged Staff Medieval Society
35 Longfield Rd
Tring
Herts HP23 4DG
Tel: 01442-824941
(A5 SAE appreciated)

Historic Scotland
Longmore House
Edinburgh EH9 1SH
Tel: 0131-668-8686

English Heritage
429 Oxford St
London W1R 2HD
Responsible for organising historical events, many of which are military re-enactments
Special Events Unit: 0171-973-3396
Concerts: 0171-973-3427
General enquiries: 0171-973-3434

Partizan Press
816–818 London Rd
Leigh-on-Sea
Essex SS9 3NH
Publishers of numerous period specific journals on military history; Renaissance, 17th–19th centuries
(A4 SAE appreciated)
Tel: 01702-73986

Medieval Siege Society
Phil Fraser
70 Markyate Road
Dagenham
Essex RM8 2LD
Tel: 0181-592-3621
(A4 SAE appreciated)

Call To Arms
Continuously updated brochure listing all societies
7 Chapmans Crescent
Chesham HP5 2QU
Tel/fax: 01494-78427
e-mail: apmin@calltoarms.com

The Company of Ordinance
Artillery 1350–1750
Keith Piggot
12 Cape Avenue
Stafford ST17 9SL
Tel: 01785-227532
(A5 SAE appreciated)

International Viking Association
Phil Burthem
46 St. John's Court
Queen's Drive
Finsbury Park
London N4 2HL
Tel: 0181-800-4013

Wulf
SFS Linksfield Hall
Linksfield Rd
Aberdeen AB2 1RW
(A5 SAE appreciated)

Commission of Array
8 Kingswick Drive
Sunnunghill
Berks SL5 7BQ
Tel: 01423-867062

The White Company 1450–85
Marketing and Events:
Mark Griffin
77 Stokefield
Pitsea
Basildon
Essex SS1 3IN
Tel: 01268-55704
(SAE appreciated)

Membership: David Chambers
56 Carkinton Road
Woollton
Liverpool L25 8TB
(SAE appreciated)

White Cockade
Michael Newcomen
Holly Cottage
David Street
Blairgowrie
Perthshire
Tel: 01250-875600

Lace Wars 1739–63
Roland Bateman
40 Middle Road
Harrow-in-the-Hill
Middlesex HA2 0HL
Tel: 01883-626439
(SAE appreciated)

NOTES

Soldiering in Anglo-Saxon Britain

1. D Scragg (ed.), The Battle of Maldon, AD 991 (Oxford 1991), pp 67–8
2. Extract from 'Byrhtferth of Ramsey's Life of St Oswald', in English Historical Documents c.500-1042, pp 912–17
3. Liber Eliensis, Cambridge Trinity College O.2.1.
4. D Scragg (ed.), The Battle of Maldon, op. cit.
5. The poem of the Battle of Maldon, in English Historical Documents c.500–1042, p 293
6. Ibid. p 295
7. Ibid. pp 320–24
8. Liber Eliensis, Cambridge Trinity College O.2.1.
9. D Scragg (ed.), The Battle of Maldon, op. cit
10. Ibid.
11. Ibid.
12. English Historical Documents, op. cit. p 296
13. 'Byrhtferth of Ramsey's Life of St Oswald', in English Historical Documents c.500-1042
14. 'Anglo Saxon Chronicle' (Manuscript C) in D C Douglas and G W Greenaway (eds.), English Historical Documents 1042-1189 (London 1981)
15. Ibid.
16. Snorri Heimskringal quoted in F W Brook, The Battle of Stamford Bridge, p 10
17. Anglo Saxon Chronicle, op. cit.
18. B Aoalbjarnarson (ed.), 'Heimskringla', (Reykjavik 1941), in A L Binns, East Yorkshire in the sagas
19. Ibid.
20. Ibid.
21. According to William of Poitiers
22. William of Poitiers
23. Guy, Bishop of Amiens
24. Guy, Bishop of Amiens
25. Guy, Bishop of Amiens
26. Guy, Bishop of Amiens

Soldiering in Medieval Britain

1. 'Chronicle of Richard of Hexham', in D C Douglas and G W Greenaway (eds.), English Historical Documents 1042–1189 (Oxford 1981)
2. Ibid.
3. Translation of 'Ailred', in Alan, Scottish Annals from English Chroniclers AD500 to 128 (London 1908), pp 188–206
4. 'Chronicle of Richard of Hexham', in D C Douglas and G W Greenaway (eds.), op. cit.
5. Translation of 'Ailred', in Alan Anderson, op. cit
6. Ibid.
7. 'The Chronicle of Henry of Huntingdon', translated and edited by Thomas Foster (1853), facsimile reprint (Lanereh Press, Felinfach 1991)
8. Translation of 'Ailred', in Alan Anderson, op. cit
9. Ibid.
10. Ibid.
11. Ibid.
12. J O Halliwell (ed.), Chronicle of William de Rishanger of the Barons' War (Camden Society, 1840)
13. Ibid.
14. Ibid.
15. 'Chronicle of Robert of Gloucester', quoted in Tufton Beamish, Battle Royal (BCA 1978), p 225
16. J O Halliwell (ed.), Chronicle of William de Rishanger of the Barons' War, op. cit.
17. Mathew Paris, Monachi Sancti Albani, Chronica Majorca, ed. H R Luard (Rolls series 1872-83)
18. 'Chronicle of Robert of Gloucester', in Tufton Beamish op. cit.
19. Ibid
20. Ibid
21. Ibid
22. William Rishanger, Chronica et Annales, ed. H T Riley (London 1865). Quoted in Andrew Fisher, William Wallace (John Donald Publishers, Edinburgh 1994), p 83
23. Ibid.
24. John Barbour of Aberdeen, The Bruce, ed. J Pinkerton (London 1870)
25. Ibid.
26. J Barbour, The Brus, ed. G Eyre Todd (1907). Quoted in Ronald McNair Scott, Robert the Bruce (Cannongate Books, Edinburgh 1995)
27. Ibid.
28. Ibid.
29. The 'Monk of Malmesbury', The Life of Edward II, tr. N Denholm-Young (London 1957), p 59
30. 'Chronicle of Lanercost', in Harry Rothwell (ed.), English Historical Documents 1189-1327 (London 1975), pp 272-3, tr. David Smurthwaite, English Heritage Battlefield notes
31. Ibid.
32. F W D Brie (ed.), The Brut or The Chronicles of England (Early English Text Society, London 1906), pp 211–12, tr David Smurthwaite, English Heritage Battlefield notes
33. Master John Barbour, Archdeacon of Aberdeen, AD 1375, The Bruce, or The Book of the most excellent and noble Prince, Robert de Broyss, King of Scots, ed. Rev Walter W Skeat (Early English Text Society 29, 1877) ii,
34. The 'Monk of Malmesbury', The Life of Edward II, op. cit. p 96
35. Ibid.
36. Ibid.
37. 'Chronicle of Lanercost', in Harry Rothwell (ed.), op. cit. pp 272–3
38. F W D Brie (ed.), The Brut, op. cit. pp 211–12
39. 'Chronicle of Lanercost', in Harry Rothwell (ed.), op. cit. pp 272–3
40. The 'Monk of Malmesbury', The Life of Edward II, op. cit. p 96
41. 'Chronicle of Lanercost', in Harry Rothwell (ed.), op. cit. pp 275-6
42. Ibid.
43. The 'Monk of Malmesbury', The Life of Edward II, op. cit.
44. Ibid.
45. F W D Brie (ed.), The Brut, op. cit. pp 217–20
46. Ibid.
47. The 'Monk of Malmesbury', The Life of Edward II, op. cit.
48. Ibid.
49. Ibid.
50. Ibid.
51. Ibid.
52. F W D Brie (ed.), The Brut, op. cit. pp 217–20
53. The 'Monk of Malmesbury', The Life of Edward II, op. cit.
54. 'Chronicle of Lanercost', in Harry Rothwell (ed.), op. cit. pp 288–90
55. 'The Cannon of Bridlington', in A R Myers (ed.), English Historical Documents 1327–1485 (London 1969), p 58
56. F W D Brie (ed.), The Brut, op. cit. p

286

57. 'Chronicle of Lanercost', in Harry Rothwell (ed.), op. cit. p 179
58. Ibid.
59. Ibid.
60. Henry Newbolt, Froissart in Britain (James Nisbet & Co., London 1900), p 85
61. Ibid.
62. 'Chronicle of Lanercost', in Harry Rothwell (ed.), op. cit. p 179
63. Ibid
64. Henry Newbolt, Froissart in Britain, op. cit. p 148–9
65. Ibid.
66. Walter Brown, Scotichronicon, Vol. 8, ed. D E R Watt (Aberdeen University Press, 1987), pp 45–7
67. Thomas Walsingham, 'Historias Anglicana', in A R Myers (ed.), English Historical Documents 1327–1485, op. cit. pp 191–2
68. Scotichronicon, op. cit.
69. Ibid.
70. Ibid.
71. Thomas Walsingham, 'Historias Anglicana', in A R Myers (ed.), op. cit
72. Ibid.
73. Ibid.
74. Annales Richard II et Henry IV, tr. E Calvert, (Transactions of the Shropshire Archaelogical and Natural History Society, 1898), 2nd series, Vol. 10, pp 295–305
75. Ibid.
76. Ibid.
77. Ibid.
78. Ibid
79. English Chronicle, (Camden Society 64, 1855)
80. Annales Richard II et Henry IV, tr. E Calvert, op. cit.
81. Ibid.
82. Ibid.
83. Ibid
84. Ibid.

Soldiering in the Wars of the Roses

1. Quoted in John Warren, The Wars of the Roses and the Yorkist Kings (Hodder & Stoughton 1995), p 50
2. Jehan de Waurin, Recuiel des Croniques et Anchiennes Istoroires de la Grand Bretagne., ed. Sir William Hardy (Rolls series 1891)
3. Jehan de Waurin, Recuiel des Croniques et Anchiennes Istoroires de la Grand Bretagne, V, op. cit.
4. Edward Hall, The Union of the Noble & Illustre Famelies of Lancastre and Yorke (1548). Reprinted as Hall's Chronicle. (1809)
5. Edward Hall, op. cit.
6. Jehan de Waurin, Recuiel des Croniques et Anchiennes Istoroires de la Grand Bretagne, V, op. cit.
7. Ibid.
8. John Whethamstead, Chroniclein Registra quorundam Abbatum Monasterii S Albani, ed. H T Ripley (Rolls series, 1876), pp 3372–4
9. Edward Hall, op. cit.
10. Ibid.
11. Ibid.
12. Jehan de Waurin, Recuiel des Croniques et Anchiennes Istoroires de la Grand Bretagne, V, op. cit.
13. Ibid.
14. Edward Hall, op. cit.
15. Historie of the Arrivall of Edward IV in England and the Finall Recouveryre of his Kingdomes from Henry VI, ed. J Bruce (Camdeb Society 1839)
16. John Warkworth, A chronicle of the first thirteen years of the reign of Edward IV, ed. J O Halliwell (Camden Society 1839)
17. Ibid.
18. Quoted in A H Burne, The Battlefields (Methuen 1951) p 113
19. A H Burne, The Battlefields, op. cit.
20. Historie of the Arrivall of Edward IV in England and the Finall Recouveryre of his Kingdomes from Henry VI, ed. J Bruce, op. cit.
21. Ibid.
22. Ibid.
23. Ibid.
24. Ibid.
25. Edward Hall, Hall's Chronicle, op. cit.
26. Polydore Vergil, Historiae Anglicae
27. Ibid.
28. Ibid.
29. Diego de Valera, A Castilian Report. Quoted in Michael Bennett, The Battle of Bosworth, (Alan Sutton, 1985)
30. Polydore Vergil, Historiae Anglicae
31. Diego de Valera, A Castilian Report, op. cit.
32. Polydore Vergil, Historiae Anglicae
33. 'Pittscottie's Chronicles', quoted in Michael Bennett, The Battle of Bosworth (Alan Sutton, 1985) p 162
34. John Rous of Norwich (1490), quoted in Michael Bennett, The Battle of Bosworth (Alan Sutton, 1985) p 159
35. 'Crowland Chronicle', quoted in Michael Bennett, The Battle of Bosworth (Alan Sutton, 1985) p 158
36. Bernard Andre, quoted in Michael Bennett, Lambert Simnel and the Battle of Stoke , Gloucester, 1987
37. 'Chroniques de Jean Molinet', quoted in Michael Bennett, Lambert Simnel and the Battle of Stoke , Gloucester 1987
38. Ibid.

Soldiering in the Anglo-Scottish wars

1. Quoted in Peter Young and John Adair, Hastings to Culloden (G Bell & Sons, 1964), p91
2. John Leslie, 'History of Scotland', quoted in A H Burne, The Battlefields of England (Methuen, 1951)
3. Calendar of State Papers … Italy, op. cit.
4. Proceedings of the Society of Antiquaries of Scotland VII I pp 147–151
5. Quoted in The Days of James IV 1488-1513, Scottish History by Contemporary Writers series, ed. G Gregory Smith (London 1900), pp 172-3
6. 'Pittscottie's Chronicles', quoted in Sir Charles Oman, Art of War in the Sixteenth Century (Greenhill Books 1991), p 312
7. Quoted in William Seymour, Battles in Britain (Book Club Associates, London, 1979), p192
8. 'La Rotta de Scocesi' (a contemporary Italian poem), translated and printed in W MacKay Mackenzie, The Secret of Flodden (Edinburgh 1931)
9. Ibid. pp 115–122
10. Quoted in A H Burne, The Battlefields of England, op. cit.
11. Calendar of State Papers … Italy, op. cit. p134
12. 'Articles of the Bataill bitwix the Kinge of Scottes and the erle of Surrey in Brankstone Feld, the 9th day of September', in the State Papers King Henry VIII Part IV, Correspondence relative to Scotland and the Borders 1513–1534 (1836) pp 1–2
13. Joseph Bain (ed.), The Hamilton Papers, Letters and papers illustrating political relations of England and Scotland in the XVI century, Vol. I 1532–1543 (Edinburgh 1890)
14. Ibid.
15. Ibid.
16. William Patten, The Expedition into Scotlande of Edward, Duke of Somerset (London 1548)

Soldiering in the Civil Wars

1. Quoted in Austin Woolrych, Battles of the English Civil War (London 1961), p 24
2. 'The Lord Conway's narrative of his conduct in the Action at Newburn', extract printed by Terry, pp 36-7

3. 'Letter of Thomas Dymock', Calendar of State Papers, Domestic series, of the reign of Charles I (London 1882) pp 38-9
4. Quoted in Austin Woolrych, Battles of the English Civil War, op. cit. p 33
5. Sir Philip Warwick, Memoirs of the Reign of King Charles I (1702)
6. Colonel Lord Wharton's speech, Thomson Tracts E.124 (32) in the British Library
7. Earl of Clarendon, History of the Great Rebellion and Civil War in England (Oxford 1888)
8. Colonel Sir Bevil Grenville in a letter to his wife dated 19 Jan 1643, Victoria & Albert Museum
9. Ibid.
10. Anonymous letter, Staffordshire Record Society, 1936 pp 181-4
11. Printed in Stebbing Shaw, The History and Antiquities of Staffordshire I (London 1798)
12. Ibid.
13. Alan Wicks (ed.), Bellum Civile, Sir Ralph Hopton's Memoirs of the campaign in the west 1642–44, (Partizan Press 1988)
14. Ibid.
15. Ibid.
16. His Highnesse Prince Ruperts Late Beating up the Rebels' Quarters at Post-Comb and Chinner in Oxfordshire and his Victory in Chalgrove field, on Sunday Morning June 18, 1642, Pamphlet, Bodleian Library, Oxford
17. Introduction by C.H. Firth, Stuart Tracts 1603–1693 (New York 1964)
18. Peter Young, The Vindication of Richard Atkyns, Journal of the Society for Army Historical Research 35
19. 'Colonel Slingsby's relation of the battle of Lansdown and Roundway Down, July 5th.' Clarendon MSS, Vol. 23, No.1738 (2) in Alan Wicks (ed.), Bellum Civile, op.cit
20. Young, The Vindication of Richard Atkyns, op cit.
21. Hopton, op. cit.
22. 'Colonel Slingsby's relation of the battle of Lansdown and Roundway Down, July 5th.', op. cit.
23. 'Colonel Slingsby's relation of the battle of Lansdown and Roundway Down, July 5th.', op. cit.
24. Young, Vindication of Thomas Atkyns, op. cit.
25. Sir John Byron's relation to the secretary of the last western action between the Lord Wilmot and Sir William Waller, York 1643
26. Quoted in Walter Money, The First and Second Battles of Newbury and the Siege of Donnington Castle during the Civil War (London 1881) p 24
27. Young, Vindication of Thomas Atkins, op. cit
28. Henry Foster, 'A true and exact relation of the marching's of the two regiments of the Trained Bands of the City of London', in Bibliotheca Gloucestrensis (1825)
29. Digby, op. cit.
30. Byron quoted in Clarendon, op. cit.
31. 'A Relation of Good Success', c.July 3/4, Thomason Tract E 54 (11). Reprinted in P. Young, Marston Moor
32. 'An Exact and full Relation of the Last Fight between the King's Forces and Sir William Waller.' Sent in a letter from an officer in the Army to his friend in London, 5 July 1644
33. Quoted in Neil Fairbairn, Battlefields of Britain (Evans Brothers Ltd, London 1983) p 111
34. Sir Hugh Cholmeley, Memorials touching the Battle of York, ed. C.H. Firth, English Historical Review V (1890) pp 347-51
35. Thomason Tract E.71 (22) quoted in P. Young, Marston Moor.
36. Quoted in Neil Fairburn, Battlefields of Britain, op. cit. p112
37. Quoted in P. Young & R. Holmes, The English Civil War, p 202
38. Lt. Col. James Somerville, 'Memoire of the Somervilles' (Edinburgh 1815) reprinted P. Young, Marston Moor, pp 258–68

Soldiering in the Stuart uprisings

1. Quoted in W MacDonald Wigfield, The Monmouth Rebellion (Moonraker Press, 1980), p 15
2. W MacDonald Wigfield, The Monmouth Rebellion, op. cit.
3. Andrew Paschall's letter to Dr James, contained in S Heywood, A Vindication of Mr Fox's History of the Early Part of the Reign of James II (1811), Appendix 4, pp xxix–xlv
4. Somerset Notes and Queries, part 273 (March 1961) pp 15–21
5. Nathaniel Wade's account contained in W MacDonald Wigfield, The Monmouth Rebellion, op. cit.
6. From an account by King James II printed in Hardwicke State Papers, 1778, Vol. II, pp 305–13
7. Somerset Notes and Queries, op. cit.
8. From an account by King James II printed in Hardwicke State Papers, 1778, Vol. II, pp 305–13
9. Captain Edward Dummer, 'A Brief Journal of the Western Rebellion', printed in J Davis, History of the Second Queen's Royal Regiment (1985), pp 48–9
10. Royal Commission on Historical Documents, Report on the Manuscripts of Mrs Stopford-Sackville, Vol. I (HMSO 1904), pp 16–19
11. From an account by King James II printed in Hardwicke State Papers, 1778, Vol. II, pp 305–13
12. A letter written by an officer in the Lifeguard, quoted in John While, Sedgemoor 1685 (Picton Publishing, Chippenham 1985), p 29
13. Quoted in W MacDonald Wigfield, The Monmouth Rebellion, op. cit.
14. Hugh Mackay, Memoirs of the War carried on in Scotland and Ireland 1689–91 (Bannatyne Club, 1833)
15. Henry Jenner (ed.), Memoirs of Lord Viscount Dundee, The Highland Clans and the Massacre of Glencoe (London 1908)
16. John Sinclair, Memors of the Insurrection in Scotland in 1715, ed. James MacKnight (The Abbotsford Club, Edinburgh 1858)
17. Quoted in John Baynes, The Jacobite Rising of 1715 (Cassells)
18. Ibid.
19. Quoted in John Sinclair, Memors of the Insurrection in Scotland in 1715, op. cit.
20. Richard Henderson to Madam Lockhart, 16 November 1715, Laing MSS, 111.375.
21. John Sinclair, Memors of the Insurrection in Scotland in 1715, op. cit.
22. Fragment of a memoir of Field Marshal James Keith, written by himself, 1714–34 (The Bannatyne Club, Edinburgh 1834)
23. General Wightman's account, printed in Rev. Robert Patten, The History of the Late Rebellion, (London 1717)